Atlanta Life
Insurance Company

Atlanta Life
Insurance Company

Guardian of Black Economic Dignity

Alexa Benson Henderson

The University of Alabama Press
Tuscaloosa and London

∞

Library of Congress Cataloging-in-Publication Data

Henderson, Alexa Benson. 1944–
    Atlanta Life Insurance Company: Guardian of Black Economic
Dignity / by Alexa Benson Henderson.
        p.   cm.
    Bibliography: p.
    Includes index.
    ISBN 0-8173-5045-4 (alk. paper)
    1. Atlanta Life Insurance Company—History. 2. Insurance—
United States—History. 3. Afro-Americans—Economic conditions.
I. Title.
HG8540.A8H46   1990
368.3'2'006—dc 19   88-34000
                                                                      CIP

British Library Cataloguing-in-Publication Data available

To Bill and my family

Contents

Tables

Preface

Shortly after the turn of the century, Alonzo Franklin Herndon, a former Georgia slave, combined personal business acumen and a modest amount of capital to create what became the Atlanta Life Insurance Company. More than three-quarters of a century later, it is an important and respected enterprise that is the nation's largest black-controlled stockholder life insurance company. The company's new corporate headquarters in Atlanta stands proudly along Auburn Avenue, the city's main black business thoroughfare, as a symbol of the long and valiant efforts of black Americans to achieve economic equality. With more than one-half million policyholders and assets of more than $108.7 million, the company is a significant force in the insurance industry.

Atlanta Life's heritage is that of a race enterprise. Historically, its main objective was to provide sick and accident and life insurance benefits to thousands of black policyholders for whom death or the loss of two or three weeks from work wreaked economic havoc. Over the years, the burdens associated with illnesses and deaths were eased by the dollars which companies like Atlanta Life paid to black families. Another important economic service was provided for blacks in the form of employment opportunities and business training. In addition, hundreds of black families received an economic boost from mortgage and policy loans that allowed them to purchase homes, build churches, and operate businesses.

Atlanta Life Insurance Company is part of the mosaic of activities initiated by African-Americans to establish an economic base within the black community. Numerous sources document the efforts of free blacks to develop business enterprises and to amass wealth in the pre– and post–Civil War eras.[1] Despite numerous proscriptions and severe handicaps that obviated business success and expansion among this class, some free blacks engaged in profitable enterprises before general emancipation. Such undertakings were generally in the personal service enterprises to which blacks were relegated and in which small amounts of capital were required to conduct operations. Whites seldom offered competition in these areas, and black business success was viewed as acceptable. Although somewhat more limited, opportunities existed for blacks, particularly in the North, to engage in other money-making efforts, ranging from farming to industrial undertakings. Similarly, free blacks in the West could be found in numerous entrepreneurial endeavors.

In the period following Reconstruction and the full ascendancy of the capitalist economy in America, an important segment of black leaders challenged black Americans to advance business efforts and to create a separate economic structure to support the black community. The ideal depicted was of an independent black economy operating within the American capitalist framework to combat the pervasive hostility and persistent racism of the American economic system, which restricted blacks to the position of a permanent underclass. Economically dependent and exploited, the majority of blacks existed largely in a state of peonage, relegated to menial jobs and economically intimidated. A significant segment of black leaders believed that the only hope to end blacks' disadvantage in American society lay in the development of a separate capitalist-employer class to create jobs and provide capital for their own group. Like Americans generally, these leaders viewed wealth as an important instrument for achieving respect and citizenship, arguing that the future of blacks in America required the growth and successful operation of business enterprises.

By nearly every measure, the possibilities of African-Americans achieving success within the expanding American capitalist system were extremely narrow. Just as in the antebellum era, certain individuals did achieve wealth and fame in a number of spheres, although their businesses generally remained small and their aggregate wealth was usually not impressive when compared with that amassed in the

mainstream American economy. Commercial and industrial undertakings that required considerable capital were the least common
ventures undertaken by blacks. These enterprises, when they existed,
usually suffered severe handicaps caused by scarce capital resources,
inefficiently trained personnel, minimal support and patronage by
blacks, and growing deterrents to black advancement resulting from
racial discrimination. Scholars such as black sociologist E. Franklin
Frazier have been extremely critical of these efforts. Indeed, Frazier
concluded that the idea of successful black business operating within
a segregated economy was a social myth propagated by the black upper class.[2]

The most important businesses established by blacks were primarily in financial enterprises, particularly banking and insurance. Even
these businesses were often unstable, springing up frequently only to
fail soon after they were organized. Confined to operating within the
so-called Negro market, these businesses were dependent on the er-
ratic patronage of blacks and frequently suffered from heavy competition with whites. The more successful of these enterprises were
usually organized as cooperatives, developing out of the efforts of established groups, associations, or societies.

Despite these shortcomings, the ideal of wealth formation and business ownership remained a dominant theme in African-American life.
Men such as Booker T. Washington and John Hope urged the masses of
blacks to eschew improvident behavior and instead to inculcate habits
of thriftiness and industry, to amass savings, and to acquire property.
Blacks were also urged to support self-help efforts and organizations
that might assist the economic emancipation of the race and to organize business concerns and enterprises whenever practical.

The Atlanta Life Insurance Company is an example of the inspiring
efforts of black Americans to build and sustain financial organizations and enterprises. As the largest proprietary life insurance company owned and operated by blacks in the country, Atlanta Life is
exemplary of the past achievements and future possibilities of black
insurance firms. From its humble beginning in 1905 as a small insurance association, Atlanta Life surmounted many obstacles caused
by economic hardships and the racial spirit of the time, weathered
bouts with epidemics, migration, depression, and wars, and
triumphed in the face of business reversals and upheavals in the industry. In spurts of expansion, the company grew until its territory
now includes twelve states in the South and Midwest. Having attained significance as one of the strongest black financial institu-

tions, the company represents important aspects of the perennial quest of black men and women to achieve economic equality.

Atlanta Life's history also proves the importance of committed, visionary leadership for black institution building. Its story emphasizes the centrality of the support and commitment of Alonzo Herndon and his associates to the enterprise's success. As builders of the company, Herndon and the men and women he selected to provide leadership for the firm worked diligently, with deep faith in its possibilities, to achieve strength and viability as a financial institution and to safeguard these achievements against unusual odds. The leadership was careful also, whether in periods of tension or triumph, always to maintain faith with the black community as the wellspring of inspiration and support for the company.

Over the years, Atlanta Life adopted a vigilant posture as guardian of the economic dignity of black Americans. Both in its relationships with the black community and with other black insurance enterprises, Atlanta Life recognized that its role as one of the country's outstanding examples of black economic development involved a responsibility to contribute leadership and resources in any number of efforts by blacks to achieve equality and to improve the quality of life. Perhaps most important, Atlanta Life viewed as a major responsibility its efforts to halt eroding business gains of black America.

Writing the story of Atlanta Life has been simultaneously a labor of love and of frustration. I received tremendous inspiration from the efforts of several generations of black leaders and entrepreneurs to develop successful and competitive enterprises despite limited capital and other resources. The formulas for survival worked out by Alonzo Herndon and contemporary blacks of the Progressive Era serve as compelling reminders of the need for economic development efforts among various groups in our own time. I have tried to provide a business history of Atlanta Life within the context of the firm's own time and setting. It was dismaying, however, in that too often bits and pieces of information that were important to the story remained elusive. I was discouraged also by the dearth of sources, printed or otherwise, on many of the significant individuals, groups, and organizations that have been associated with black business development in Atlanta and elsewhere. Sadly, many of these inspiring stories are lost forever. I hope, however, that some who read this book may be stimulated to research these important chapters.

The development of black enterprises has until very recently been sadly neglected. Records were often discarded, and people with valuable and important insights into entrepreneurial history passed from the scene without leaving recorded data. In recent years, however, historians have begun invading dusty company files to ferret out source materials for this important area of research. The files and official minutes of Atlanta Life Insurance Company, the extensive correspondence files of longtime company secretary Eugene Martin, and the relatively small amount of materials on the company in the Herndon Family Papers have been the primary sources for this study. In addition, I have examined the papers of several of the leading advocates of black business development around the turn of the century, including Booker T. Washington and Robert R. Moton. Other sources include newspapers and publications of the period; the reports of the Georgia insurance commissioner, as well as other official agencies and groups; and the proceedings of the National Negro Business League, the National Negro Insurance Association, and other organizations. Interviews with persons with intimate knowledge or firsthand observation of Atlanta Life and business development in the period also formed an important source for this study.

This story could not have been told without the assistance of a number of persons. I especially acknowledge the kind cooperation of Jesse Hill, Jr., other officers, and the staff of Atlanta Life Insurance Company. President Hill graciously gave support and guidance throughout the months of research and writing of an earlier version of the study. Company Secretary Henry N. Brown made voluminous files, minutes, and financial records available, and the late Edward L. Simon, company auditor and chairman of the board of directors, became an invaluable oral history source and assisted in searching out much pertinent data. My appreciation is also extended to many others, inside and outside the company, for time and assistance in conducting interviews, compiling statistics, and generally helping with this project.

In such an undertaking, moral and financial support are also important. This study began under the direction of Merl Reed at Georgia State University. Professor Reed, along with Jack Blicksilver of the Economics Department, gave me initial encouragement and have been supportive all along the way. The staffs of a number of libraries, especially the Robert W. Woodruff Library of the Atlanta University Center, the Hollis Burke Frissell Library of Tuskegee University, and the Library of Congress in Washington, D.C., deserve special praise for their assistance in the research phase of the study. Over the years, financial assistance to complete the study was provided from several sources, including the Ford Foundation, Clark College, the United Negro College Fund, and the National Endowment for the Humanities.

Finally, I am especially grateful to my family and to my husband, Bill, the greatest source of inspiration and support throughout the years of research and writing of this book, to whom this book is dedicated.

Atlanta, Georgia   A.B.H.

Atlanta Life
Insurance Company

1

A Heritage of Mutual Aid

Everywhere the Freedman is noted for his efforts to ward off
accident and a pauper's grave by insurance against
sickness and death.
—W. E. B. Du Bois, ed., *Some Efforts of American Negroes*
for Their Own Social Betterment

On 1 July 1927, Alonzo Herndon convened a memorable session of the board of directors of the Atlanta Life Insurance Company. Unable to travel to company headquarters on Auburn Avenue in Atlanta because of ill health, he arranged for the meeting to take place at his magnificent home on University Place adjacent to the campus of Atlanta University. Lush shrubbery and a gentle breeze added to the pleasantness of the surroundings on this warm July morning as Herndon, wearing pajamas and accompanied by the family's pet dog Cuffie, welcomed the directors onto the west veranda of his home overlooking the city. In this serene setting, the president conducted his final meeting of the board of directors of the company he had founded and nurtured for twenty-two years.

Despite health problems, the sixty-nine-year-old Herndon conducted the meeting in his usual affable, dignified manner. He showed only slight indications of the severe heart condition that would soon claim his life as he "entered into the meeting in the finest of spirit, interested in all that was said and done."[1] Herndon's customary good humor added an aura of lightheartedness to the meeting as he shared jokes from his vast storehouse of witty tales and stories.

On a more serious note, however, the founder-president of Atlanta Life followed his usual habit of reminiscing about the struggle that had been waged to build the company. He recounted difficulties experienced by Atlanta Life in the early years, emphasizing the efforts to secure qualified agents and managers, to expand territory and increase the number of policyholders, and to earn the confidence and approbation of the black public. He spoke also of his personal sacrifices of time and resources in building the enterprise and indicated his pride and pleasure in the many ways it had repaid him. In his usual cautious manner, he also reminded the men of the many failures sustained by black businesses generally and urged them to be vigilant in the future.[2]

The directors listened eagerly to the president's words, for they understood that Herndon spoke out of the rich experience of a pioneer in the organizing of a successful insurance enterprise among African-Americans. His success was built upon early business ventures extending back to slavery and the Reconstruction period conducted by Richard Allen, William Washington Browne, John Merrick, Maggie Lena Walker, Thomas Walker, and hundreds of other black men and women. The enterprises initiated by these pioneers were intended to harness the spirit of solidarity and mutual cooperation which blacks exhibited in bondage and in freedom. Developing through successive stages, the enterprises evolved from mutual aid societies, to church benevolence and burial associations, to secret and fraternal organizations with numerous affiliated enterprises, to full-fledged industrial and legal reserve insurance companies with millions of dollars in assets and insurance in force. In nearly every instance, the enterprises were organized to provide for the collective support and protection of black people and to promote the independent economic and social advancement of the race.

Alonzo Herndon did not recover from his illness and died on 21 July, just three weeks after the board meeting. Following his death, an article in the *New York World* compared Herndon's life to that of Booker T. Washington, stating, "It was another whimsical tale of adventure and conquest, another graphic story of a spectacular rise from abject poverty to a position of financial security and unquestioned influence, another arresting and gripping 'Up From Slavery.' "[3] Although portions of the *World*'s tribute may have been apt, neither man had come by success and influence through whimsy. Like Washington, Herndon had come up by toil and thriftiness, and his most consequential undertaking, the founding and development of Atlanta Life, was the result not of fanciful dreams and conquest but of the strong traditions of self-help and mutual aid that had sustained African-Americans for more than a century.

Black insurance companies are descendants of the mutual aid and benevolence tradition that extended as far back as the antebellum period. In nearly every community, there existed numerous voluntary associations, generally referred to as mutual aid or benevolent societies, aimed primarily at alleviating some of the problems that affected the black population. Along with the church, these societies represented the most effective form of social and economic cooperation among African-Americans, and they helped to promote the ideals of community interest and racial solidarity among the group. Indeed, these associations aided significantly in the advancement of a group that was systematically isolated from the mainstream of American society. Within the black community, these organizations provided an important underpinning for institutional life.[4]

Mutual aid societies existed on some southern plantations. As slaves, blacks often expressed their group consciousness by banding together to care for the sick and to provide assistance until they were well again. As early as 1833 every community or village of any size in Virginia had some such association among the slaves.[5] Robert Smalls of South Carolina, in testimony before the American Freedmen's Inquiry Commission in 1863, referred to the church societies that existed on some plantations, whose members helped one another in sickness and distress.[6] Such organizations were usually tied closely to the church, for as Carter Godwin Woodson has noted, "Whenever Negroes had their own churches benevolence developed as the handmaiden of religion." In urban communities throughout the South, bondsmen also attempted to organize for mutual support and improvement of their social life. The collective activities involving slaves were usually carried out in secret, for as Woodson observes, "Such could not develop very far without drifting into antagonisms to the interests of the slaveholders."[7]

Mutual aid societies were most successful among free blacks in the North. Among the earliest known associations was the African Union Society of Newport, Rhode Island, formed by free blacks on 10 November 1780 to provide for the collective social needs of blacks in the community. The efforts of the African Union Society included recording births, deaths, and marriages, apprenticing black youths to useful trades, and generally fostering the moral and economic welfare of Newport's blacks. The society also promoted the idea of emigrating and attempted to organize northern free blacks to work toward the establishment of an independent black nation in Africa.[8]

Pennsylvania, the first state to abolish slavery (1780) and the state which, along with Maryland, Virginia, and New York, contained more than half of all free blacks, provided another early example of mutual associations and cooperative strides made by African-Americans. Like members of their group everywhere, Pennsylvania's free blacks had few rights of citizenship and were subjected to restrictions similar to those prescribed for slaves. Despite the restrictions placed on their caste, free blacks in Philadelphia had gradually gained an economic foothold, and as early as 1780 a significant number owned property and engaged in business enterprises. This group, like Americans generally, seemed to place a high priority on the ownership and control of businesses and institutions. According to Charles Harris Wesley, "This group, having solved its economic problem of making a living, needed only an aggressive leadership and an organization of its weak individual efforts in order to make its group life socially more effective."[9]

Philadelphia's free blacks found effective leadership in Richard Allen and Absalom Jones, two black churchmen. On 12 April 1787, they organized the Free African Society for the purpose of looking after the social, moral, and economic needs of the group. As too few of the interested persons initially expressed a desire to participate in a strictly religious organization, and as those who did belonged to different denominations, the organizers formed the Free African Society as an independent association "without regard to religious tenets, provided the persons lived an orderly life, in order to support one another in sickness and for the benefit of their widows and fatherless children."[10]

The Free African Society was one of the earliest efforts of free blacks to cooperate for economic unity. Among its major aims was the mutual protection of members against sickness and death.[11] The responsibilities and benefits associated with membership were set forth in the articles of the organization. To carry out its benevolent and beneficial aims, members were required to pay monthly "one shilling in silver, Pennsylvania currency." After one year's membership, the needy of the society would receive "the sum of three shillings and nine pence per week . . . provided, this necessity is not brought on them by their own imprudence."[12] Although the society did not include a specific burial payment, it did provide for widows to receive benefits as long as they did not remarry and complied with the rules of the society. Children of deceased members also came under the care of the organization, which, if necessary, assumed responsibility for their education and saw to it that they were apprenticed in a suitable trade.

Strict rules of conduct governed the members, and slothful living or improper behavior was not tolerated. A member could be removed from the society's roster for neglecting to pay dues for more than three months or for failing to attend meetings except in cases of sickness. At the monthly meetings, responsibility for the oversight of the membership was assigned to a committee of stalwart souls charged with the task of visiting members to "give such advice as may appear necessary." In this manner, the Free African Society sought to advance the social and moral life of the community and to disprove the widely held contention that free blacks were "an idle and slothful people, and often proved burdensome to the neighborhood and afford[ed] ill examples to other Negroes."[13]

In contrast to the idea of blacks as an idle and slothful group, the African Union and the Free African Society served as important examples of mutual helpfulness among blacks. Moreover, such organizations had a tremendous and far-reaching impact on the social and economic development of African-Americans. The Newport and Philadelphia examples inspired free blacks in other northern cities to organize mutual aid societies to advance their common good.[14] Because of the economic insecurity and social isolation which free blacks experienced in northern cities, mutual aid organizations performed important social and economic functions and were able to lessen the burden of poverty for at least some black families. In general, these associations "outstripped even the church as the predominant structure among free blacks."[15]

Even in the South, where their activities were guarded closely, free blacks often attempted to organize for mutual support and helpfulness, especially in a few communities where free blacks existed as "a respectful, economically independent, class-conscious group."[16] Charleston, South Carolina, provides a notable example. From the late 1700s, free blacks in Charleston were independent artisans, owners of property, promoters of businesses, and supporters of churches, schools, and associations. On 1 November 1790, a group of free mulattoes in Charleston organized the Brown Fellowship Society, stating as their purpose the need to alleviate "the unhappy situation of our fellow creatures, and the distress of our widows and orphans, for want of a fund to relieve them in the hour of their distress, sickness, and death."[17] Eligibility requirements were high, and membership was limited to fifty persons aged twenty-five and over. Each person paid a membership fee of $50 along with specified monthly dues. The benefits, based on need, included a sick payment of $1.50 weekly and a small funeral stipend for members without a sufficient estate for burial. The Brown Fellowship was also obligated to assist needy widows and children of deceased members. In addition, the society maintained a cemetery for its members and any other baptized black persons. Among its unique provisions was a "credit union," which permitted the members, a large number of whom were entrepreneurs, to borrow from the treasury to make improvements to homes or businesses. The organization spearheaded a number of activities that stressed companionship and promoted social relations within the group. It also required members to visit sick brothers and to attend the funerals of deceased members.[18]

Another important mutual aid association also existed among free blacks in Charleston. Organized on 19 June 1843, this group adopted the name Humane Brotherhood. Its constitution, similar to that of the Brown Fellowship, provided for monetary assistance to members and their families at times of sickness, accidents, and death. Another benefit resulting from membership in the organization involved the payment of a $12 annual benefit to widows of deceased members. The Humane Brotherhood also provided for other contingencies likely to affect the black group. The constitution specified that "should they [the members], through the natural course of events fall into prison, without injuring or rendering impeachable their moral character, but by real misfortune, their families shall receive the amount of one dollar and fifty cents per week, the same amount when members are sick."[19] Generally less well off economically than the Brown Fellowship Society, the members of this association nevertheless emphasized social occasions and companionship within the group. They also maintained a separate cemetery plot for members and stressed the importance of providing for the education and apprenticeship of children of deceased members.[20]

After emancipation, mutual aid efforts remained an important avenue of self-help. Among the freedmen, the major portion of relief and benevolent work centered in the church. With growing memberships, composed largely of poor working people, appeals for relief were generally heavy in most congregations. On numerous occasions, churches were called upon to assume responsibility for the burial of indigent members, which soon became a serious burden for most churches. In addition to the legitimate appeals for aid coming from within a large congregation, abuses often accompanied this form of relief. In some cases, indigent families sought to increase the size of the donation received by appealing to several churches for burial assistance, usually claiming that the deceased was a member of all of them. These abuses, along with the large number of legitimate appeals, made a voluntary church relief system impractical, but the situation provided incentive for black leaders, usually churchmen, to formulate a different kind of relief program. Within churches, ministers frequently promoted the idea of mutual aid organizations as a means of meeting the growing economic problems among freedmen. And, recognizing that blacks must learn to look out for themselves and make plans for their economic survival, the freedmen widely supported mutual aid organizations. For the majority of this class, the small sum acquired during an illness or at the time of a death was extremely significant.

By the 1880s, benefit or benevolent societies could be found in practically every church of any size throughout the South. The associations often required that in addition to paying dues and attending meetings, individuals engage in social intercourse of a charitable nature. The announcement of a member's illness was usually followed by visits with food or money given by the visiting brother or sister to augment the association's small sick benefits. When the ill member was female, the other women attended to the nursing and household duties. For example, in New Orleans among members of the Union Band Society, a person designated as the official "mother" of the organization assumed responsibility for delegating individuals to carry out nursing chores for ill members.[21] The social nature of these groups also extended to deaths. In addition to paying an extra assessment for the burial of a deceased member, the survivors banded together to attend the funeral and did not forget the widow and children.

Mutual aid societies were precursors of the early insurance companies that developed in the South. In general, these societies followed simple business procedures and made little pretense at adhering to sound insurance principles. Unlike the Free African and Brown Fellowship societies, most of the organizations operated without a formal constitution, although specific and often very strict rules governed the membership. No formal contracts existed, all ages and both sexes received the same benefits, and the organizers generally paid little heed to the physical condition of individuals admitted into the organizations. All members paid a small initiation fee and periodically made payments into a common treasury. The major feature that connected the societies with insurance was that for a stipulated payment each member received specified benefits when ill and families were given a small payment to defray burial expenses. Such enterprises, therefore, represented one of the first attempts by blacks to form social devices for shifting the problems of certain unforeseen crises from the shoulders of the single individual to the group. In short, these black organizations typified "the economic efforts of the weak to find strength in unity."[22]

One of the earliest efforts to expand the concept of mutual aid beyond simple provisions for the sick and for burial occurred in Virginia. Georgia native William Washington Browne, head of the True Reformers, a leading fraternal association in Virginia, advanced the idea of offering a benefit that would permit members to create estates for the benefit of surviving relatives. Browne's plan called for the True Reformers to establish an endowment or benefit fund composed of a specified percentage of monthly dues, initiation fees, fines, money raised from suppers, festivals, and excursions and any other receipts of the organizations. In this manner, Browne sought to increase the benefits members could receive from the organization. The True Reformers' plan provided that "any member's heirs or assigns holding a certificate ... after the first of November 1881 ... shall draw five hundred dollars from the Benefit fund; provided they are members in good standing at the time of death."[23] In addition, members were permitted to increase the benefits they were able to receive by paying supplementary assessments. The introduction of these features, stressing the insurance and savings provisions, marked an important milestone in the development of insurance among blacks.

An effective organizer and businessman, Browne also introduced principles of management into the operations of the True Reformers. He was careful in the selection of members, paying close attention to the adequacy of rates and aware of age classifications. He also required that members be issued certificates or policies, that trustees be elected to oversee the endowment fund, and that a reserve fund be established to supply money when needed by chapters, also known as fountains, throughout the system. To provide a depository for the growing funds of the True Reformers, Browne took another step in the advancement of the group as an business enterprise, organizing a savings bank in 1888. Established in Richmond, the enterprise was among the first banks in the country to be founded and administered by blacks.[24] Under Browne's management, the True Reformers operated several additional enterprises, including a real estate department that invested in a good deal of property, a commercial department that operated several stores, a hotel, an old folks home, and a weekly newspaper. Unfortunately, the True Reformers fell into disrepute after Browne's death on 21 December 1897, and much of his work was undone by his successors, who made unwise policy changes and failed to adhere to the procedures he had established. After losing the bank and other assets, the True Reformers ceased to be an effective organization.[25]

As the True Reformers declined in membership and significance, a number of people who had been associated with Browne established independent insurance enterprises in Virginia, Maryland, North Carolina, and the District of Columbia. Although some of these firms were short-lived, several made important contributions to the development of insurance as a major commercial enterprise among blacks. Indeed, Walter B. Weare claims that "virtually every insurance association founded in the Upper South during the late nineteenth and early twentieth centuries can be traced to ex-True Reformer agents who organized their own societies, each aspiring to become another William Washington Browne." Among this group were men who founded several of the companies that became prominent in the twentieth century. In Durham, John Merrick, a prosperous barber and former agent of the True Reformers, organized a small mutual assessment company in 1899, which became the North Carolina Mutual Insurance Company.[26] Another former agent, Samuel Wilson Rutherford, organized the National Benefit Insurance Company of Washington, D.C. Chartered in 1898, this firm was one of the most widely known companies among blacks until its demise in 1932 in the throes of the Great Depression. In Virginia, Booker Lawrence Jordan, a former official of the True Reformers, was a significant force as secretary-manager in the development of the Southern Aid Society of Richmond.[27]

The influence of the True Reformers seems to have been confined primarily to the upper South. In the lower South, Alabama was touted as the center of benevolent societies among African-Americans, possessing more of these organizations than any other locale.[28] Like Browne, Thomas Walker of Birmingham appeared to provide the spark that ignited conventional insurance enterprises in the lower South, particularly in Alabama and Georgia. A former slave and a preacher, Walker had by 1881 initiated several churches in the black community. In his pastoral capacity, Walker was often called upon to assist members of his congregations in pressing matters that affected their general welfare. The frequency of these intercessions soon led him to conclude that blacks in Birmingham needed broader avenues of racial support than the church alone could provide. Assessing the needs of the community, Walker organized several businesses in the area, including a coal company, brick manufacturing firm, shoe store, drugstore, livery stable, newspaper, funeral home, and cemetery. To assist black families in becoming more self-sustaining economically, Walker also organized a bank and a mutual aid association. The latter, called the Afro-American Benevolent Association, was a small, church-related organization.[29]

In December 1894, the Afro-American Benevolent Association expanded into a full-fledged business enterprise, the Union Central Relief Association of Birmingham. As the primary promoter, Walker attempted to conduct the organization in a businesslike manner. He established benefit rates that were tied closely to premiums, setting the maximum death payment at $100. He hired salaried agents to solicit clients, collect premiums, and pay sick and death claims, and he issued contracts or policies that specified rates and benefits. Walker also petitioned the state legislature to secure a charter for the organization, and in February 1901, after several failed attempts, Union Central became the first black insurance association to be chartered officially in Alabama.[30]

In addition to the relief provided to black families, Union Central offered other benefits to the community. Important to the long-term economic benefit for African-Americans was the opportunity the company offered for employment as agents. Walker was particularly incensed that white companies did not employ blacks even to solicit black clients. He was also outraged by the behavior of white agents, who, upon entering black homes to service policyholders, frequently failed to give proper respect to the inhabitants, especially black women, whom they addressed by their given names or referred to as "Auntie." Walker viewed the opportunity to earn a living as a matter of "first importance," and he perceived that the promotion of Union Central was a way of providing an alternative to the discrimination and discourtesies faced by blacks in this area.[31]

As the enterprise developed in the late 1890s, Walker initiated a period of expansion. Moving throughout the state, he hired solicitors in many towns in Alabama. In 1897 he crossed the state's eastern boundary into Georgia and organized the Union Mutual Relief Association of Atlanta. Walker served as president of the Georgia organization, and in 1902 Union Mutual became the first black insurance association to be chartered in Georgia, receiving authorization to write policies for a maximum benefit of $500. The enterprise expanded from Atlanta into other Georgia cities and was frequently pointed to as an example of the potential of black businesses, especially insurance, on the development of blacks.[32] The oldest officially chartered black insurance association in Georgia, Union Mutual represented the earliest effort of blacks in Atlanta to advance economic relief beyond the benevolent and mutual aid societies.

The historic roots of mutual aid and benevolence among blacks in Atlanta are found in the city's black churches. Independent churches, the earliest institutions established by blacks, were formed in Atlanta a few years before emancipation, with at least two black congregations formed before the Civil War.[33] The first independent congregation of black Baptists organized the Friendship Baptist Church in April 1862 when a little group of bondsmen and bondswomen withdrew from the white First Baptist Church and formed their own congregation. Led by the Reverend Frank Quarles, the black Baptists obtained a plot of land and arranged with the American Missionary Association to share a railway boxcar as a place of worship until the congregation was able to move to a building in the southwest quadrant of the city. The membership grew steadily, and by 1870 some members living in the northeast section became weary of having to travel to worship at Friendship. With the consent and blessings of Pastor Quarles, this group broke away and organized a second Baptist church on the East Side. Unable to acquire a building, the group held services in the pastor's yard until they organized the Mt. Pleasant Baptist Church in a small wooden building on Fort Street. Ten years later, with a membership of approximately two hundred persons, the church relocated to Wheat Street (now Auburn Avenue) and changed its name to the Wheat Street Baptist Church.[34]

The membership of Wheat Street Church increased rapidly after emancipation, and it grew from two hundred to four hundred by 1894. Among its members were some of the most prosperous blacks in the city, although a large segment was composed of poorer families and individuals. Like other congregations in the city, Wheat Street recognized early the need for mutual assistance among freedmen and organized a number of societies that operated "for the good of the church and its members."[35] Among these societies, the Sisters of Love, organized in 1880, had a large membership and appears to have been one of the most prosperous. According to a report on secret and beneficial societies in Atlanta, the Sisters had an annual income of $570 and in 1898 had $600 in the bank. Wheat Street's other societies including the Rising Stars, the Ailing Brothers of Love, and the Woman's Mission, the latter providing relief specifically to widows and orphaned children. Like similar organizations in other churches, these societies generally provided benefits to sick members, gave donations to the poor, and provided cemetery lots for paupers.[36]

The church societies undoubtedly rendered good services, although requests for aid were frequently greater than they could meet. Despite the benevolent effort of these groups, poverty and illness persisted in the black community, which had experienced a tremendous swell in population in the decades after emancipation. In 1900 blacks in Atlanta numbered 37,727 or 39.8 percent of the total population in the city, which ranked forty-third in population in the nation. By 1910 this figure had risen to 51,902, with the largest concentration of black residents in the fourth ward in the vicinity of Wheat Street Church.[37]

A growing population meant growing need in the areas of health and economics. Hoping to find jobs and to improve their living conditions, the migrants flowed into Atlanta from small towns and rural areas in the state, but most were fortunate if they could eke out a living on a day-to-day basis. With few resources, they had little to put aside for periods of illness and unemployment or the expenses associated with dying. Inadequate public charity failed to meet the needs of the masses of blacks and whites and, when available, was usually pitiable and discriminatory.

For many residents of the black community, obtaining any form of insurance or relief was difficult. Poverty and a low social standing made them unacceptable as members of some of the fraternal organizations that operated insurance units or departments. White insurance companies generally refused insurance to blacks, charging that they were high risks because of their poverty, greater exposure to diseases, and shorter longevity.[38] The heavy burden of handling the problems of the black needy fell largely to black organizations, especially black churches. On numerous occasions Wheat Street members were called upon to make donations to families in the growing pauper class or to contribute to the burial of the church's poorer members. As the appeals for alms increased, and as the number of persons needing assistance with burials grew in a congregation as large as Wheat Street's the need became clear for independent insurance programs, such as Union Mutual, that would assist the black masses in becoming more self-sustaining and economically independent.

In 1904 the Reverend Peter James Bryant, then in his sixth year as pastor of Wheat Street, organized the Atlanta Benevolent Protective Association. An independent business enterprise, it was not connected organizationally with the church, and church groups continued to carry out visitations to the sick and to engage in general relief work. This organization, set up along the lines of an insurance society, was promoted as a way of helping African-Americans to meet their most pressing needs in economic crises. For individual members, the enterprise provided a sum of money varying from one to five dollars for a specified number of weeks of illness. It was essentially a burial association, providing a death payment that ranged from ten to fifty dollars. The members were required to pay an assessment, generally weekly, of five to twenty-five cents. The organization was largely devoid of social features, the rules specifying only that any member whose dues fell in arrears for more than one month was out or, at least, would receive a reduced burial benefit.[39]

Bryant's popularity aided in the early development of the new association. A respected member of the Atlanta community, he had been only twenty-five years old when called to the pastorate of Wheat Street Church and was soon one of the leading preachers in the community. Intelligent and very witty, he frequently spoke for the clergy on various issues and often represented blacks in interracial meetings in the city. A powerful orator, who entered the ministry at age fifteen, he was gifted with a fluent command of the language and with a strong delivery. He could usually move audiences whether speaking from the pulpit or some other podium on matters of economics, disfranchisement, or other issues affecting the race. An associate editor of the *Voice of the Negro*, a monthly magazine that started publication in early 1904, Bryant could also move individuals with his pen, and he sometimes used this medium to express his opinions on issues or to appeal to public sentiment.[40]

As president of the Atlanta Benevolent Protective Association, Bryant primarily handled publicity for the organization. He used his public skills to attract members into the association, offering it as an enlightened way to alleviate the economic burdens associated with sickness and death. The enterprise was managed by the Reverend James Arthur Hopkins, a businessman and preacher who was well known in the community. The business of the association was conducted in Hopkins's home at 162 Edgewood Avenue until the organization obtained a small office in the newly constructed and more centrally located Rucker Building at the corner of Auburn and Piedmont avenues. Millie Harris, a member of the Wheat Street congregation, served as secretary. William C. Alston, a coal and wood dealer with an establishment on Auburn Avenue, was treasurer, and three young doctors, Alfred D. Jones, Lewis P. Walton, and Thomas H. Slater, functioned at various times as medical directors. The association ran smoothly under this team for several months.[41]

Before 1905, the activities of groups such as the Atlanta Benevolent Protective and Union Mutual Relief associations were not closely regulated. Georgia had no laws to monitor the activities of these organizations, and there was no specified legal entity to oversee their management. The first insurance law enacted in the state in 1869 did not apply to burial organizations, secret societies, or insurance associations. Consequently, almost anyone could start such an organization with little or no capital. Again and again, people were victimized by the hastily organized and nearly insolvent associations. Indeed, whenever a difference arose within one of these groups, it seemed that the final result would usually be the birth of yet another organization, often making even more liberal promises and with no capital to meet its obligations. As an indication of the magnitude of the problem, the third Atlanta University Conference, meeting in 1898, issued a resolution emphatically warning against "unstable insurance societies conducted by irresponsible parties."[42]

A good deal of support existed in Georgia for a formal system of insurance regulations to weed out the irresponsible groups and to make insurance a safer investment for policyholders. Blacks believed that regulatory legislation would guarantee that companies carried out their part of the insurance agreement and would place "the insurer and the insured upon mutual grounds."[43]

The initiative for strict regulatory legislation, however, came from another source. It is reported that John N. MacEachern, cofounder and first president of the white-controlled Industrial Life and Health Insurance Company, "had much influence in shaping and directing the insurance laws of the state of Georgia." It is estimated that "as many as 75% of the insurance laws made during his active participation in the field of insurance originated with him."[44] Although Industrial Life was white-owned, virtually all its policyholders were black, which may have motivated MacEachern to support the 1905 law as a way of eliminating the black associations as competitors for the nickel-and-dime premiums of black policyholders.

The bill to regulate the business of industrial life insurance was introduced in the Georgia General Assembly on 6 July 1905 by Robert B.

Blackburn, representative from Fulton County. The act, approved on
22 August 1905, specifically defined industrial life insurance as "that
insurance for which the premiums, advanced assessment or dues are
regularly payable and collectible weekly or bi-weekly, and the policies
or benefit certificates . . . are for sums of not more than five hundred
dollars on a single life, and . . . weekly benefits for disability, caused
by sickness or accident, not greater than twenty dollars per week." To
secure the small but essential investments of policyholders, the act required that all companies deposit $5,000 with the state treasurer on
or before 1 January 1906. The deposit, made in negotiable securities,
was to be held by the state as a guarantee that claims would be paid in
case of a company's failure.[45] Organizations such as the Atlanta Benevolent Protective Association, insurance societies, and fraternal or-
ders that operated insurance units or departments, whether black or
white, came under these provisions because the act specified that all
such enterprises were to be characterized as doing an industrial insurance business.

Historically, industrial insurance was designed for and promoted
among the working classes. Unlike ordinary insurance, which carried
larger premiums that were payable annually, semiannually, or
monthly, industrial insurance was suited particularly to the great majority of people who made up the industrial or wage-earning population. Copied from the British concept, it was introduced in the United
States with the founding of the Prudential Insurance Company in
1875 and was designed originally to meet the needs of factory workers
and their families. The proponents of industrial insurance in America
argued that it constituted an inexpensive form of life and health protection and could be obtained by the masses for as little as three cents
a week. Workingmen generally received their wages in small install-
ments so agents called at their homes weekly and collected premiums
before the money could be spent on other items. As another plus, this
form of insurance required no medical examination for most policyholders. John Fairfield Dryden, Prudential's founder, was a passionate
advocate of industrial insurance, seeing it as a way of alleviating the
plight of the pauperized masses in many urban areas.[46]

Industrial insurance was not accepted immediately as a legitimate
enterprise in America. Indeed, some individuals perceived it as little
more than a street-corner flim-flam game. Bitter objections came
from insurance reformers such as Elizur Wright, often called the
father of life insurance in America, who vigorously opposed industrial
insurance for several reasons, including the contention that it encour-

aged infanticide by parents who insured the lives of their infants and then murdered them for the money.[47] Industrial insurance was supported, however, by a number of sources, including Connecticut Insurance Commissioner Ephraim Williams, who saw it as socially useful and recommended it as an "antidote to poverty." The acceptance of industrial insurance was further increased when the market for ordinary insurance weakened as a result of the severe depression that followed the Panic of 1873, leaving many families unable to pay large premiums. By the end of the decade, industrial insurance had created a boom in the insurance business. Wage earners and their families quickly realized that this form of insurance was suited to their pattern of life. Unable to afford ordinary life insurance, which usually sold in multiples of $1,000, they were glad to buy insurance in smaller amounts and to pay premiums weekly to the agent who came to their homes to collect.[48] With wider acceptance, however, came the need for tighter regulations and controls, and by the early 1900s this concern had reached a critical point.

The insurance industry in general went on trial in 1905. On 6 September a joint committee of the New York State legislature began a sensational public hearing which investigated insurance companies operating in the state. Dubbed the Armstrong Investigation, it resulted from the growing public demand for a thorough probe of the insurance industry, which had grown to undreamed-of size and wealth. Accusations of mismanagement, risky investments, and other malpractices and abuses were made frequently against the large companies. The hearings, chaired by New York State Senator William W. Armstrong, looked into alleged evils and abuses in the industry. Many of the top executives of the top companies appeared as witnesses, testifying about the procedures and practices of their firms. Out of these hearings emerged a picture of widespread business ineptitude, extravagance, and wastefulness among the top corporations.[49]

Insurance suffered a damaging blow in the eyes of the public. As a result of the Armstrong Investigation, however, steps were initiated to tighten state regulation of the industry, to limit investments and expenses, and in general to begin to eradicate the abuses that were uncovered. The Armstrong Committee offered no specific recommendations regarding the industrial segment of the industry but did call attention to the worst abuses. The hearings also prompted some states to take a closer look at practices within their jurisdictions. Throughout the country, according to Morton Keller, "a great new surge of state lawmaking followed on the heels of the Armstrong Investigation, and the already developing system of state insurance regulations gained strength from the events of 1905." In Georgia, legislation subjecting industrial companies to certain requirements preceded the Armstrong hearings by only a few weeks, when, in the summer of 1905, the state took steps to initiate a deposit requirement and to strengthen reporting and oversight activities regarding insurance.[50]

The 1905 regulation had an important impact on the Atlanta Benevolent Protective Association. In midsummer, just before the legislature's approval of the new insurance law, the association was reorganized under new management. As talk about the new regulation crystallized into reality, the Reverends Bryant and Hopkins realized that $5,000 was more capital than the association could secure. They also concluded that two busy ministers could no longer run a competitive business as a sideline. Acting promptly on the decision to sell the small enterprise, they agreed that Hopkins would seek a buyer. The organizers felt that the association should remain in the hands of African-Americans so Hopkins looked for potential purchasers only in the black community. He later wrote that "in the final meeting . . . [the organizers] placed all the assets of the company in my hands and asked me to sell it. When there were bids by white institutions, [we were] fully decided to let this institution remain as it began, a race institution."[51] The prosperous black entrepreneur Alonzo Herndon offered a splendid alternative to white purchasers. When Herndon was offered the chance to buy the business, he purchased its assets for $140 and began plans immediately for its reorganization as the Atlanta Mutual Insurance Association.[52]

On 6 September 1905, the same day the Armstrong Hearings convened in New York, the state of Georgia granted a charter to Atlanta Mutual. Thirteen days later, on 19 September, Herndon and Henry Lincoln Johnson, the noted black attorney, went before state officials and deposited $5,000 in bonds and other securities that Herndon had acquired with his personal funds. In an editorial on the event, the *Atlanta Independent* pointed out, "While the deposit was not compelled to be made under the law until January . . . the Atlanta Mutual thought it fair to offer its policyholders absolute protection from the start."[53] Raising $5,000 was not an easy task for any black insurance association, and for some it was impossible. Therefore, Herndon's prompt response to the new ruling in 1905 put Atlanta Mutual, the newest black association, in the front rank among enterprises in the state.

Alonzo Franklin Herndon, Founder and first President, 1905–27 (Courtesy of Atlanta Life Insurance Company)

In promoting Atlanta Mutual, Alonzo Herndon joined the long line of economic and religious leaders whose efforts helped advance the ideals of self-help and race independence. Although affected by the traditions established by Richard Allen, William Washington Browne, and many others, Herndon belonged to the group of black capitalists whose activities transformed mutual aid societies, church and secret societies, and other benevolent endeavors into more efficient secular operations. Influenced by Booker Washington and the movement to expand black business involvement, Herndon joined men like John Merrick and Samuel Rutherford in solidifying the new link between mutual aid and capitalism.

In view of some observers, Herndon's promotion of Atlanta Mutual confirmed his role as a race leader, especially in Atlanta and Georgia. For some, his timely placing of $5,000 on deposit distinguished him as "the savior of black enterprise." One contemporary described the event as "a critical hour," when Herndon "came forward to the help of the race and to the succor of the enterprise of his people. With the dollars he had accumulated by toil and sacrifice . . . he deposited $5,000 with the state and restored the confidence of the people. By that act he averted a crisis which might have swept all our race enterprises out of existence."[54]

These were high words of praise for the man and for his actions, but Herndon's effort had not saved every black enterprise, nor did his actions end the prevailing skepticism of black consumers. His purchase of the small association in no way reduced the competitive edge enjoyed by white firms in the state and region, which always maintained a larger share of policy sales in the black market and whose more powerful leadership allowed them to influence decision making in the state regarding insurance. Herndon did not possess any magic wand, and he would face numerous obstacles in reorganizing and running the company. Nevertheless, Herndon's sound judgment, ability, and money put him in the role of an angel for the new Atlanta Mutual Insurance Association, paving the way for the development of an important firm with far-reaching impact on the economic and entrepreneurial development of black America.

2

Alonzo Herndon:
Barber and Businessman

---

*Some of us sit around and wait for opportunity when it is
always with us.*
—Alonzo F. Herndon

People who knew Alonzo Franklin Herndon found him witty and gregarious. Samples of a seemingly inexhaustible supply of homespun philosophy and folksy tales flowed smoothly from his lips, and people genuinely liked to be with him. In conversations and meetings, he inevitably recounted some experience or story that imparted bits of the knowledge and wisdom he had acquired over the many years of his life from slavery to his position as the wealthy and respected head of the Atlanta Life Insurance Company. Another part of Herndon's personality showed an uncommon insight into the possibilities inherent in business opportunity. Although his formal training was limited, Herndon sometimes seemed to have a sixth sense for business, and he seldom missed a chance to expand his holdings whenever an opportunity arose.

Herndon's growing wealth and involvement in business ventures placed him among a group of progressive blacks in Atlanta. Most were only a few years removed from slavery when they began establishing businesses in the service and retail trades, which found a thriving market among white customers. As southern race relations worsened in the late nineteenth century, these individuals spearheaded movements to develop enterprises geared to the black market, especially cooperative endeavors aimed at promoting self-help and economic advancement among African-Americans.[1]

Alonzo Herndon, perhaps more than any other person in Atlanta, exemplified the goal of the black entrepreneurial class to blend ventures of racial self-help and independent business. In 1884, as a newcomer to the city, Herndon became involved in a number of cooperative endeavors. In one such venture, he worked with black mortician David T. Howard and several other men to establish the Southview Cemetery Association. Organized in 1885, it was the first stock-venture, privately owned cemetery for blacks in the city. He also joined Georgians Richard R. Wright and Wesley C. Redding in forming the Atlanta Loan and Trust Company in 1891 to provide loans for land and home purchases.[2]

People in Atlanta generally viewed Herndon as a man of great influence and power. His influence rested primarily on his money, his relationship with influential whites, and his involvement in cooperative, social, and civic endeavors. His character and personality also stood him in good stead with many blacks, and for some they were the most important traits upon which his influence was grounded. Atlantans frequently spoke of his honesty and willingness to deal fairly with people in business and otherwise. Added to these qualities was the unassuming manner and affability he displayed in his contacts with others, especially his pleasant disposition when people met him on his frequent strolls along Auburn Avenue. In short, Herndon was approachable, he seemed without guile or pretense, and people believed that he could be trusted. Such traits were considered very fine ones for the promoter of the Atlanta Mutual Insurance Association.

An early life of poverty motivated Herndon in his determination to grasp opportunity and turn it into success. Born on 26 June 1858 in Walton County, Georgia, near Social Circle, he spent seven and a half years of his life as a slave, and, in his own words, he "was very near it for twenty years more."[3] The son of a slave woman and a white man, Herndon grew up on a farm with his mother, Sophenie, a younger brother, Thomas, and his grandparents, Carter and Toma Herndon. When freedom came, his family, like so many newly emancipated blacks, was destitute with only "a corded bed and a few quilts" among their possessions. Barely eight years old, young Alonzo went to work to help earn money for the family, and at the age of thirteen he arranged to work full time as a farmhand at wages of $25 for the first year, $30 for the second, and $40 for the third. He spent his meager

spare time engaging in such entrepreneurial endeavors as selling pea-
nuts, peddling homemade molasses candy, and making axle grease
from burnt pine knots. All of his earnings, with the exception of a
small portion set aside as savings, went toward the support of his family. His savings, however, were earmarked for a specific purpose, for he
had decided early to get away from farm work and go to the city.[4]

At age twenty, Herndon left Walton County determined to improve
his economic condition. With $11 in his pockets, he walked to Cov-
ington, Georgia, where he stopped in a farming community called
Senoia. Once again, Herndon worked as a farmhand, supplementing
his meager pay by cutting hair on Saturday afternoons. He rented a little space in the town's black section and, with a pair of scissors and an
old-fashioned razor, began learning the barbering trade. After a few
months in Senoia, he migrated to Clayton County, where he opened
his first barbershop in the small town of Jonesboro, near Atlanta, em-
barking on a career that would eventually bring him fame and
fortune.[5]

Herndon developed a thriving business in Jonesboro, and his reputation as a barber spread rapidly. But he soon left Jonesboro, migrating
as far north as Rome and Chattanooga before settling in Atlanta in
early 1883. Once in Atlanta, he found work as a barber in a shop on
Marietta Street owned by Dougherty Hutchins, a black man who had
operated a barbering establishment since before the Civil War. Herndon's skill and reputation as an efficient and respectful barber spread
quickly among the white customers, and they began requesting his
chair. At the end of six months, he had acquired enough capital to purchase half interest in the shop, which was renamed Hutchins and
Herndon. From this time until well into the twentieth century, a
Herndon barbershop could always be found in the downtown business
section of Atlanta.[6]

As trade increased, Herndon expanded his barbering business, opening the first A. F. Herndon Barbershop on Whitehall Street in 1886. He
remained in this location for one year until the white owner of the
Markham House, then Atlanta's leading hotel, offered him space to re-
locate his shop. Catering to the hotel trade, Herndon operated a successful twelve-chair establishment until the hotel burned in 1896.
After the fire, he opened another barbershop in the Norcross Building
on the corner of Marietta and Peachtree streets. When a fire in 1902
damaged this shop, he moved to 66 Peachtree Street, where for many
years he operated one of the leading barbering establishments in the
city.[7]

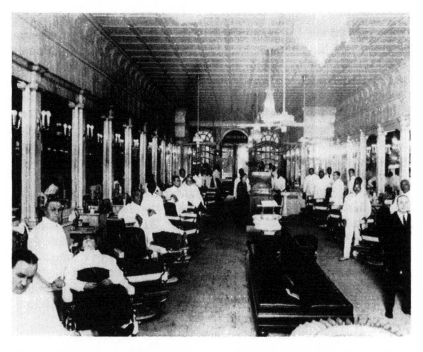

Herndon Barbershop at 66 Peachtree Street, Atlanta, Georgia (Courtesy of Herndon Foundation, Atlanta, Georgia)

A good businessman as well as a good barber, Herndon was proprietor of three shops by 1904. The largest and best equipped was the shop at 66 Peachtree Street. First opened in late 1902, the famed Herndon Barbershop was considered one of the finest barbershops in the country. Remodeled and enlarged in 1913, it was outfitted with chandeliers and elaborate gold mirrors and fittings which Herndon had purchased during his travels in the United States and Europe. He had also acquired architectural and decorating ideas in his travels which he incorporated into the remodeled shop. Measuring 24 by 102 feet, the Peachtree Street shop extended an entire block in length, boasted twenty-five chairs and eighteen baths with tubs and showers, had the finest furniture, fixtures, and equipment available, and was set off by handsome sixteen-foot front doors of solid mahogany and beveled plate glass which Herndon had copied from a pair he had seen on the Avenue de l'Opera in Paris.[8]

Herndon was immensely successful as a barber, becoming widely respected among his customers. According to newspaper reports, Herndon and his all-black barbering staff were "known from Richmond all the way to Mobile as the best barbers in the South."[9] Barbering, traditionally an area where black entrepreneurs could achieve success, was a service-oriented trade, which, like catering and tailoring, permitted the master-servant relationship to be maintained. During slavery, blacks had dominated such trades, and this tradition continued in freedom with many black businessmen and women operating successful establishments that served white patrons exclusively.[10]

Because of their economic status and extensive acquaintances with whites, barbers were usually well-respected figures in the black community. Herndon was not an exception in Atlanta. Indeed, some Atlantans viewed him as the "king of boss barbers."[11] His shop at 66 Peachtree Street served an all-white clientele made up of some of the state's leading judges, lawyers, politicians, ministers, and businessmen. As proprietor, Herndon saw personally to the tonsorial services provided to some of the most important figures in the state, earning their acquaintance and goodwill.[12]

Not unexpectedly, Herndon sometimes experienced the envy and resentment of white competitors who attempted to drive him out of business either by violence or legal maneuvers. A 1906 report on the vicious race riot in Atlanta indicated that "the finest shop in the whole country had the glass front smashed because the owner [Herndon] was colored." Moreover, as "racial violence exploded during the riot, four of the barbers in the shop were shot and a bootblack was kicked to death." It was widely believed in Atlanta that the violence inflicted upon the black barbers was carried out by white barbers who used the riot as a cover to destroy their black competitors.[13] In 1926 Herndon's barbering business was again threatened by a bill passed by the Atlanta City Council, which prohibited black barbers from serving white customers, especially women and children. Herndon's position in the community and the commitment of some whites to maintaining the Negro barbershop as part of the southern tradition led to support for his efforts to have the ordinance repealed.[14]

Barbering was only the initial source of Herndon's eventual fortune. Thrifty, smart, and, many believed, well advised by some of the white customers in his barbershop, he invested some of his earnings from the barbering business in real estate, acquiring some valuable property. He purchased his first piece of property in the early 1880s and continued adding to his holdings until he eventually owned more than one hundred houses, a large block of commercial property on Auburn Avenue, and a large estate in Tavares, Florida. Just before the depression set in during the 1920s, Herndon shrewdly sold his Florida property, with the exception of the family's winter home.[15] Property acquisitions such as the Auburn commercial block and the Florida deal greatly boosted his fortune over the years. At Herndon's death in 1927, the value of the real estate he owned was assessed at $324,107. Herndon was considered the wealthiest black man in Atlanta; his entire estate was worth more than one-half million dollars.[16]

Besides his wealth, Herndon's prominence was enhanced by his family and community life. On 31 October 1893, he married a beautiful and cultured graduate of Atlanta University. His bride, the former Adrienne Elizabeth McNeil, was born in Augusta, Georgia, on 22 July 1869. As a child, she moved to Savannah with her family, where she attended public schools. In 1886, at the age of seventeen, she entered Atlanta University, where she continued to pursue her studies, excelling particularly in dramatics. Graduating in 1891, she entered the teaching profession.[17]

Adrienne Herndon spent most of her professional career as a teacher, devoting herself to the education of black youth in Georgia. In 1891, with fellow Atlanta University alumnus Richard R. Wright, she began her work in education, teaching for four months as a member of the first faculty of what was then referred to as the black branch of the University of Georgia, which opened for a summer's session in Athens before its formal establishment as the State College of Industry for Colored Youth in Savannah (formerly Georgia College for Negroes and presently Savannah State College).[18] At the end of the appointment, she returned to Atlanta and, following her marriage to Alonzo Herndon, taught for two years in the Gray Street Public School. In the fall of 1895, she returned to her alma mater, where she and Professor George Alexander Towns became the first black faculty members at Atlanta University.

Adrienne Herndon had a far-reaching impact on her husband, introducing him to culture, refinement, and education. Adrienne, beautiful, sylphlike, and slight in stature, became acquainted with the courtly young mulatto barber while she was a boarder in the home of the grandmother of Walter White (who later became executive secretary of the National Association for the Advancement of Colored People [NAACP]). When Herndon proposed marriage, she accepted on the condition that she could continue her training in dramatics in the

North.[19] Herndon apparently agreed to her condition, and before beginning her first year of teaching at Atlanta University, Mrs. Herndon spent the summer studying at the Boston School of Expression. She enrolled for several additional summers and completed the course of study during a winter's sabbatical in 1904.

Mrs. Herndon excelled in her studies and developed impressive skills as a dramatic artist. In Boston, her teachers quickly recognized her potential as an actress, informing her husband that "with the advantage of training she will make one of the greatest platform artists that is before the country today." School officials even suggested that if, after completing her studies in Boston, Mrs. Herndon went to London for her professional debut as a stage actress, she could return to America and "command almost any price for her services."[20] At the conclusion of her work in Boston, using the stage name of Anne Du Bignon, Mrs. Herndon gave a highly acclaimed one-woman public reading of Shakespeare's *Anthony and Cleopatra* in Boston's Steinert Hall in which she performed all twenty-two roles. According to the *Boston Daily Advertiser*, "the characterization of any one of [these] would have marked her as a mistress of the profession."[21]

The heady reviews notwithstanding, Mrs. Herndon did not travel to London for a professional debut. Despite her talent and training, she did not pursue a career on the stage or in film. Following the completion of studies in Boston, she returned to her family and to Atlanta University's Department of Elocution and Dramatic Arts, where her remarkable abilities as a teacher became evident in the excellent training she gave her students. In 1907 she spent another year studying in the North; this time she enrolled in the School of Dramatic Arts in New York City. As the crowning point of this period, in May 1908 she received the Belasco Gold Medal for excellence in expression. Throughout her studies, in Boston and in New York, Mrs. Herndon's racial background apparently went undetected, especially by the critics, who described her as "a beautiful Creole." In general, she received very high praise for her performances, and her vocal quality and expression were compared favorably to Sarah Bernhardt.[22] Indeed, W. E. B. Du Bois reported that Thomas Dixon, "in blissful ignorance of her Negro descent," once offered Mrs. Herndon the leading female role in *The Klansman*.[23]

Mrs. Herndon brought culture and refinement into the Herndon household. Their marriage broadly expanded Alonzo's horizons. At his wife's urging, they traveled in many regions of the United States. In 1900, on their first tour abroad, they traveled through Europe, going,

Mrs. Adrienne McNeil Herndon and son Norris, c. 1908 (Courtesy of Atlanta Life Insurance Company)

as Herndon wrote later, "from Paris across the Alps into Switzerland and down to Milan . . . enjoying some of the most beautiful scenery in all the world."[24] At home again, they enjoyed theater and other cultural events.

Herndon's formal education was expanded under his wife's tutoring for, as one biographer states, "It was Adrienne who filled the gaps in her husband's education."[25] Hampered by the evils of slavery and poverty, Herndon had been able to acquire only a few months of formal schooling. But he was an eager student, and with his wife's encouragement, he easily absorbed the skills and polish to enhance his public image and business position. In turn, he boasted of his wife's accomplishments and supported her efforts in teaching and in the theater.

The Herndons were a popular couple in Atlanta. In addition to her work at Atlanta University, Mrs. Herndon used her talents as an actress and dramaturge to enhance the cultural life of blacks in Atlanta and in other southern cities. She gave dramatic readings and recitals in Atlanta, usually performing at the university or the First Congregational Church. She also traveled to other cities to give dramatic performances for worthy social causes, appearing in Chattanooga to benefit the local public school libraries, in Augusta to benefit the Haines Institute, in her hometown of Savannah, and in several other locales in the region.[26] Through these efforts to carry dramatic entertainment beyond the university's walls, theater and other cultural activities reached the black community. Blacks were usually barred from attending theater and other cultural events in southern cities, and the performances by Mrs. Herndon filled an important cultural void.

The Herndons' involvement in the Atlanta community extended largely from their connection with Atlanta University. For the first two years of their marriage, the Herndons lived at 70 Ivy Street, close to the downtown business district. Following Mrs. Herndon's employment at Atlanta University, they moved into South Hall, the boys' dormitory on the campus of the university. Later, the couple and their only child, a son, Norris, who was born on 15 July 1897, resided in Bumstead Cottage at 169 Vine Street, which the unversity had built for its second president.

In these early years, as Mrs. Herndon pursued educational and career goals, the family had delayed building the grand home they planned to construct in Atlanta. As they traveled in America in these years and during their trip to Europe, Mrs. Herndon collected furnishings and objects to be displayed in the house. Their plans were interrupted by the Atlanta race riot of 1906. Faced with the violence and the devastation the riot had wreaked on Herndon's barbering business and the city in general, the Herndons, like some other Atlanta families, considered moving away permanently. In the immediate aftermath of the riot, the Herndons took Norris to the North, enrolling him temporarily in a school in Philadelphia while they returned to Atlanta. Mrs. Herndon's pessimism about the city, the South, and indeed, the country is reflected in a letter she wrote to Booker Washington following the 1906 riot: "The riot and the unsettled conditions here make us feel that we can never hope to have [a home] in this ungodly section. Some times I doubt if there is any spot in this country where one with Negro blood can plant a home free from prejudice scorn & molestation. The sanctity of the Negro home is to the majority (the vast majority) of the white race a thing unrecognized.[27]

As Atlanta recovered from the worst effects of the riot, Mrs. Herndon's pessimism apparently subsided, and she began planning a mag-

Herndon Family Home at 587 University Place, constructed in 1910 (Courtesy of Atlanta Life Insurance Company)

nificent new home for the family. Built adjacent to Atlanta University, overlooking the city from the west, the house she designed contained every comfort for the family as well as an elaborate setting for entertaining. The Herndons' new home promised to be one of Atlanta's showplaces. Among its unique features was a terraced roof garden where Mrs. Herndon planned to stage plays and to entertain university colleagues and her husband's business associates. Perhaps the showpiece of the mansion, however, was the magnificent frieze which she had placed in the library. Located near the ceiling, the frieze contained a series of panels depicting the life of Alonzo Herndon from slavery to freedom.

Unfortunately, just as work on the house neared completion, Mrs. Herndon became gravely ill. Her illness persisted for several months, and she was forced to give up her work at the university in February 1910. This was a tragic period for the family, and in March, just before the Herndons left for Philadelphia to consult with specialists, Mrs. Herndon commented poignantly to Mrs. Edward Twitchell Ware, wife of the university's president, "We have only just got ready to live, now I must die."[28] Shortly after returning from Philadelphia, Mrs. Herndon died of Addison's disease on 6 April 1910, only a week before the completion of the beautiful new mansion she had planned as the family's first real home.

Mrs. Herndon's untimely death brought to an end the promising career of an artist and teacher of unusual talent and ability. Her students and colleagues at the university were saddened at the loss of such an outstanding faculty member who had brought important recognition to the school. The Atlanta black community was distressed at the passing of one who was so important to the educational and cultural life of the city. The greatest loss, however, was experienced by her family. Her husband mourned deeply the loss of his spouse, and their son, now twelve years old, was distraught at the death of his mother.

Shortly after the funeral, Herndon and his son moved into the new home which his late wife had planned with such pride. For a while, Mrs. Herndon's mother lived with them and, along with a housekeeper, helped to care for Norris, who was now enrolled in the Normal Department of Atlanta University. Work in Atlanta Mutual and his barbering enterprises consumed the bulk of Herndon's time in the period immediately following his wife's death, but he did not neglect his duties as parent and devoted a great deal of time to Norris.

Although firm with his son, Herndon was a doting father and found it difficult to refuse Norris anything; he admitted to friends that he

Alonzo Franklin Herndon and son Norris, c. 1908 (Courtesy of Atlanta Life Insurance Company)

spoiled "everyone that I have anything to do with." He exhibited a fatherly pride in his young son's performance as a student. He was perhaps strictest with him in the matter of schoolwork, taking measures to ensure that Norris did not engage in too many activities that distracted him from his studies. Indeed, Norris was generally allowed to attend shows or other activities only on weekends. Herndon conferred with his son's teachers, however, who confirmed that attending shows was fine as long as they were "good and wholesome." On Sundays, Norris was often allowed to travel with the housekeeper to visit her family in a small community outside Atlanta or to attend the "big meetings" at her church when baptisms were held. Frequently, too, Herndon and his son took excursions to McDonough or Walton County to visit with family and friends.[29]

In 1912 the Herndon household once again became a full family unit. While visiting friends in Chicago, Herndon met Jessie Gillespie and began a courtship that ended with their marriage on 20 May. Following their marriage, the couple sailed to Europe for a honeymoon, taking Norris along to enjoy the sights and other intellectually broadening experiences of travel.[30] At the end of the European honeymoon, the Herndons returned to Atlanta and settled into their home on University Place.

As Herndon continued to develop his varied business interests in Atlanta, especially the expansion of Atlanta Mutual, the new Mrs. Herndon assumed the role of a wealthy matron. She became active in social clubs and community activities. In addition to membership in the exclusive Twelve Club, she became involved actively in social uplift organizations, working with the Phillis Wheatley YWCA and the Herndon Day Nursery. As in his first marriage, Herndon displayed an unusually progressive attitude toward the activities of his second wife. He believed she should occupy herself as she saw fit. Indeed, before their marriage he had indicated his awareness of and sensitivity to the change marriage would bring to her lifestyle. As a beautician, she had operated a shop with her sisters on West Madison Avenue in Chicago. In correspondence with the Gillespie sisters, he had indicated his willingness to "give her a business training . . . so as not to have a lonely life for her."[31] She apparently rejected the idea of an independent business career and, over the years, became the grande dame of Atlanta's black society, entertaining the black elite on numerous social and business occasions.

In addition to her social skills, Jessie Herndon's background included political and religious activism that made her an ideal partner for Alonzo. Born in 1872 in Milwaukee, Wisconsin, she was the daughter of Ezekiel Gillespie, a former Tennessee slave who became a civil rights figure, and Catherine Lucas Robinson Gillespie. Her parents were active in both politics and religion and were instrumental in establishing the African Methodist Episcopal Church in Wisconsin. When Ezekiel Gillespie was refused the right to vote in the gubernatorial election of 1865, he initiated a landmark test case for the state of Wisconsin, suing on the grounds that an 1849 suffrage referendum had made blacks eligible to vote. In *Gillespie* v. *Palmer*, as the case was known, the state supreme court of Wisconsin ruled unanimously in favor of Gillespie, and after April 1868 blacks went freely to the polls in that state.[32] This background coupled with experience in business placed Mrs. Herndon in good stead to influence and support her husband in his business and social life.

Like many other black leaders, the Herndons found that their growing wealth and their business and family positions brought a great deal of social responsibility. As a man of money and influence, Alonzo Herndon was looked to for leadership in any number of areas. He was acquainted with some of the leading black intellectual and political

Herndon Family—Alonzo Herndon, Mrs. Jessie Gillespie Herndon, and Norris Herndon
(Courtesy of Herndon Foundation, Atlanta, Georgia)

leaders in the country and participated in several organizations with national political or economic focus.

On a national level, between 1900 and 1905, Herndon met on several occasions with different groups to set agendas for black advancement. Although he did not view himself as a race leader or as having any particular expertise on race problems, he was deeply interested in the economic and social welfare of African-Americans. He seemed to be greatly influenced by the prevailing gospel of progress through hard work, thriftiness, and business activity. His conversations often echoed the ideas of black leaders such as Booker T. Washington, John Hope, Du Bois, and others who espoused business development as an important aspect of race progress. As race leaders, these men emphasized the significance of business ventures among blacks. They despaired at the growing poverty affecting so many African-Americans and were distressed because blacks remained at the bottom rung of the economic ladder. They were also disturbed by the exclusion of college-trained black men and women from the nation's businesses and industries. The black advocates of business development, taking cues from the success experienced by white capitalists and industrialists in the late nineteenth century, talked of creating economic structures to advance the position of the race and to gain a measure of acceptance and respect for blacks.[33]

The black leaders rejoiced that some blacks, hardly a generation removed from slavery, had already established successful enterprises. In 1899 Atlanta University, in its annual study of the condition of blacks, conducted an investigation to gauge the progress blacks had made in business and to determine the number and kind of existing businesses, to assess the amount of capital invested by blacks in business enterprises, and to analyze the impact of these enterprises on overall black economic development. The findings, reported at the Fourth Annual Atlanta University Conference to Study the Negro Problem, which convened in May 1899, indicated that blacks were largely a wage-earning class. The report emphasized that although blacks were developing the nation's resources, whites received the benefits of black labor. It pointed out further that blacks were losing their monopoly on the labor market as whites replaced them in many jobs. The report underscored the necessity for wage earners to turn a portion of their earnings into capital to provide employment of thousands of black workers. Concerns for race security and economic independence were also addressed, with the conferees lamenting the helplessness of a "race that cannot speak its mind through men whose capital can help harm those who would bring oppression."[34]

Based on these findings, the 1899 conference adopted resolutions encouraging blacks to enter business life in greater numbers and to patronize establishments conducted by African-Americans. The conference participants deemed it important to continue agitating in churches, schools, newspapers, and other media concerning the necessity for business careers for young people and to encourage savings and thriftiness so as to amass capital among blacks. Finally, the conferees recommended that business leagues be organized in various towns and hamlets and that these leagues be gradually federated into state and national organizations.[35]

The first steps toward forming business leagues were taken in Tuskegee. Although Du Bois had gathered data on black business efforts, he did not organize a federation. Du Bois failed to interest the Afro-American Council, of which he was head of the business bureau, in forming an organization of business leaders on the basis of the information gained through the 1899 conference. Rather, it was Booker T. Washington who issued a call in June 1900 for a meeting to be held in Boston on 23 and 24 August, "to organize what will be known as a National Negro Business League."[36] More than four hundred delegates from thirty-four states representing a variety of enterprises from bootblacking to banking attended the two-day conference in Parker Memorial Hall to share inspirational stories about their experiences, successes, and problems in business, as well as to describe how their enterprises were started and conducted. Washington was acknowledged as the pivotal figure and was elected president of the new organization.[37]

Alonzo Herndon was among the Atlanta delegates attending the founding meeting of the league. Records indicate that he did not make speeches or give testimonials regarding his own success in business. Herndon was not one to dwell publicly on his personal achievements, and he said little at the meeting.

Herndon reacted favorably, however, to the doctrines espoused by league promoters. Sometime later, in an address before the students and faculty at Tuskegee Institute, he emphasized the need to support business endeavors by blacks, extolling the possibilities within the group for amassing capital and providing job opportunities for youth. He also stressed the theme of self-help and talked about the need for patronage and business cooperation among blacks. Echoing the

Alonzo Herndon (*left*) with Booker T. Washington (*right*) and unidentified man in motorcade on Auburn Avenue, 1914 (Courtesy of the author)

league's theme, he told the audience, "My aim has been for several years to get as many of our people together to cooperate in business and along all lines as possible. If we wish to do anything of importance in a business way, we must have the cooperation of other people."[38]

Although Herndon apparently agreed with the league's philosophy, he did not regularly attend the annual meetings held in Chicago (1901), Richmond (1902), Nashville (1903), Indianapolis (1904), and New York (1905). Although Herndon assured league officials of his continuing interest in the organization, his failure to involve himself actively distressed the leaders, causing them to question his commitment. A comment in the margin of a letter Herndon wrote explaining his absence from one of the meetings says, "We have tried hard to get him [involved]."[39]

Herndon briefly attempted a second involvement in an effort to organize for race progress at the national level. When Du Bois called a meeting of selected black leaders from throughout the country to organize the Niagara Movement, Herndon was among the twenty-nine men who attended the founding meeting in July 1905 near Buffalo, New York.[40] Demonstrating his concern for progress among blacks in areas other than business, Herndon joined with representatives of the black "talented tenth" to found an organization aimed at arousing African-Americans to work toward general liberation.

Again, Herndon's involvement was brief. He came to the attention of Booker Washington and other Tuskegee officials, who vigorously attacked the Niagara Movement and its participants. They tied the movement to Monroe Trotter of the *Boston Guardian*, Washington's bitter foe, and to a general malice toward the Tuskegee forces. In an editorial in the *New York Age*, Emmett Scott named Alonzo Herndon as one of the "aides of Trotter." In a thinly veiled threat, Scott announced, "In the future we shall hold to a strict account those who have respect for Trotter and Trotterism."[41] Through contacts in Atlanta, Washington obtained information about supporters of the movement, including Herndon, J. Max Barber of the *Voice of the Negro*, George Alexander Towns of Atlanta University, and others, inquiring about the political and other involvements of these men.[42] Washington's supporters in Atlanta assured him that Du Bois and the others had not incited much interest in the Niagara Movement among the general population and that the "agitators" would soon lose stock.[43]

There is no evidence that the criticisms of influential people in Tuskegee or Atlanta dissuaded Herndon from participating further in

Alonzo Herndon (*third row, second from left*) and son Norris among delegation to first Niagara Conference in 1905 under leadership of W. E. B. Du Bois (*second row, second from right*) (Courtesy of Atlanta Life Insurance Company)

the Niagara Movement. He may have thought that the movement would not be well received in Atlanta. It is likely also that he was advised by conservative black and white friends to refrain from further involvement in an organization that forthrightly demanded social, political, and economic equality for blacks because of the potential effect of such action on his business dealings. Herndon was not heavily involved with the talented tenth, and he may not have understood the significance and timeliness of the Niagara Movement or identified fully with all of its aims and principles. The 1906 Atlanta riot had upset both his business and family life, and though Herndon probably shared the aims of the militant black leaders, he may have differed with them as to the appropriate methods or procedures for attaining the desired end.[44]

The breach with the Tuskegee forces was soon healed. Herndon's example of black entrepreneurship was important to the National Negro Business League, and his value to the organization was indicated by the efforts of Scott and others to draw him into an involvement with the league. Du Bois also continued to view Herndon as "a man of integrity and power." He clearly recognized Herndon's limitations in matters "of broad sympathies and knowledge of the world." Nevertheless, he respected Herndon's achievements and efforts to aid charities and provide opportunities for blacks at the local level. Du Bois described Herndon as "an extraordinary man [who] illustrates at once the possibilities of American democracy and the deviltry of color prejudice."[45]

In addition to his work at the national level, Herndon was also involved in the petition movement of Georgia blacks to foil the disfranchisement efforts of the Georgia legislature in 1907. During the extremely Negrophobic gubernatorial campaign in 1906, the issue of black disfranchisement came to the fore when some members of the Georgia legislature pushed for the legal elimination of the black vote. With the support of Tom Watson and other advocates of legal disfranchisement, Hoke Smith, a former secretary of the interior, won the governorship, and on 29 June 1907, in his inaugural address before the general assembly, he outlined a disfranchisement law designed to eliminate blacks from the political scene. Despite protests from blacks in the state urging the defeat of any disfranchisement scheme, by July the Felder-Williams Disfranchisement Amendment reached the floor of the general assembly.

Black leaders held mass meetings to protest this action and presented memorials to the legislature. Alonzo Herndon joined other black leaders in Atlanta, Augusta, Savannah, Macon, and other Georgia cities in signing an eleven-page memorial protesting the action of the legislature. Organized under five headings, the petition argued that disfranchisement was unnecessary, unjust, undemocratic, unconstitutional, and would have a morally degrading effect on black youth in the state. The protest, however, went largely unnoticed as the disfranchisement measure passed the Georgia Senate 37 to 6 and the House 159 to 16. The governor signed the bill on 21 August 1907, and in the general referendum the amendment carried by almost a two-to-one majority.[46] Herndon's protest against the measure along with Judson W. Lyons and Henry W. Rucker, two of Georgia's leading black politicians, and a host of other black leaders ranging from ministers to business and professional men indicated his stature and influence in the community as well as his progressive position on voting and disfranchisement.

Herndon's efforts to improve the social and economic status of blacks in Atlanta earned him great admiration and respect. Herndon tended to support "charities which he knew and . . . movements which he understood."[47] His business success permitted the Herndon family to maintain a vigorous philanthropic posture in the community. He gave financial support to local institutions and charities such as the YMCA, Atlanta University, the First Congregational Church, the Leonard Street, Carrie Steele, and Diana Pace orphanages, and the Herndon Day Nursery. Although he manifested generous support and zeal for all of these programs, it was the Leonard Street institution that perhaps claimed his greatest devotion. For some years, Herndon served actively as the chairman of the board of directors of the orphanage, and he provided funds to build a new facility for the young girls housed there.[48]

Although the Herndons lived within the relatively secure environs of Atlanta University, they were aware of and concerned about the poverty and suffering that engulfed much of the black community. When several Atlanta University Conference reports confirmed the dire need among black working mothers in the city for day nurseries and kindergartens, Herndon and his first wife joined with Mrs. John Hope, wife of the president of Morehouse College, and other progressive black women in organizing the Gate City Free Kindergarten Association in 1905. The Herndons took a deep interest in promoting the work of this organization and donated a building in one of the most deprived sections of the city for its work. In addition, they provided salary for a teacher and free milk for children attending the unit. As a tribute to their generosity, the facility was named the Herndon Day Nursery. Donations from the Herndons, it was said, "put the [Gate City] Association on a solid basis," and the family's unfailing support allowed the organization to continue its work for thirty years.[49]

Herndon was a steady supporter of the aims and causes of the First Congregational Church, of which he was a leading trustee and treasurer. The pastor, the Reverend Henry Hugh Proctor, pioneered in the development of innovative church programs to uplift and advance the black community. Called to the pastorate of First Congregational Church in 1894, he established a wide range of social ministries "that soon marked the church as one of the most progressive centers of Christian social actions in the nation." The programs included one of the earliest health centers to serve blacks in the city, a home for girls, a community gymnasium for males, an employment bureau, and a temperance society. Reflecting its interest in the welfare of all groups, the church also operated a prison mission.[50] A zealous promoter of church ministries to support community welfare, Proctor joined in the criticism of the early insurance associations, believing them to be "greatly overdone and [a] hinder to thrift and benevolence." In Proctor's opinion, "the church could in many ways do away with the necessity of so many of these societies."[51]

Herndon manifested a good deal of interest and support for these church programs. As treasurer of the church, he was close to its ministries, and he frequently augmented support of one or another of the causes through his private benevolence, giving several hundreds of dollars annually to civic organizations and groups.[52] When the First Congregational Church curtailed and eventually discontinued many of its programs in the 1920s, Herndon continued his private support of a few of them. One may surmise that Herndon's promotion of Atlanta Mutual stemmed from his philosophical connections with Proctor and First Church.[53]

It was for his involvement in and support of local endeavors for charitable, cultural, and economic uplift that Herndon gained a reputation among blacks in Atlanta. Widely admired for his thriftiness and business acumen, he was considered a leader in business and uplift activities in the city. As an employer of more than fifty black men in his barbering establishments, as supporter of day nurseries and orphan homes, and as promoter of black involvement in various cooperative endeavors to advance the race, Herndon was viewed as providing an important avenue of self-help for blacks. Black Atlantans perceived Herndon to be "a race man without playing up the fact . . . or discussing the race problem." In describing Herndon's attributes of racial leadership, the *Atlanta Independent* noted: "He has sought to prove his faith in his people by providing opportunities for them in home and education for their families that they may find useful and profitable employment. He thinks he can do the race more good by creating jobs for them and furnishing them opportunities to help themselves than by discussing the race problem."[54]

In July 1905, Alonzo Herndon had not yet reached the pinnacle of success, wealth, or power, but he enjoyed a stable position in Atlanta. Rising from slave origins, he had earned the respect and admiration of large numbers of people, including some of the most reputable whites and blacks in the state. He was hardworking and thrifty, his assets were expanding rapidly. He owned a good deal of urban real estate, much of it commercial property along Auburn Avenue. His interest in promoting local business and civic enterprise had been demonstrated. He and his wife were well-known supporters of educational and cultural advancement in the community. At her urging, they had traveled widely, visiting Europe and enjoying numerous cultural pursuits. His formal education, which because of slavery and a poverty-ridden childhood totaled less than one year, was expanding as he absorbed knowledge and skills through these experiences.[55] Herndon participated in a number of local efforts to advance blacks economically and socially.

Herndon enjoyed a good reputation in Atlanta. His associates could find little to criticize about his business or personal character and habits. He was held in wide esteem by Atlantans, who praised his business acumen and willingness to support opportunities to advance African-Americans. Even *Atlanta Independent* editor Ben Davis, though admitting no personal liking for Herndon, praised his interest and success in providing economic opportunities for blacks.[56]

Following overtures by the Reverends Bryant and Hopkins in July 1905, Herndon purchased the Atlanta Benevolent Protective Association. This deal represented an entirely new venture for the longtime barber and investor in real estate, but few people doubted his ability to mobilize the necessary resources and personnel to promote the enterprise effectively. In taking over the business, however, Herndon made no secret of the fact that barbering was his first love and for many years he remained actively engaged in his barbering business. Nevertheless, he stepped into the new business determined to "make good [this] opportunity."[57]

3

Faith in the Enterprise

If I thought that anything with which I was connected would
always be small, I would not want to be in it.
—Alonzo F. Herndon

Herndon was a shrewd and successful entrepreneur as evidenced by his sizable personal fortune and the success he achieved in business. But he had very little knowledge, if any, about insurance. Nor could he devote a great deal of time to learning the business because of other demands on his time and energy. Indeed, few African-Americans possessed any skills in the technical requirements of insurance work because opportunities for blacks to train or to engage in apprenticeships with soundly managed firms seldom arose. Nevertheless, Herndon viewed his investment in Atlanta Mutual as an opportunity to play a part in building a reliable enterprise that would provide an important service to blacks and advance the community economically.

From the outset, Herndon's personal reputation as an honest, self-made man was the organization's strongest feature. Too often black families had been cheated by insurance groups that promised big benefits only to find numerous loopholes to avoid paying claims or to have someone abscond with the organization's funds. For many prospective policyholders, Herndon's personal backing meant more than the $5,000 he had placed with state officials. Some years later, Ben Davis, the controversial editor of the *Atlanta Independent*, put the matter succinctly: "When the people buy a policy in Atlanta Life they are buying Alonzo Herndon."[1] Robert W. Chamblee, a former agent, direc-

43

tor, and home office executive, agreed, noting that in the early days "that's about all we had to sell—his name."[2] In 1905, then, with little more than his reputation and the goodwill of the public, Herndon undertook a new business opportunity developing Atlanta Mutual.

By July 1905 the sale of the Atlanta Benevolent Protective Association to Herndon was complete. Articles and advertisements began appearing in the local black paper calling attention to the enterprise's new ownership and setting forth its operating procedures, indicating that sick and accident claims would be paid at the end of each week. Death claims would be paid to beneficiaries as soon as notification reached the association's office. Although the association did not intend to pay every claim filed regardless of its merit, it announced the intention "to establish and maintain the policy with its policyholders of investigating reasons why a sick or accident claim should be paid, instead of digging up some loopholes to slip out."[3] These ads, however, appeared in only two or three editions of the *Atlanta Independent*, for plans were soon under way to reorganize the enterprise and expand its operations into other areas of the state.

The plans for reorganization went into effect swiftly. In August, Alonzo F. Herndon, John H. Crew, Monroe W. Woodall, Wade Aderhold, and William H. Jackson petitioned the state for a charter to operate the Atlanta Mutual Insurance Association.[4] This new enterprise resulted from a merger of the Atlanta Benevolent and Protective Association with two other small insurance organizations, the Royal Mutual Insurance Association and the National Laborers' Protective Union. Like Bryant and Hopkins, the men associated with the latter two groups recognized their inability to raise $5,000 to meet the state's deposit requirement, and they joined forces to organize a stronger enterprise. Alonzo Herndon, Wade Aderhold, John Crew, W. L. G. Pounds, and Edward Howell formed a five-man board of directors to oversee the new association.[5]

Although a newcomer to the insurance business, Herndon assumed the presidency of the new enterprise. Among the members of the newly formed board of directors were men who had acquired some knowledge of the fundamentals of operating an insurance company. Wade Aaron Aderhold had worked for the Union Mutual Relief Association, the first chartered insurance association organized by blacks in Georgia, for a number of years and was reputed to be proficient in the trade. Aderhold was a self-taught insurance wizard, and much of the business done by Union Mutual was credited to his knowledge of insurance and organizational skills. Herndon wanted the most astute persons available, and he brought Aderhold into the new organization as first vice-president and treasurer. On 23 September, the *Atlanta Independent* reported that Aderhold would have "entire control as treasurer of the financial end of the concern." Furthermore, the paper announced, "he will be the personal representative and confidential man of the president whose interest in other concerns will prevent him from personally conducting the insurance office."[6]

In John Crew, Atlanta Mutual gained another of the individuals known as "founders of Negro insurance in the South." By the time Crew affiliated with the new enterprise in 1905, he had already spent more than ten years in insurance work among blacks, having worked with the Reverend Thomas Walker in organizing Union Mutual in Atlanta in 1897. When he joined Atlanta Mutual, he assumed the position of secretary and general manager with major responsibility for overseeing the operation.[7]

In the remaining board members, W. L. G. Pounds and Edward Howell, the enterprise gained men with rudimentary knowledge of insurance. Pounds had founded and managed the Royal Benevolent Insurance Association and was named second vice-president in the Herndon organization. As head of the National Laborers' Protective Union, Howell had also acquired some insurance training, and his experiences were put to use as assistant general manager of Atlanta Mutual. Henry Lincoln Johnson, recorder of deeds for the District of Columbia and one of the ablest black lawyers in the country, acted as attorney for the company.[8]

With the reorganization completed and a new charter in hand, Atlanta Mutual's next move was to find more suitable quarters than the one-room office the association had occupied in the Rucker Building. The office equipment, consisting of an old typewriter, two second-hand desks, one table, several badly worn chairs, and a few writing instruments, was also outdated and inadequate. Within a few weeks, the company had set up a new office a few blocks away at 202 Auburn Avenue in a building owned by Herndon.[9]

Atlanta Mutual seemed almost ready to launch a thriving new business, but before it could begin full operation it was necessary to expand the field and office staff beyond the three agents and one clerk employed by the old Atlanta Benevolent Protective Association and to find competent men and women to act as solicitors.[10] This was not an easy task, for few African-Americans possessed even the basic skills needed to sell insurance. Nonetheless, between 19 September and 31 December 1905, President Herndon and his associates hired agents throughout the state, covering territory from Rome in the north to Bainbridge in the south. The company experienced a great deal of success in the soliciting end of the business, and the weekly earnings increased quickly from the $40 debit brought over from the old association. As of 31 December, Atlanta Mutual's insurance in force in the state amounted to $180,962 with 6,324 policyholders.[11]

Much of this remarkable growth after only a few months can be attributed to one of the early developmental strategies employed by the company. An important characteristic of the period involved expansion through the acquisition of other small associations. Herndon and the other officers began with the idea that one strong, reliable firm with ample assets to protect the investments of black policyholders would be more profitable and beneficial to the community than a dozen or more smaller, less efficient organizations. Beginning with a core of three small associations, Atlanta Mutual expanded gradually by acquiring several other struggling enterprises. In December 1905 it reinsured the Empire Industrial Insurance Association, an organization formerly headed by two African Methodist Episcopal churchmen, Bishop Joseph S. Flipper and the Reverend H. N. Newsome. By the end of 1907, Atlanta Mutual had also acquired the Metropolitan Mutual Benefit Association and the Great Southern Home Industrial Association. The latter was among the fifteen firms that met the state's deposit requirement but later found it expedient to turn over its policyholders to Atlanta Mutual. By taking over these weaker competitors, the directors of Atlanta Mutual hoped to strengthen the enterprise and, at the same time, build confidence in insurance firms operated by African-Americans by saving the business of the less stable groups.[12]

Reinsurance deals made for great advertising for Atlanta Mutual, and the firm quickly gained the public's confidence. In addition, the officers made an appeal to black pride, urging that the race support a race institution. In advertisements and other contacts with the public, they seldom failed to mention the number of black men and women the company employed. The company highlighted particularly the splendid opportunity it provided for college men to earn money during the summers by working as agents and the unique chance it afforded young women to work in a business environment as typists, clerks, and cashiers. The public relations strategy also included a heavy emphasis on the company's early motto, "An Honest Account of Every Dollar Collected," stressing the integrity of the principals and the honest business practices in relations with policyholders and the general public. Herndon and the other officials showed clearly their real-ization that in the company's infancy, at least, the chief asset was the goodwill of the people.[13]

Despite the firm's apparent success, difficulties occurred in the early years which taxed the ingenuity and spirit of company person-nel. In spite of favorable publicity, the sterling reputation of the foun-der, and the unusual experience of the firm's managers, the ultimate success of the insurance enterprise rested with the agents. It was es-sential that Atlanta Mutual develop an agency force capable of in-creasing policy sales and maintaining good debits. Outlining a series of districts within the state, the company hired special agents and sent them to organize sales in various locales. These agents opened of-fices in the more populous areas and began hiring solicitors to work in the districts. Working under the direct supervision of the special agent, the solicitors went into homes and churches in the cities and hinterlands of the state offering Atlanta Mutual policies.

The agents worked on a commission basis, retaining the application fee from each policy and 20 percent of their weekly collection or deb-its.[14] An agent hired to work in the Gainesville, Georgia, district around 1908 recalled his early compensation arrangements: "I re-ceived as an agent my first premium, which we called the application fee. . . . If it was a five cents policy . . . I got the first premium, the first five cents. Then on the debit . . . [I] got 20 percent of collections." After advancing from the position of agent to supervisor of the district, which encompassed much of northeast Georgia, the agent continued to receive the commission, which was supplemented by a salary of $78 a year in 1911.[15]

Even with the employment of special men, agents, and supervisors, problems plagued the production end of the business. One constant source of worry was the inexperience of the agents. Untrained in the insurance business, most agents did not have even rudimentary skills or knowledge of the techniques of insurance sales. They could not keep good records or select good risks and were apt to make huge blunders in their efforts to develop new business and bolster their earnings. Good sales techniques were practically nonexistent. In some cases, inexperience and a clumsy sales approach were the lesser of the evils as dishonest agents sometimes attempted to defraud the com-pany and the policyholders. The policyholders were another frequent source of despair as many tended to allow their policies to lapse either because of their penurious financial condition or dwindling confi-dence in black insurance. This situation doubled the efforts of agents, who were required to visit the lapsed policyholders and repeat the task of trying to convince them of the value of carrying an Atlanta Mutual policy.

Another problem related to the general racial spirit of the South and the social milieu of the Georgia communities in which the agents operated. Travel between rural towns was often a precarious experience for black insurance agents. Rail travel was both uncomfortable and undignified because they were forced to wait in filthy Jim Crow waiting rooms and to ride in dirty, overcrowded Jim Crow coaches. They frequently met with cold and curious stares from whites unaccustomed to the sight of black men with business intentions. Upon finally arriving at his destination, the agent usually found hotels for blacks to be nonexistent or, when available, intolerable. In many of the rural towns and backwoods communities, where the insurance agent was viewed as atypical of the stereotyped black man and therefore a threat to the status quo, whites sometimes forbade agents to solicit on their property, refused them business licenses, or even ran them out of town.

Even when allowed to engage in business among blacks in the community, insurance agents encountered many humiliations and restrictions. Fearing the antagonism of local whites, blacks sometimes refused to be seen talking to black insurance agents.[16] As they traveled about the state, a number of agents witnessed lynchings and other acts of violence, although none of Atlanta Mutual's agents were lynched or suffered serious physical harm. Recalling the repressive atmosphere in some areas, a former agent explained that "in a number of places they did have a lot of trouble," adding that "every time you pick[ed] up a paper every week there was one, two or three lynchings. Many of those lynchings . . . were framed up. The courts were built up for white men and not for Negroes. Did not allow a Negro to dispute a white man's word. . . . Agents had to be careful."[17]

Atlanta Mutual initiated business in an era characterized by a serious deterioration in southern race relations as white supremacy propaganda raised race hatred to a dangerous level. Indeed, 1906, the company's first full year of operation, was one of the worst in the history of race relations in the state. Lawlessness prevailed in many communities as lynch law, becoming increasingly a southern and racial phenomenon, "took a savage toll of Negro life."[18] Not fully satisfied with the results of the white primary, which effectively eliminated black voting power, southern extremist politicians were obsessed with maintaining white supremacy at all costs and led vituperative

campaigns against blacks, urging their disfranchisement by state law.
The 1906 Georgia gubernatorial election highlighted the level to
which racial hatred had risen as both candidates engaged in race-bait-
ing tactics. The campaign exacerbated the already deteriorating race
relations, and Hoke Smith's election portended even greater racial
polarization.[19]

In Atlanta, the election was followed by an outbreak of mob violence, which gripped the city for four days near the end of September
1906. Blacks were murdered and maimed, and their homes and businesses were destroyed as white mobs carried out senseless acts of fury
and terrorism. In blind hatred the mob recognized no distinctions of
character and class among blacks in carrying out its violence and attacked workers, entrepreneurs in their establishments, and idlers
alike. Some observers believed that the frustration of white groups at
their inability to halt the growing examples of progress and upward
mobility exhibited by a large number of prosperous blacks in the city
had been one cause of the riot and that these whites used the upheaval
as a pretext to destroy what some viewed as "the eyesore of black
achievement." Among certain blacks, the leading opinion was that the
mob's chief aim and command had been to "humiliate the progressive
Negro." As a consequence of the riot, a number of progressive blacks
considered leaving Atlanta and the South, and though many eventually found the fortitude to stay in the city, some, like Jesse Max Barber
of the *Voice of the Negro*, left for other regions.[20] Clearly, the spirit of
multiracial cooperation and harmonious relations, so well publicized
in the 1960s, did not exist in Atlanta in the early years of the century.

Racial animosity also caused death and destruction in rural regions
of the state. After 1900 lynchings in Georgia defied the national pattern as more blacks died at the hands of lynch mobs between 1900 and
1920 than in the previous two decades. Determined to keep African-
Americans in virtual peonage and total subservience, whites permitted no threats to the system of white domination and tolerated no
breach in racial etiquette as ordained by their group. To maintain tight
control over blacks, whites frequently attempted to suppress examples
of black uplift and progress. In 1907, for example, black secret societies
became the object of white enmity in Georgia. Representative E. H.
McMichael of Marion County introduced a bill in the General Assembly requiring all secret societies in the state to obtain a license upon
payment of a bond ranging from $5,000 to $20,000. Vilifying the purposes of such organizations, McMichael emphasized the harm done
by black lodges, which he described as being made up of "a few mean

rascals who think themselves leaders of their race . . . and organize the innocent, satisfied Negroes into secret societies."[21] The very existence of lodges with secret doctrines, rituals, and closed-door meetings among blacks incensed whites, and wild rumors circulated in some rural districts of the subversive activities of "Be-Fo-Day Clubs," which plotted to kill whites, fix wages, and plan boycotts. Whites responded violently to such perceived threats, and in Early County alone, seven black lodges were dynamited in one week, representing a pattern of violence that extended to black schools and churches in that county.[22]

In this atmosphere, black insurance agents walked on the proverbial eggshells, a feat that sometimes required extraordinary wisdom and deft manners. Only time and the steadfastness of individuals and groups working to achieve first-class citizenship for African-Americans would remedy the worst of the problems, but most agents learned to accommodate the situation in Georgia's cities and rural communities and built debits in these places. Assessing this period in a 1940 report, a company officer found a rainbow in the early storm and concluded that although "the early years were filled with hardships and trials of many kinds and descriptions . . . after all is said and done, these hardships and trials were but stepping stones. . . . They taught by experience many problems that it was not given to learn through access to schools and colleges having to do with business." Conditions were made bearable as agents found homes where they arranged to stop overnight and restaurants that served tolerable food. Anxious to perform well in a new business endeavor, the black agents stayed in the field and worked diligently to make a living. As one agent recalled, "We stayed out there . . . and got a lot of enjoyment out of it, a lot of pleasure, met a whole lot of fine people, [and] maintained a friendship with them for a long time."[23]

By 1909, after four full years of operation, there were clear signs that Atlanta Mutual was indeed weathering the storms of bigotry and financial woes which had forced many small black companies into bankruptcy and absorption by healthier firms. As the agents' experience and level of proficiency increased, aided by rudimentary training in salesmanship and techniques of selecting good risks and record keeping provided by supervisors and special agents, the company showed a modest growth in policy sales and amount of insurance in force during the 1905–9 period. And, though the number of lapsed policies was a major hindrance to growth in the early years (see Table 3.1),

Table 3.1. Growth of Business in Force, 31 December 1905–31 December 1909

Policies	Number	Insurance in force
In Force 31 December 1905	6,324	$180,962
1906		
Written during year	14,791	421,373
Ceased to be in force	5,764	211,292
In Force, 31 December	15,351	390,043
1907		
Written during year	12,829	334,284
Ceased to be in force	9,359	258,419
In force, 31 December	18,821	465,908
1908		
Written during year	14,487	360,000
Ceased to be in force	14,700	356,068
In force, 31 December	18,608	469,840
1909		
Written during year	24,817	605,580
Ceased to be in force	21,193	514,316
In force, 31 December	23,304	567,904

Source: *Report of the Insurance Department of the Comptroller-General's Office, 1905–9.* According to the law of 16 August 1909, "the amount of insurance in force shall be estimated by adding to the amount payable under any policy as a death benefit, the amount of one week's sick or accident benefits payable under said policy."

the firm's annual report showed nearly $600,000 of insurance in force on 31 December 1909.

Atlanta Mutual experienced several changes in management during its early years. After incorporating the firm, Herndon depended largely on Crew and Aderhold to run the enterprise. In June 1907, however, John Crew resigned as secretary and general manager, and his duties were assumed by Wade Aderhold. For over a year, Aderhold ran the day-to-day operations of the company almost single-handedly, fulfilling his own responsibilities as well as carrying on the duties of secretary and general manager. In the fall of 1908, Aderhold announced his departure from Atlanta Mutual. The loss of both men at the home office was compensated by the promotion of Edward Howell to secretary, and Herndon himself spent more time in the enterprise, taking over as general manager in 1908.[24]

One of the earliest issues confronting the new home office team of Herndon and Howell concerned the insurance law enacted in August 1909. The Georgia General Assembly approved additional regulatory legislation fixing the amount of solvent assets that each mutual aid association, benefit society, or industrial insurance company was required to maintain as a policy reserve indicating that after 1 January 1910 these companies must at all times have solvent assets equal to $1.50 for each $100 of insurance in force.[25] For industrial companies such as Atlanta Mutual, estimates of the amount of insurance in force were made by adding the total amount of death benefits and the amount of one week's sick or accident benefits payable under each policy. The law deemed 1.5 percent of this sum a sufficient cash reserve or amount of net solvent assets for a company to maintain to meet expected obligations. The new legislation was not especially burdensome for Atlanta Mutual because the company set aside the required reserve fund and until 1922 always kept a surplus of reserves ranging from $5,127 in 1911 to $25,204 in 1921 (see Table 3.2).

Table 3.2.   Net Solvent Assets of Atlanta Mutual, 1911–1921*

Year	Insurance in force	Net solvent assets	Surplus	Assets plus surplus
1911	$ 389,327	$ 5,839	$ 5,127	$ 10,967
1912	472,740	7,091	6,455	13,546
1915	1,200,549	18,008	17,294	35,303
1916	1,377,775	20,667	24,650	70,317
1917	1,235,318	18,530	27,070	70,600
1918	2,325,124	33,527	13,784	72,311
1919	4,523,723	67,855	42,840	135,696
1920	7,592,816	113,892	10,256	149,148
1921	9,464,493	141,967	25,204	192,171

Source: Report of the Insurance Commissioner of the Comptroller-General's Office, 1911–21; Examination of Atlanta Mutual Insurance Company; 1 January 1917–31 December 1919, 1920–21, in ALCF.

*Data for 1913–14 not available.

With the 1909 legislation also came closer scrutiny of firms by the insurance commissioner. The new law made industrial companies subject to an examination by an independent actuary at the order of the commissioner. William A. Wright, Georgia's insurance commissioner, had long pressed the legislature to enact a law that would force insurance companies to adhere to more diligent bookkeeping practices and hold them to a stricter accountability for management aspects. The passage of the new legislation in the summer of 1909 signaled all industrial companies to begin adhering to sounder business practices.[26]

Atlanta Mutual's books were in excellent shape, although a technicality arose concerning the management end, and Herndon was advised to adhere strictly to the insurance regulation. Because it was a mutual company, the policyholders theoretically owned Atlanta Mutual and ultimately controlled its management. In practice, they had not been consulted regarding any aspect of company operations during its entire existence. Therefore, at the behest of Commissioner Wright, Herndon convened the first meeting of the policyholders in May 1910. At this time, a board of directors was elected composed of Herndon, Edward Howell, Charles A. Faison, Edgar S. Jones, and Solomon E. Pace. The directors, the latter three of whom were barbers, in turn elected Herndon to the position of president-treasurer and Howell as secretary-auditor. Faison, a business partner of Herndon and Faison, a downtown barbershop, became first vice-president.[27]

Atlanta Mutual thus acquired its first board of directors duly elected by the policyholders in the company's five-year history. The number of policyholders attending the meeting was not indicated by even the *Atlanta Independent*, which usually reported such details, and it is therefore difficult to know how seriously the meeting was viewed by any of the parties involved. With no other recourse for addressing what was probably an action precipitated by more powerful competitors, or at least an unfairly administered regulation, it is likely that this action was merely a perfunctory response to the commissioner's requirement.[28] Nevertheless, the convening of this session illustrated the company's early attempts to comply with state regulations of the industry.

Another section of the 1909 Insurance Act held significance for Atlanta Mutual. The legislation authorized an insurance company to raise a guaranty fund for the purpose of paying operating expenses, making deposits that might be required by state agencies, or promoting the company.[29] Pursuant to this provision, the board took steps to begin repaying the money Herndon had put into the company in its first years. In addition to the initial $5,000 which he had advanced to make the state-required deposit, Herndon had used personal funds from time to time over the years to pay expenses. In 1910 the amount of the company's indebtedness to him was around $12,000. As permitted by the 1909 legislation, the board issued certificates in denominations of $100, which Herndon, as bearer, could redeem at the rate of $1,000 per year with interest at the high rate of 8 percent. Within seven months, the company was able to use its profits to begin retiring the certificates. Herndon was now finally able to get out of the firm the money he had put into it. The repayment of these loans reaffirmed Herndon's early belief in the enterprise, which, he had expressed confidently, "would grow old and become strong and would be able to reimburse me for all the aid I afforded it, when it was not able to care for itself."[30]

With regulatory and fiscal matters settled, the company turned its attention to other concerns. The first five years had been characterized by efforts to put Atlanta Mutual into full operation across the state, ensure its compliance with state laws and official requirements, and, in general, to make it a substantial business entity that was trusted and respected by the population it served. In 1910 a movement began to expand the business beyond Georgia. In early January, Herndon conferred with Howell on the matter of entering the adjoining state of Alabama. On 7 January, the two men drew up a contract which called for Howell to resign his position as secretary and to assume a new assignment as manager of operations in Alabama. At its May meeting, the board ratified the agreement, and by the end of the year Herndon reported with pride in his quarterly review to the board that "Secretary Howell was marching forward in Alabama and would soon cross the line."[31]

By the end of its first year of business in Alabama the insurance in force amounted to $71,692. The company enjoyed particular success in the prosperous urban area around Birmingham, but business lagged throughout the state until the early 1920s. One reason for the sluggish sales may have been that Howell's relations with the home office became sour, and he was fired amid charges of taking business from Atlanta Mutual and into another insurance society which he had organized. Herndon canceled Howell's contract on 11 October 1911 and paid him $3,220 for his work in developing business in Alabama. In retaliation, Howell brought suit in the Alabama courts seeking to enjoin Atlanta Mutual from operating in the state. Howell's efforts failed, but the matter was not settled until June 1917, when the Alabama State Supreme Court ruled in favor of Atlanta Mutual.[32] Meanwhile, James Tunno Harrison had been dispatched to Alabama and given the task of reclaiming policies and stabilizing business there.

When Howell left the home office for Alabama, his duties as company secretary had been assumed by Truman Kella Gibson, a young Harvard-educated man working as an agent with Atlanta Mutual. Born in August 1882, Gibson grew up in Macon, Georgia, where he attended Ballard Normal School. Coming to Atlanta around 1900, he entered Atlanta University. When he graduated in 1905, he decided to continue his education and entered Harvard College, where he studied for two years. Following his graduation in 1908, he worked as a teacher in Lawrenceville, Virginia, for two years. A former teacher persuaded him to enter the field of insurance, and in 1910 he became an agent with Atlanta Mutual. Gibson's education made him a logical choice for an executive position, and he was quickly tapped for the position of secretary. He worked closely with Herndon, and the two men continued to look for ways to expand the company from its Georgia base.[33]

The attention of the Atlanta Mutual officers soon shifted to Kentucky, where yet another benevolent society was struggling to survive. Henry E. Hall, a native Kentuckian and a graduate of Hampton Institute, organized the National Benevolent Union in 1904 following the departure from the state of a fraternal organization for which he had been an agent and state manager.[34] When the fraternal went out of business, he organized the National Benevolent Union to keep intact the business then under his supervision. The small enterprise developed smoothly until 1911, when Hall, unable to meet the state's requirements, was threatened with arrest for operating without a license. Hall immediately appealed for help to a number of black insurance companies, and Atlanta Mutual responded with an agreement to reinsure the Kentucky business.

The board of directors of Atlanta Life met in March 1911 and voted to apply to the Kentucky Insurance Department for a license to operate in that state. Kentucky law required that an industrial company have $10,000 on deposit, an amount that was twice Atlanta Mutual's assets. To secure the money and meet Kentucky's requirement, the board once again obtained a loan from Herndon, issuing to him the appropriate certificates to cover the amount of the loan. Therefore, on 14 June 1911, Atlanta Mutual was able to make the $10,000 deposit and to begin acquiring the business of the National Benevolent Union in Kentucky. Lemuel H. Haywood was transferred from his position as supervisor of business in the state of Georgia to assist Hall in Kentucky.[35]

A native of Stephens County (Toccoa), Georgia, Haywood had worked with Atlanta Mutual since 1907. Beginning as an agent in the district around Gainesville, Georgia, he demonstrated extraordinary ability and enthusiasm for insurance work and quickly advanced in the agency. His style and knack for selling insurance made him especially suited for opening new areas for the company. Haywood frequently used an unusual mass sales approach, which involved coaxing prospective insurance buyers onto their front porches to listen to his sales pitch. As he fervently argued the merits of an Atlanta Mutual policy, his dramatics usually attracted people from the neighborhood Prepared to sell policies to the entire gathering, Haywood generally had a fellow agent along to help enroll all who wished to join.[36]

When Haywood and Hall began their work in Kentucky, the home office heralded the event with a grand promotional campaign. A big Atlanta Mutual Jubilee on the first Sunday of September celebrated the occasion, and several churches saluted the company for the $10,000 deposit and its entrance into a new state. Some proclaimed the achievement a great step in the development of black business. Atlanta Mutual's deposit was $5,000 more than any other company had been able to raise and was good advertising. More than one hundred thousand copies of Herndon's personal check for $5,481.64, advertised in the *Atlanta Independent* as "the largest bank check ever signed by an individual member of our race," were distributed as souvenirs and as evidence of the company's prosperity.[37]

The ballyhooing subsided quickly, however, when Atlanta Mutual learned that it could not continue operating in Kentucky. Soon after agents began developing business in the state, Kentucky passed another law requiring all insurance companies to have a deposit of $100,000. Atlanta Mutual believed that it was inexpedient to try to comply with so onerous a requirement and sought to arrange a plan whereby the policyholders it had acquired in Kentucky would not lose and the company's reputation would be preserved.[38]

In 1911 only one black company, the Mississippi Life Insurance Company of Indianola, Mississippi, had an authorized capitalization of $100,000, although only a portion of this amount had been sold. Organized in September 1908 as the Mississippi Beneficial Insurance Company, this enterprise initially raised $25,000 and secured a charter on 9 January 1909 authorizing the sale of industrial insurance. In 1910, however, desiring to expand beyond the $500 risks permitted an industrial company, the stockholders voted to increase the amount of capitalization to $100,000 and became the first legal reserve company organized by African-Americans.[39] In spite of its status as a legal reserve firm and the backing of substantial black citizens such as Wayne W. Cox, a schoolteacher, large landowner, and founder of the Delta Penny Savings Bank in Indianola, Mississippi Life experienced many problems and sustained a great many losses in the years between 1909 and 1914. Until 1917 the company confined its operations to Mississippi, where it was ridiculed and threatened by white competitors and an insurance commissioner who once declared frankly that the firm's ability to operate in the state depended on the goodwill of white agents and white companies.[40] The company's prospects for boosting black insurance thus were poor for several years.

In Atlanta, however, the prospects for negotiating an arrangement with a new black company appeared somewhat more hopeful. In 1908 Heman Edward Perry, a native of Houston, Texas, had organized the Standard Life Insurance Company, the first legal reserve company among blacks in Georgia. Perry was very enthusiastic about the insurance profession, and he observed that most small black insurance

Alonzo Herndon (*right*) in business meeting with Heman Perry and Harry Pace (stenographer unidentified) (Courtesy of the author)

companies were on very shaky ground with little or no capital and that they were restricted solely to writing industrial policies. He hoped to establish an enterprise that would put blacks into the mainstream of the insurance business by selling only ordinary insurance and proposed to capitalize the firm at $100,000.

In 1908 such a capitalization was not achieved easily. Blacks were skeptical of their ability to raise such a large amount of money for an insurance venture. Most remembered that only three years earlier many of the black mutual aid organizations had been forced to disband because of their inability to raise $5,000 to meet the Georgia deposit requirement. Therefore, when Perry revealed his plan in Atlanta the reactions ranged from concern for his sanity to shocked disbelief and a snort that "even Alonzo Herndon couldn't raise that amount of money."[41]

The skepticism of many of his contemporaries notwithstanding, Perry spent the next four years traveling throughout the southern states, from Virginia to Texas, selling Standard Life stock among blacks who were asked to demonstrate their faith in black entrepreneurship by investing in the project. In 1911 he nearly conceded defeat after failing to raise the required $100,000 within the stipulated two-year period. He was disappointed with this failure to launch the company, and he returned approximately $70,000 to the investors as promised. Perry recovered quickly from this defeat, however, and by early 1913, after another two years of arduous work, he had collected over $50,000 in cash and took notes for approximately $30,000, but he still needed $50,000 to comply with state's deposit requirements and begin operating the company.[42]

As Atlanta Mutual looked for a way to hold onto its business in Kentucky, Standard Life seemed to offer a solution. As a legal reserve company with $100,000 capital, it would meet Kentucky's requirements for licensing a firm. A reinsurance agreement with Standard Life would save Atlanta Mutual's business from predatory white companies. Heman Perry wished to sell a large chunk of Standard Life stock to Alonzo Herndon. With a prodigious talent for arranging deals, Perry proposed to take over Atlanta Mutual's business in Kentucky in return for Herndon's subscription to a block of Standard Life stock and a loan endorsement.

The board of directors agreed to Perry's proposal, and on 29 January 1913 the directors formally authorized Herndon to withdraw the $5,000 held by the state treasurer, which the officers now designated as a "voluntary deposit," and to invest that money in Standard Life stock. At this meeting, the board also empowered Herndon to subscribe for additional stock in such amount as he deemed appropriate and ratified any arrangements Herndon wished to make for the management of the business in Kentucky. Herndon withdrew $5,000 which he had earlier deposited with the Georgia Insurance Department, leaving only the original deposit as required by state law, and finalized the details of the agreement with Standard Life.[43]

The arrangement enabled Perry to move ahead with plans for initiating Standard Life. With the endorsement of Herndon and several of his associates, Perry secured a loan for $50,000. With the full amount in hand, he deposited $100,000 with Georgia insurance officials, acquired a charter on 22 March, and began operating Standard Life Insurance Company in June 1913. With its home office on Atlanta's Auburn Avenue, Standard Life became the first black company organized for the express purpose of conducting solely an ordinary life insurance business. As the third black life insurance company to achieve legal reserve status, it followed Mississippi Life (1910) and North Carolina Mutual Life Insurance Company (January 1913).[44]

Herndon's agreement with Heman Perry called for an interesting arrangement between the two Auburn Avenue enterprises. Because Perry had from the outset announced his intention to devote full attention to ordinary insurance, the agreement stipulated that Atlanta Mutual would continue operating its own industrial business in Kentucky in the name of Standard Life. To effect this arrangement Standard Life merely added an industrial department headed by Atlanta Mutual Secretary Truman Gibson, and, in Kentucky, Henry Hall was retained as state manager and placed in charge of operations. The agreement also called for Atlanta Mutual to participate in the administration of Standard Life, and, in June 1913, at the first meeting of Standard Life stockholders, Herndon was elected to the board of directors and made treasurer of the company.[45]

The efforts at mutual cooperation between these two firms ended unsuccessfully after only a few months. Although there is no concrete evidence, it appears that disagreements between the two men led to the conclusion of the arrangement.[46] The industrial agents were withdrawn from Kentucky, and the business developed through Atlanta Mutual's efforts was transferred to the Mammoth Life and Accident Company, a new firm organized by Henry Hall and W. H. Wright, a Louisville lawyer. Severing all ties between Atlanta Mutual and Standard Life, Herndon also withdrew from the administrative team and by December 1914 was no longer a member of Standard Life's board of directors.[47]

Following the second exodus from Kentucky, Atlanta Mutual turned its attention homeward. For a time, its efforts were confined exclusively to Georgia and Alabama, where the agents continued to build the firm's business and reputation. In 1915 another insurance deal demonstrated Herndon's attempt to augment his company's business and, at the same time, to preserve the reputation of black insurance companies. In February, Atlanta Mutual reinsured the Union Mutual Relief Association, which succumbed to mismanagement and unfavorable publicity. Organized in December 1894 by the Reverend Thomas W. Walker, a former slave, Union Mutual was the oldest black insurance association in the state and had done a substantial business in Georgia for nearly twenty years; its reports showed over $1 million in business in 1911. Union Mutual had also trained many black pioneer insurance agents, and other associations had for years drawn upon the company for managers and agents.[48]

For a time, Union Mutual's financial outlook had been rosy and the company presented a favorable public image. Even Ben Davis, the hard-biting Atlanta newspaperman and self-appointed custodian of the public good, had often given the company enthusiastic reports in the *Atlanta Independent*. Conditions in the firm deteriorated rapidly, however, and it began a devastating decline around 1912. In June 1913, in a well-publicized effort to recoup, the officials attempted to amend the charter and reorganize the company from a mutual to a stockholder corporation. Following this failed effort and a major personnel change, Union Mutual continued to decline, beset by discord and financial insolvency.[49] All further action came too late to save Union Mutual, and in early 1915 the business was reinsured by Atlanta Mutual.

The reinsurance of Union Mutual was a significant factor in the overall growth of Atlanta Mutual. With this acquisition it became the largest industrial insurance company owned by African-Americans in the lower South. Since 1906, Atlanta Mutual had lagged behind the two largest industrial companies in the city, Union Mutual and Industrial Life and Health Insurance Company, a white-owned firm with a large black clientele (see Table 3.3). As the company neared the end of its first decade of operations, the $1 million mark seemed well within reach as the officers reinsured Union Mutual and then launched an aggressive ten-year anniversary campaign to push insurance sales over the symbolic mark. In achieving this goal, Atlanta Mu-

Table 3.3. Growth of Assets and Insurance in Force of Atlanta Mutual Compared with Union Mutual and Industrial Life and Health, 1906–1915*

Year	Atlanta Mutual	Union Mutual†	Industrial‡
Comparison of assets (ledger)			
1906	$ 10,138	$ 12,856	$ 25,348
1907	10,414	10,543	56,458
1908	12,729	14,913	56,749
1909	15,111	17,389	56,763
1911	22,302	24,656	66,958
1913	27,494	18,290	96,503
1915	32,411		126,860
Comparison of insurance in force			
1906	$ 309,043	$ 518,672	$ 996,576
1907	465,908	637,113	919,779
1908	469,840	775,877	1,173,768
1909	567,904	839,850	1,222,352
1911	389,327	1,073,249	1,899,265
1913	472,740	427,535	1,583,302
1915	1,200,549		1,588,800

Source: *Report of the Insurance Department of the Comptroller-General's Office,* 1906–15.

*Data for 1910, 1912, and 1914 not available.
†Incorporated in 1897; reinsured in Atlanta Mutual in 1914.
‡Incorporated in 1891. Although white-owned and operated, the company had a predominantly black clientele.

tual made tremendous progress in closing the gap with Industrial Life in the amount of insurance in force.

Along with the excitement of an anniversary sales campaign went the more sobering responsibility of reassessing the progress of the enterprise. It had survived its first decade and even showed signs of prosperity but not without a struggle. The lapse rate had been large and the growth of insurance in force agonizingly slow, and in 1908 the number of policies lapsed exceeded by 213 the number of new policies written. These had been lean years financially, and the company had required "frequent doses of medicine and nourishment" from the founder-president. Expenses were high in these early years; expenditures exceeded income in both 1908 and 1912 (see Table 3.4). In the

Table 3.4. Total Income and Disbursements of Atlanta Mutual, 1906–1915*

Year	Total income	Total disbursements	Operating gains/losses
1906	$ 37,117.00	$ 35,586.32	$ 1,530.68
1907	47,359.85	46,485.20	874.65
1908	58,130.70	58,367.87	−237.17
1909	109,056.67	108,649.49	407.18
1911	162,766.67	159,690.67	3,076.00
1912	196,314.82	198,811.23	−2,496.41
1915	348,199.00	333,408.92	14,790.08

Source: Report of the Insurance Commissioner to the Comptroller-General's Office, 1906–15.
*Data for 1910, 1913, and 1914 not available.

first three years, approximately 60 percent of the total company income went to policyholders in payment for claims, although the ratio decreased to between 35 and 42 percent. Other than claims of policyholders, commissions to agents and salaries for employees and officers constituted the largest expenditures. The assets consisted almost wholly of the bonds held as deposit by the state insurance officials along with several small bank accounts and the agents' balances.

In spite of the gloomy financial picture in these early years, which would have undoubtedly led observers from the financial and corporate world to predict doom for the company, the officials rejoiced at the progress that had been made. Compared to other industrial companies, both black and white, Atlanta Mutual had made a good showing in the industry in Georgia and had earned a reputation among blacks as a safe and reliable company, consistent in its efforts to reinsure faltering insurance associations and thereby to augment the worth of black enterprises in the public's estimation. As the company moved into its second decade, now in the vanguard among black industrial insurance firms, it had begun to vindicate the faith the founder had placed in the small enterprise in 1905.

4

A Matter of Survival

In one form or another it [insurance] has played an important part in the progress of the Negro race. Negroes have made their greatest commercial successes and have suffered their greatest financial failures in this field.
—Merah S. Stuart, An Economic Detour

Like Atlanta Mutual, any number of insurance associations had emerged from mutual aid or fraternal organizations or business ventures, with the entrepreneurs expressing optimism that these firms would prosper. Expecting success and commendations, many of them met with failure and criticisms. With limited capital and virtually no business training or tradition, the entrepreneurs encountered numerous deterrents to business growth and wealth formation.

Even when black enterprises survived, they were frequently unable to expand their capital or their territory. Too often the enterprises were tied to the interests and whims of one individual or family, and they passed into oblivion when the primary benefactor died or incurred personal misfortunes. Most businesses, including insurance, faced stiff competition from white firms that secured a larger portion of black patronage. Despite pleas for race solidarity and support of black enterprises, too many black patrons seemingly "could not easily abandon the thought that the white businessman was more reliable and could give the most in return for one's money."[1] Considering the reality of the situation surrounding black businesses, it is not incongruent that the more pragmatic and discerning entrepreneurs exhibited pessimism even while they rejoiced in their accomplishments.

63

Although not a pessimist by nature, Herndon was a pragmatic and sagacious businessman, and a prudent and cautious optimism pervaded his outlook for the company. Since 1913, growth in income among blacks had translated into increasing policy sales and augmented the business of black companies. Nevertheless, a realistic assessment of Atlanta Mutual's true position in the industry left Herndon gravely concerned about its ability to grow and expand in the rising American economy.

Herndon was particularly concerned because assets were small and the company continued to operate in the category of a mutual assessment organization. Although insurance sales were expanding generally, Atlanta Mutual offered only one policy contract, an industrial health and accident policy, sometimes called "sick benefit," which carried a small death payment. Herndon knew that without substantial capital, Atlanta Mutual might succumb to the forces of adversity and stagnation. Furthermore, with only $5,000 paid-in capital, it was unlikely that it could expand into other states, and the danger remained that the company might be forced to close in Georgia and Alabama by legislative changes similar to those enacted in Kentucky. Anxious to put the company in a position to achieve greater viability, Herndon took steps in 1916 to increase the capital and improve its standing among industrial companies.[2]

The initial step occurred when Atlanta Mutual adopted a new organizational structure and increased its capitalization to $25,000. In part, changes in the Georgia insurance laws prompted a major modification in the method of raising new revenue. In August 1912 the Georgia General Assembly repealed the 1909 law, which had allowed insurance companies to issue guaranty certificates as collateral for loans obtained for operating purposes or for maintaining reserves and deposits.[3] Repeal of the legislation ended this practice after 1 January 1913, making it difficult for Atlanta Mutual to raise new funds or to reimburse Herndon for his loans to the company.

Another drawback derived from the company's limitations as a mutual assessment organization. The primary concern was that the majority of the revenue came from the policyholders, who theoretically shared in both profits and losses. The problem was that policyholders generally paid only a stipulated premium, although under the mutual assessment plan they could be assessed additional dues annually to meet certain obligations. The experiences of earlier mutual aid groups and insurance associations sustained the view that economic conditions made extra assessments unfeasible for most policyholders, who were already strained to pay their regular premiums. The assessments coupled with regular dues frequently compelled many of the younger and more fit members to lapse their policies, leaving the older and ill members to deplete the resources further. Increasing sick and death claims forced the organizations into financial reverses from which they could not be saved.[4]

In contrast to the frailties of a mutual assessment organization, a stock corporation offered greater potential for security and advancement. It was controlled by stockholders, and resources could be obtained through the sale of stock. The responsibilities and obligations of stockholders matched those of policyholders under the mutual arrangement, and policyholders shared neither in any profits nor in any losses arising from the operation of the business. In addition, a stock company's financial basis was strengthened by the requirement of a specified amount of capital beyond the statutory deposit and reserves Georgia required of mutual assessment associations.[5]

The practical-minded Herndon undoubtedly saw the advantages of a stock corporation and deemed it an appropriate way of solving the twofold problem of raising additional capital for expansion and protecting his own investment in Atlanta Mutual. One provision of the Georgia Insurance Act approved 19 August 1912 permitted the reorganization of a company such as Atlanta Mutual as a stock company. Specifically, Section 16 provided that any mutual, industrial, life, health, or accident insurance company could become a stock company by filing a certificate with the secretary of state showing that three-fourths of the policyholders approved of the proposal and that the capital was fixed at not less than $25,000. The act provided that the new corporation "shall have all of the power and authority as though it had been originally organized as a stock corporation."[6] This provision suggests that reorganization was a relatively painless process, especially because policyholders in mutual companies were allowed to vote by proxy, a power Atlanta Mutual policyholders gave to the president at the time of application, empowering him to act in the interest of the company.[7]

Herndon, Gibson, and the other officers took steps to create a new corporation, filing a petition in early September 1916 to incorporate the Atlanta Mutual Insurance Company as a stock corporation with capital of $25,000. The state allowed the petition, and the capital stock, divided into 250 shares at a par value of $100 per share, sold for $105 cash. In an apparently little-advertised stock sale, Herndon and a few business associates purchased the entire subscription with approximately 90 percent coming under the president's control. The remaining stockholders acquired from one to five shares for which some paid cash and the others gave Herndon notes. With the funds in hand, the Atlanta Mutual Insurance Company paid in the entire authorized capital of $25,000 and was granted a charter on 27 September 1916.[8]

Without publicity or fanfare, the new company began operating officially on 8 November 1916. As its first order of business, the new enterprise reinsured the policyholders of the old association and assumed all its assets and liabilities. This action followed a resolution by the officers of the old Atlanta Mutual Insurance Association to "reinsure business in the Atlanta Mutual Insurance Company, which in reality is one."[9] All officers and directors of the old association remained in their positions and continued to manage the new company. In contrast to the publicity that surrounded the earlier voluntary deposit which raised the company's paid-in capital to $10,000 and in view of the importance of favorable reviews to insurance firms, it appears that little or no publicity accompanied this transaction. Surprisingly, the *Atlanta Independent* failed to give any account of the reorganization; the first reference to the new Atlanta Mutual Insurance Company appeared as a semiannual report in February 1917.

Another effort to propel the company forward centered around Atlanta Mutual's attempt to expand into Arkansas, a state the officers judged as a fertile field for insurance because of the large influx of African-Americans in the last half of the nineteenth century. As market conditions improved, it appeared that there might be a substantial insurance market in the region. In 1914, Dr. J. H. Barabin, a physician, had attempted to organize a legal reserve company in Arkansas, the Negro National Insurance Company of Little Rock. He failed to sell the required amount of stock to raise the initial capital, and the cash collected on stock sales for this company was later taken over by Standard Life of Georgia.[10] Other than white companies, fraternals dominated the insurance field among blacks in Arkansas. Projecting booming sales for an industrial company, Scipio Africanus Jones, a Little Rock attorney and friend of Truman Gibson, urged Atlanta Mutual to expand into Arkansas.[11]

A dynamic lawyer and leader in Republican politics, Jones was an important contact for Atlanta Mutual officials. An expert in fraternal law, he had been admitted before the Arkansas Supreme Court on 26 November 1900 and the United States Supreme Court five years later on 29 May 1905. Jones was active in national politics and served as a delegate to the Republican National Convention in 1908 and 1912. A businessman as well as lawyer and politician, Jones was then president of the Arkansas Negro Business League and a vice-president of the National Negro Business League. He also owned a hotel in Little Rock and was president of the Arkansas Realty and Investment Company. Gibson acted quickly to arrange a deal with Jones, and in March 1916 the board authorized Jones to act as the company's legal representative in Arkansas. With his assistance, Atlanta Mutual obtained a license to operate in Arkansas and, in early April, sent Robert Chamblee, then state supervisor in Georgia, to Little Rock to launch a program for the "Atlanta Mutual-i-zation" of Arkansas.[12]

This move was Atlanta Mutual's first effort at expansion since the ill-fated Kentucky venture in 1911. But, as in Kentucky, the effort to expand into Arkansas was unsuccessful. The difficulties centered primarily around Atlanta Mutual's reorganization as a stock company and the amount of capitalization specified by the new firm. The statutes of Arkansas required a stock or proprietary company to have an authorized capital of $100,000 with at least 50 percent paid in.[13]

When Atlanta Mutual officials learned of this situation, they began immediately to explore ways of preserving the business Chamblee had already developed. In Arkansas, Herndon and Scipio Jones conferred with officials in an effort to solve the problems. Despite Jones's expertise and influence in the state, no legal avenues could be found by which Atlanta Mutual might continue under its present organization without depositing at a minimum an additional $25,000. Instead, Herndon was advised to organize a mutual assessment company in Arkansas as a subsidiary of Atlanta Mutual and later to convert it into a stock company when the required funds were available. The board approved this plan, and Herndon hastily organized a new firm, the Atlantic Mutual Insurance Company, with himself as president and Robert Chamblee as vice-president and secretary. Chamblee assumed primary responsibility for developing Atlantic Mutual in Arkansas.[14]

Unfortunately, the attempt to conserve the early inroads in Arkansas did not work, and Atlantic Mutual was soon embroiled in difficulties with the state. Once again, the insurance officials called Herndon to Little Rock and this time notified him of the requirement that a portion of Atlanta Mutual's capital and reserves be transferred from Georgia to Arkansas. Georgia officials would not permit the firm to comply with Arkansas's demand, and the company was forced to give up operations in Arkansas. At a meeting in Memphis, Herndon, Chamblee, and John A. Copeland, a white actuary employed by Atlanta Mutual, negotiated for the reinsurance for Atlantic Mutual.[15]

With this deal concluded, the parties returned to Atlanta to reassess Atlanta Mutual's strengths and weaknesses. The Arkansas episode reinforced Herndon's concern for the company's future growth. This concern had been enhanced by correspondence from an Arkansas official, which noted, "We have been aware from the beginning that your capital stock of $25,000 would be a stumbling block to your admittance into the state."[16] For a time following this setback, Atlanta Mutual confined its operations to Georgia and Alabama and concentrated on expanding its policy contracts and physical facilities in the home office.

Several factors indicated that the time was propitious for the company to expand from the limited health and accident contracts, especially since no legal obstacles existed to hinder such a move. Under its license, Atlanta Mutual could write only industrial policies that did not exceed $500. Agents' reports indicated the need for expanded contracts for even small improvements in the economic conditions of some black families during the war years resulted in an increased demand for insurance policies paying larger benefits. Furthermore, company officials were aware that several other companies in the field were already marketing larger-benefit-paying industrial life contracts. Therefore, in 1918, with the country in the midst of World War I, Atlanta Mutual prepared to add this new feature to its portfolio.[17]

Chamblee's relocation to the home office in Atlanta also helped stimulate expansion. There had been many discussions about the folly of continuing to operate the company on income derived from the health and accident business alone, and the officials agreed that an industrial life plan would offer better coverage for individuals who could afford higher premiums. Chamblee had already begun to plan to implement this feature in Arkansas. These plans were not discarded when the Arkansas venture failed and Chamblee came to Atlanta. In August 1918, soon after Chamblee arrived, the company created a straight life department, with him in charge. The first applications for the new policies were written on 19 August.[18]

With the addition of industrial life insurance, Atlanta Mutual took another forward step. By 1 November, the new department was functioning fully, and Chamblee was assisted by Eugene Marcus Martin, a capable young graduate of Atlanta University. The immediate task of the new department was to set up a bookkeeping system and organize a clerical department. It was also necessary to organize a medical department and to have a medical examiner on the staff. For some time, Dr. Thomas Heathe Slater, a local black physician, served as a part-time medical examiner for the company, but an epidemic of influenza that hit the city in 1918 so occupied his attention that he could no longer devote time to insurance examinations. The company was likewise besieged by victims of influenza, and sick and accident claims were heavy. The high number of industrial claims coupled with the anticipated rise in new applications for straight life policies made it necessary to have a full-time medical director. Upon Dr. Slater's recommendation, the company hired Dr. Lyndon M. Hill, a graduate of Meharry Medical College, as its first full-time medical director.[19]

The anticipated rise in new business in the straight life department was not achieved immediately. After two months, the department showed a debit over the entire system of only $65.40, ranging from $26.05 in Atlanta to $0.10 in Anniston, Alabama. Therefore, in early November, the department launched its first New Business Campaign, which lasted for thirteen weeks. Interest had appeared to lag among the regular field force, accustomed to selling only health and accident policies, so the campaign aimed at increasing the amount of business in force as well as arousing the enthusiasm of district managers and agents for selling the new industrial life contracts. By the campaign's end in February 1919 an increase of $346.35 had been achieved in the weekly debit of the department. After a year, the straight life department was holding its own with over $3,400 in weekly premiums.[20]

Although the company actuary had approved the plans to initiate industrial straight life insurance, he had exhibited concern that a life insurance debit, though profitable in the long run, might be expensive to put into operation. Initially, a cost of twenty to thirty-five times the premium income had been projected to place the first $2,000 or $3,000 of industrial life on the books. Therefore, the officials were justifiably proud to find that the straight life department had cost the company less than two times the premiums in the initial stages of its work. Some of the savings no doubt occurred because the straight life department did not maintain a separate force of agents. Instead, the special agents already canvassing the states selling the smaller-premium health and accident policies handled the new contracts. Both the company and the agents benefited from the arrangement, which spared the expense of hiring additional agents and at the same time allowed agents to increase their commissions. The growth of the straight life department also illustrated the value of using special campaigns for promoting insurance sales and increasing business in force. Special campaigns soon became an important and effective pro-

Atlanta Life "Million Dollar Team," c. 1916, an early team of special agents sent to open
new sales territory (Courtesy of Atlanta Life Insurance Company)

motional technique of Atlanta Mutual, and they were put into widespread use throughout the system in the next decade.[21]

The addition of the straight life department and the general growth of the company soon made larger home office facilities a necessity. Since March 1915, following the acquisition of Union Mutual, Atlanta Life had maintained its headquarters on the second floor of the Odd Fellows Building, a magnificent five-story structure on Auburn Avenue built by the Georgia Odd Fellows in 1912.[22] As the need for space became more acute, in November 1918 the directors voted to acquire their own headquarters building, and they purchased an old two-story frame house and lot at 132 Auburn Avenue. Originally a private residence, the structure had for years housed the local black YMCA. In the midst of the Y's campaign to build a more commodious structure a few blocks east on Butler Street, Herndon purchased the old house and began extensive overhauling. The company occupied the remodeled two-story brick building in 1920, setting up its operations on the first floor. The upper level, unused initially by the firm, was rented to several other businesses and organizations.[23]

In 1920, when Atlanta Mutual moved into its newly remodeled home office on Auburn Avenue, the street had become the commercial hub of a growing black community. Contiguous to the downtown business district and adjacent to a fashionable residential area that was inhabited by some of the leading black citizens, this east-west corridor was the location of the city's most vital black enterprises and institutions. Along this thoroughfare were the real estate and contracting firms, the newspapers and funeral homes, and the insurance companies and financial institutions that had been organized by blacks. Here, too, were the offices of black professionals as well as the establishments operated by master black craftsmen and artisans. In addition, any number of smaller enterprises such as florists, grocers, cleaners, and restaurants were located along the avenue and its intersecting streets. Churches, hotels, entertainment establishments, and fraternal organizations added to the vitality of this area, which contained a significant portion of the capital, industry, and intellect in black Atlanta.[24]

The virulent racism that dominated Atlanta at the turn of the century unwittingly inspired the formation of this dynamic area. For African-Americans, the infamous Atlanta race riot of 1906 and its aftermath contributed to a growing awareness of the perils blacks faced in the nation and helped generate greater race consciousness. Manifestations of the new consciousness were a move to consolidate the business community in the northeastern sector of the city along Auburn Avenue and a stepped-up campaign by black leaders to increase financial support and patronage of black enterprises. In a period of rigid social segregation, the Auburn Avenue area developed into a community of unusual distinction in the South. Some believed that segregation nurtured rather than starved blacks on Auburn Avenue and that this area was illustrative of the ability of African-Americans to survive against racial hostility and a restrictive economic and social environment.[25] In 1956 an article in *Fortune* magazine cited Auburn Avenue as "the richest Negro street in the world," a description it attributed to the wealth and achievement of businesses such as the Atlanta Life Insurance Company, Mutual Federal Savings and Loan Association, and Citizens Trust Company—all located along this famed thoroughfare.[26]

Before 1900 most of the property along Auburn Avenue was owned by whites. Primarily a residential area, it was home to only 52 of the 28,098 African-Americans residing in the city in 1890. As the turn of the century approached, more and more blacks were attracted to the area. By 1900 ten black businesses and two professionals operated on Auburn Avenue alongside white firms, which continued to dominate the area. The riot of 1906 stirred racial hostilities in a way that profoundly influenced racial separation in the city. Recognizing the need to develop their own communities, influential African-Americans led the movement to establish businesses and homes in the area of Auburn Avenue. As large numbers of blacks took up residence in the area, whites responded by leaving this sector of the city. By 1909 black families were in a majority along the street, with 117 black residences and 74 white residences. There were 64 black business establishments and 7 black professionals. Most of these enterprises were located within eight blocks of the downtown business sector.[27]

Several building efforts along the Auburn Avenue corridor greatly facilitated the settlement of the area by black businesses. In 1904 Henry Allan Rucker, a black man whom President William McKinley appointed as Georgia's collector of internal revenue in 1897, built the Rucker Building at Piedmont and Auburn. The Odd Fellows Building, constructed between Butler and Bell streets in 1912, and the adjacent Odd Fellows Auditorium, built the following year, also aided in the dramatic rise in the number of black businesses in the area. By 1920 the number of black businesses along Auburn Avenue had reached seventy-two, and twenty black professionals had offices on the street.[28]

Four years later, in 1924—the same year Alonzo Herndon erected the Herndon Building across the street and in the same block as the Odd Fellows Building—the *Classified Negro Business Directory of Atlanta* reported the existence of three legal reserve life insurance companies with a combined capital and surplus of more than $10 million and insurance in force of $75 million. Several industrial health and life insurance companies also operated in the area with more than $10 million of insurance in force. There was also one bank (with reported capital and surplus of $500,000 and resources of $1 million) and a hundred merchants, restaurants, barbershops, and other enterprises.

Although these figures were perhaps exaggerated, Auburn Avenue was the locus of the city's most vital black institutions. As the community's leading thoroughfare, it pulsated with activity. Early black firms such as the Georgia Real Estate Loan and Trust Company and the Atlanta Loan and Trust Company were now joined by enterprises such as the Atlanta State Savings Bank and the Service Enterprises associated with Standard Life Insurance Company to provide financial resources to blacks in Atlanta. A leading black newspaper, which served as the voice of the Georgia Odd Fellows, the *Atlanta Independent,* was published from its office on Auburn Avenue. Located here, too, were the headquarters of the YMCA, YWCA, the National Urban League, and other agencies aimed at improving the health, civic consciousness, and living conditions of Atlanta's black residents. In addition, numerous outlets for entertainment were part of the Auburn scene, where blacks enjoyed a variety of attractions including traveling shows, vaudeville acts, orchestral pageants, and concerts.

Other institutions drew African-Americans from across the city to worship and to engage in social and religious activities. At least three of the leading black churches were located along this corridor. The Bethel African Methodist Episcopal Church, the oldest black church in the city, was perhaps the street's most important religious edifice. In addition to the religious meaning it held for the community, Bethel's significance extended to other areas. Morris Brown College, Standard Life Insurance Company, and a number of other secular organizations that undergirded African-American life in Atlanta were launched from its sanctuary. As the only place in the area where public meetings of any size could be held, the church was called the People's Church. Along with Wheat Street, Ebenezer, and First Congregational churches, Bethel served as an important social agency and augmented the progress of the developing black community.[29]

By the 1920s, Auburn Avenue was socially and economically the most dynamic area in the city for blacks. With resources unmatched elsewhere in the country, except possibly Durham, North Carolina, many of the institutions and enterprises along Auburn Avenue were progressive and fairly prosperous. In addition, the area provided the setting for much of the intellectual flowering among blacks in the city. Atlanta Mutual, therefore, in its move to 132 (later 148) Auburn Avenue seemed to have positioned itself at the westernmost entrance to a vigorous and thriving area.

Despite the good omen of its new location and its expanded policy contracts, Atlanta Mutual faced a series of difficulties in this period which threatened its very existence. Over the next months, a number of external and internal problems affected the enterprise, forcing it to retreat from the growth pattern experienced a few years earlier. These issues also claimed the full attention of the leadership and prevented the company from sharing fully in the economic promise of its new status and new location.

Events during the decade following 1910 had far-reaching effects on African-Americans. World War I brought talk of freedom and democracy and rekindled hope for improved social and economic conditions. The unprecedented demand for labor in the urban industrial centers, brought on by the war's demands and the sudden reduction in European immigration, sparked one of the most remarkable migratory movements in the history of blacks in the country as thousands left the southern states seeking better-paying, more attractive jobs in the North. At the same time, oppressive conditions in the southern states pushed black families out of the region. In 1915 and 1916, boll-weevil-damaged crops and unusual floods resulted in economic depression in large sections of Georgia, Alabama, Mississippi, Florida, and Louisiana.

Like the social proscriptions and economic peonage that engulfed black lives, violence continued unabated in these states. Between 1911 and April 1917, when the United States entered the war, at least three cases of violence in Georgia stood out in the public mind. These cases ranged from the brutal hanging of a black father, his young son, and two daughters in Monticello in 1915 to a reign of terror in southwest Georgia that resulted in the burning of homes, churches, and society halls, and the hanging of at least eleven people in Early, Worth, and Lee counties in late December 1915 and January 1916.[30]

For these reasons, the migration's full impact was soon felt in Georgia. Following movements from Florida, which was one of the first states entered by northern labor agents, southeastern Georgia became the second district to feel the drain of the exodus as large numbers of workers headed into Pennsylvania, New York, and New Jersey. Striking a blow for full economic and social freedom, large numbers of people joined the movement, which carried skilled and unskilled workers as well as black professionals into the North. This situation was phenomenal in some locales, and numerous illustrations may be found of professional men following their clients northward, of pastors watching their congregations melt away, and of families, struck by migration fever, selling homes and furniture at a loss in order to join the exodus.[31]

Black businesses were directly affected by the exodus of more than fifty thousand blacks from Georgia. The migration not only depleted churches and drained laborers from farms, it also cut down the business of black doctors, lawyers, dentists, and merchants and reduced deposits in black banks and insurance companies. Georgia's black insurance companies reported a 20 percent loss in membership. In Alabama, which blacks also left in floods, similar reports were heard.[32]

Atlanta Mutual showed overall growth through 1920. With increasing policy sales, reflected in a steady growth in insurance in force, the company's income reached $1 million for that year (see Table 4.1). Within a year, however, the full impact of migration along with other difficulties caused premium collections to sag and led to a decline in income. Two years later, total income had been reduced by nearly a quarter of the 1920 level; the records show an even more dramatic de-

Table 4.1.   Growth of Atlanta Mutual, 1917–1922

Year	Total income	Total paid to policyholders	Admitted assets	Insurance in force
1917	$ 491,961	$179,759	$ 92,158	$1,235,318
1918	550,710	245,631	136,497	2,235,124
1919	828,955	358,667	169,536	4,523,723
1920	1,165,517	512,020	201,348	7,592,816
1921	973,442	406,141	243,814	9,464,493
1922	881,825	344,704	405,810	9,745,978

Source: Report of the Insurance Department of the Comptroller-General's Office, 1917–22 (Atlanta: Franklin Printing and Publishing Company, 1918–23); Atlanta Life Insurance Company, Examination of Atlanta Mutual Insurance Company, 1 January 1917–31 December 1922, in ALCF.

crease in the amount paid to policyholders in 1922. An examination of six Alabama branch offices of Atlanta Life in June 1923, ordered by the Alabama insurance commissioner and conducted by an accounting firm in Birmingham, showed that premiums collected in 1921 were $47,607 less than those collected in 1920 and that 1922 premiums netted $38,428 less than in 1921. The report explained these differences as resulting from the exodus of blacks to the North.[33] The sick and accident division was particularly hard hit by reduced collections, and the company considered discontinuing this business in districts that operated at a loss.[34] Disbursements increased with the occurrence of the flu epidemic, and even when heavy claims subsided as the epidemic ended, other expenses drove disbursements to an all-time high in 1920–21. Nevertheless, Atlanta Mutual registered an increase in the gains/losses column each year after 1919 (see Table 4.2).

World War I also had a heavy impact on black policyholders and agents. Draft statistics for Georgia showed "statewide discrimination, as a forty percent black population supplied over half of the state's conscripts. This induction rate was well above the percentage of blacks drafted nationally."[35] Leaving homes and families, usually for the first time, the recruits often allowed their insurance policies to lapse when they were called up to active duty. On the home front, black agents were affected by the compulsory "work or fight" legislation passed in several states. Following the national work or fight order, which required every able-bodied male of draft age to engage in necessary employment, a number of southern states, including Geor-

Table 4.2. Total Income and Disbursements of Atlanta Mutual, 1917–1922

Year	Total income	Total disbursements	Operating gains
1917	$ 419,961	$ 396,926	$23,035
1918	550,719	499,744	50,975
1919	828,955	811,239	17,716
1920	1,165,517	1,134,694	30,822
1921	973,442	920,103	53,339
1922	881,825	799,015	82,809

Source: *Report of the Insurance Department of the Comptroller-General's Office,* 1917–22; Examination Report of Atlanta Mutual Insurance Company, 1 January 1917–31 December 1922, in ALCF.

gia, passed compulsory work laws designed to control labor. Although selling life insurance was declared an essential occupation by the provost marshal of the United States Army, black agents were sometimes forced by officials in small communities to give up this employment to work in local plants. In the Georgia town of Pelham, an insurance agent was ordered by the town marshal to "get a job as he [the town marshal] did not consider the selling of life insurance an essential occupation for a Negro." In the same town, a part-time agent was ordered by the same marshal to stop selling insurance and devote his full time to the plant. In another Georgia county, a similar law forbade one black person to work for another black person. These compulsory labor ordinances allowed many white employers of black labor to use the national emergency to force blacks into a condition bordering on peonage and caused black insurance companies to lose policyholders who could not maintain premiums on low prewar wages as well as forcing agents to abandon employment with black firms.[36]

In addition to the drain on agents, policyholders, and premium collections caused by migration and war regulations, Atlanta Mutual experienced internal problems that contributed to and sustained the postwar difficulties. The root of the problem stemmed from a division of managerial responsibilities within the company and the alleged dishonesty of one of the managers. In 1918, with the addition of the industrial life feature, two separate departments operated under two general managers. In the straight life department, Robert Chamblee had complete managerial control. Joseph C. Lindsay held a position of similar authority in the sick and accident department. Unfortunately, separate factions soon developed around these administrative divisions and discord became pronounced.[37]

At the beginning of 1920, insurance officials in Georgia ordered the independent state examination of Atlanta Mutual covering a three-year period from 1 January 1917. The examiner reported his findings on 6 May 1920, noting the company's assets, liabilities, and other pertinent data as well as the friction and disharmony at the managerial level. To resolve the problem, the examiner recommended that a single directing head be placed in charge of both departments. Atlanta Mutual officials studied the recommendations, and in November the board ordered a reorganization of the managerial staff. The reorganization plan called for the retention of both managers but divided their responsibilities by states. On 18 November, all district managers and agents were notified that Chamblee was state manager of Georgia and Lindsay had charge of Alabama. Each manager, therefore, controlled both the straight life and the sick and accident business in his respective state.[38]

Before the decision of the board could be fully implemented, more troublesome matters surfaced. It was alleged in the *Atlanta Independent* that a routine audit of the books had revealed a shortage which the independent examiner apparently had not uncovered. Accounts in the newspaper indicated that Christopher C. Shanks, the company secretary, and an unnamed cashier had given affidavits tying the alleged shortages to Lindsay. It was alleged, too, that Shanks had admitted making false entries in the company ledgers to cover up the shortages, and though he initially denied having received any of the funds, the newspaper report indicated that he later confessed to embezzlement and resigned his position. The *Atlanta Independent* further charged that the cashier had also admitted having received a portion of the "loot." Follow-up reports on the alleged collusion among the three employees appeared in several issues of the *Atlanta Independent*. The paper called for a speedy prosecution of the culprits.[39]

Undaunted by this public challenge, Herndon and the other company officials proceeded at their own pace, even as rumors spread that Atlanta Mutual was seriously threatened and that the policyholders might lose. Amid talk of impairment, however, the state Insurance Department initiated another investigation of the company. In early 1921 the state insurance commissioner ordered the company's bonds sealed by the state auditor, and a second, more prolonged examination of the company began.[40]

This examination sorely tested the leadership of Atlanta Mutual. A series of meetings occurred between President Herndon, Commissioner Wright, Robert Chamblee, John A. Copeland, and W. Carroll Latimer, at which time the company's financial condition was laid out and Atlanta Mutual was given ninety days to prove its solvency. Unfortunately, as the meetings proceeded, the black officers came to feel that there were some within the group who did not wish to see the black company succeed. They suspected that Copeland and Latimer, the white consulting actuary and company attorney, were attempting to show that the black firm was insolvent and to convince the insurance commissioner that Herndon and the other officers had no chance of pulling it out of this crisis. Sadly, Herndon and the others came to believe that these former supporters' tactics were part of a scheme to bring about the downfall of Atlanta Mutual and take over its operations.[41]

The company's friends and supporters were scarcely more encouraging. White friends advised Herndon to sell the company before it wrecked him. Herndon, however, expressed his genuine commitment to seeing the company through this crisis. In his usual polite manner, he responded to those who encouraged him to sell with a firm "I don't think I will let it go." "I am willing to sink everything I have in order to save it and make it the kind of institution I want it to be" were his final words on the subject.[42] Once again, Herndon took the role of angel, and in this decision he brought about a major turning point in the company's history.

The future appeared to hinge on the firm's ability to increase its capital stock. To save the enterprise, additional funds had to be secured to comply with a new Georgia insurance law enacted in August 1920. This statute required that any new life insurance company, whether organized on the mutual or stock plan, must have $100,000 fully paid in before receiving a license to transact business in Georgia. Another provision applied to companies already chartered whose deposits were less than $100,000. It specified that such firms annually increase their deposits by 10 percent of the required amount until the deposit aggregated not less than $100,000.[43]

The new law applied to legal reserve and industrial companies alike, and it obligated Atlanta Mutual to begin augmenting its $25,000 deposit by 31 December 1921. As the Insurance Department concluded its investigation of Atlanta Mutual, Herndon was once again summoned to a meeting with William Wright, the insurance commissioner, and informed of the findings. By all indications, the company was financially solvent, and the investigation had not uncovered impairments or major irregularities in its assets or reserves. Nevertheless, the insurance commissioner ordered Atlanta Mutual to comply fully with the 1920 law under terms specified for new companies. Herndon was told that the firm needed to increase its deposit by $75,000. This was a tremendous sum even for Alonzo Herndon, but he seemed prepared to meet almost any condition. He responded to the request for $75,000 with a simple and straightforward, "I can't have it [the money] before morning."[44]

This response may have shocked the commissioner, and it undoubtedly dismayed Herndon's white friends, who chided him about foolishly putting his money into the company. But Herndon moved forthrightly to increase the capital stock and to reorganize Atlanta Mutual as a legal reserve company. After careful study and preparation, in November 1921 the officers of Atlanta Mutual petitioned the state to amend the company's charter by changing the name to Atlanta Life Insurance Company, increasing the capital stock to $100,000, and changing the status to a legal reserve company authorized to write all classes of life insurance. A new charter reflecting these amendments was granted on 29 September 1922.[45]

With the new charter in hand, the president moved swiftly to sell the new stock. Time was extremely important to the enterprise, especially because of the need to recover its reputation for public honesty and exemplary management, which had been blemished by the allegations against Lindsay and Shanks. A growing fear also existed among the officials that unfriendly whites were waiting in the wings to take over should they flounder. Herndon concluded that the company could ill afford to wait two or possibly three or more years before enough stock could be sold through public subscriptions to increase the capitalization to $100,000. Furthermore, a public sale offered the opportunity for unfriendly forces to purchase shares in the firm. Therefore, on 20 October 1922, when the books opened for cash subscriptions, Herndon immediately presented a check for $78,750. This amount covered the entire cost of the new stock and paid-in surplus of Atlanta Life. To permit the other stockholders to obtain a portion of the new issue, a thirty-day stock option was offered on a limited scale. Within this period, the old Atlanta Mutual stockholders had an opportunity to purchase as much of the new stock as they wished at $125 per share—the same price Herndon had paid for it. As this option was taken advantage of, on 7 December Herndon transferred 16.28 shares of the new stock to other purchasers. In addition, each of the stockholders, upon surrendering obsolete Atlanta Mutual stock, received 1.48 shares of Atlanta Life stock at a par value of $148 and 1.48 percent interest in the surplus at a value of $37.[46]

The company thus weathered a potentially serious crisis and reached an important milestone in its history. Those who had labored to save the enterprise rejoiced in the good news that in addition to achieving legal reserve status the company's assets had more than doubled in the two years since 1920, the entire income from new stock sales had been invested in state and municipal bonds, and the capital stock had increased to $100,000. Although the outcome of the internal investigation into the alleged embezzlement of company funds was never reported publicly and the issue disappeared from the newspaper after February 1921, both Lindsay and Shanks were promptly replaced. The two managerial positions were eliminated, and Chamblee became general manager and Eugene Martin secretary.

Because the firm's internal problems had not been publicly debated, its achievements were not overly publicized or its successes too loudly proclaimed. Within the company Herndon frequently complimented the officers and staff members for the hard work each had exerted on behalf of the company. In spite of the optimistic outlook indicated by growing assets and the new legal reserve status, Herndon remained prudent and ever cautious to avoid too much publicity. He frequently warned of criticism of and opposition to the company and to black endeavors generally, which made it necessary for Atlanta Life to "keep our own council until fully and completely out of the woods."[47]

5

An Emphasis on Expansion

The Ox and the mule work but men ought to think. If our race wishes to control Negro Business, we have got to scheme and think and plan.
—Alonzo F. Herndon

Race relations in America did not improve substantially as a result of the country's involvement in a war fought ostensibly to preserve democracy. In the South and in many other parts of the nation, segregation continued unabated. Nevertheless, World War I and the earlier race riots and lynchings stimulated a renewal of black business activity. Despite the preachments of the National Negro Business League and other groups and individuals that encouraged blacks to organize businesses and urged support of race endeavors, most black businesses before World War I did not enjoy high status. Such enterprises were frequently discouraged by whites and belittled by blacks, who failed to support them either through financial investments or patronage.

Following World War I, however, as John H. Harmon put it, large numbers of blacks "became not only racially conscious, but economically conscious," and "from this realization began to enter business in a large measure."[1] Indeed, notable achievements were made in certain lines of business with black investors pooling their resources and forming corporations to render services to African-Americans. Unfortunately, many of these corporations were short-lived, and times were generally perilous for black enterprises, which were limited almost exclusively to the black market.[2]

Amid the turmoil and the promise of the 1920s, Atlanta Life recovered from the reverses it had experienced in the early years. Seeking to move the enterprise to greater heights, the company's leaders worked to establish an image of strength and social responsibility. As a legal reserve company, Atlanta Life joined a select group among insurance companies owned by African-Americans, which in 1922 included Mississippi Life (Indianola), Standard Life (Atlanta), North Carolina Mutual (Durham), and National Benefit (Washington, D.C.). Dubbed the golden years of the company, this decade of relative prosperity for Atlanta Life saw the laying of a secure foundation for growth and development.

In the fall of 1922, the company set up an ordinary department and expanded from the restricted industrial basis with no policies in excess of $500 to twenty-one new broad-ranging policy contracts which included all classes and kinds of ordinary insurance to $10,000. Because the new department required additional space, the company expanded its physical facilities by occupying the entire Atlanta Life Building on Auburn Avenue. And though conservative restraints continued to guide the founder-president, an emphasis on growth dominated the next few years.[3]

In early 1923, Atlanta Life moved vigorously to expand its operations. After careful deliberation, the company officials decided initially to enter states nearest to Georgia to save time and money as well as to permit greater efficiency in managing new districts. Accordingly, at its February meeting, the board of directors approved plans to enter Florida, Tennessee, and Kentucky. Herndon scouted several additional states in anticipation of further expansion over the next months. Determined to move forward with this endeavor, company officers were soon engaged in the greatest bout of expansion fever in the company's history, rapidly entering a half dozen new states in the twenty-two months between February 1923 and December 1924.[4]

The company expanded first into Florida, where Herndon was initially highly optimistic about insurance sales. Florida had many positive features. The climate was good, and it was ideally suited for the production of some crops each season of the year. There were numerous progressive towns, and as the Florida land boom grew to sensational proportions in 1924, the state experienced the most delirious fever of real estate speculation in recent history. Based on far-flung reports that from Miami to Palm Beach Florida's coast was being developed into an American Riviera, many Americans were scrambling to purchase land in the state. The fever soon spread across the state to

Tampa and other cities along the west coast. Reports circulated throughout the country that whether through legitimate or fraudulent means, a great deal of money could be made in Florida.[5]

Herndon had purchased a large tract of land in the state where he built a comfortable winter home set picturesquely amid a large orange grove in Tavares. In the midst of the land boom, he sold the bulk of his holding for a substantial sum, although he maintained the family's winter home on a smaller tract. From Tavares, he traveled frequently about the state observing the advancements in jobs and living conditions among the nearly 330,000 blacks, whom he believed would contribute positively to the company's development. In April 1923, with Herndon's strong approval, the board voted unanimously to enter Florida, and by July, Atlanta Life had set up branch offices at Jacksonville, Tampa, Pensacola, Gainesville, Palatka, and Orlando.[6]

Although sales in Florida did not skyrocket immediately, the old industrial business progressed smoothly from the outset. In Florida, as elsewhere, Atlanta Life adhered to the previously successful practice of expanding business through acquisitions whenever practical, and company officials immediately entered into negotiations to reinsure Union Mutual of Jacksonville, Florida's second oldest black company. The firm, controlled by the widow of the former president, was on the verge of bankruptcy caused partly by the ill health and inexperience of the hapless owner. Unable to liquidate the firm's debts, she sought to reinsure the company in a healthy one. Although Atlanta Life made an offer for the business, its bid was not accepted, and Union Mutual went to People's Industrial, another small black-owned firm in Jacksonville. Contending that this business should be merged with a Florida-based enterprise, the former president's widow accepted a more generous offer, involving a lifetime salary and a stock merger.[7] Although disappointed at the company's failure to acquire this ready-made business, Herndon remained optimistic as Atlanta Life developed satisfactorily in the state. By the end of the first quarter of 1924, Florida headed the lineup of new states with over $16,000 in premium income.[8]

Tennessee also appeared to offer opportunities for insurance sales among the more than 451,700 blacks in the state. Economic conditions were favorable in some sections, especially in urban areas, where blacks worked in the lumber industry or on railroads. Blacks in Tennessee also showed a tremendous entrepreneurial spirit following World War I and had established numerous businesses in cities such as Memphis, where the famed Beale Street literally beat to "the thriving pulse of capitalism" as black Memphians initiated cooperatives, department stores, and manufacturing plants.[9]

Atlanta Life entered Tennessee in July 1923, several months before a dramatic upheaval in black insurance in the state involving Mississippi Life Insurance Company. Although domiciled legally in Mississippi, this firm had moved its headquarters to Memphis in 1920 and was one of the largest black businesses in Tennessee. By 1924, however, Mississippi Life had experienced a series of difficulties which led to a sale of the majority of the company's stock to Heman Perry of Atlanta. Following this highly publicized sale, several events occurred which led to the realization of one of the greatest fears of black Tennesseans, who watched helplessly as the first black firm to achieve legal reserve status passed out of control of African-Americans. Many of the agents, officials, policyholders, and supporters of Mississippi Life had initially perceived Perry's takeover as a merger between the Atlanta-based Standard Life and Mississippi Life. This hope was dashed when, following the takeover in December 1923, a reinsurance deal was arranged with the white-owned Southern Life Company of Nashville. Blacks in Tennessee were angered by this turn of events, and their reaction was to heap the harshest of insults upon the perpetrators of the deed and to protest vigorously.[10]

George Washington Lee, an Indianola, Mississippi, native and veteran lieutenant of World War I, was cast in a central role in the protest against the sale of Mississippi Life to a white firm. As a vice-president and manager of the Memphis district, Lee had worked with Mississippi Life for four years and had pointed with pride to the enterprise as proof of African-Americans' ability to develop and sustain viable businesses. Lieutenant Lee, as he was known widely, censured Heman Perry for his part in the demise of Mississippi Life and charged publicly that whites had conspired to take over the firm. Moreover, he contended that they "had made Perry an unwitting dupe in their scheme to sap the black man's economic strength."[11]

Angered and alarmed by the deal, which he believed represented "the white rape of a black company," Lee joined several officials of the black firm in taking their protest to the Mississippi insurance commissioner. When they failed to obtain redress, Lee sought a court injunction to prevent Southern Life agents from collecting premiums from Mississippi Life policyholders. He also convinced managers from the several states that constituted the company's territory to converge in Memphis, where they marched to the old home office of Mississippi Life. In an audience with the officials of Southern Life, the managers protested the sale and refused to sanction or support it. When the Mississippi court ruled in favor of Southern Life, Lee organized the field representatives in a walkout, leaving Southern Life without agents to collect the weekly premiums. Opposition to the transfer of Mississippi Life to a white firm widened further when Southern Life put white agents in the field to collect from black policyholders. Lee and the others rejoiced heartily when the policyholders realized how the reinsurance deal affected the jobs and income of African-Americans and some refused to pay their premiums to the white collectors.[12]

From Atlanta, Alonzo Herndon followed the events in Memphis with intense interest. In April 1924 he visited Tennessee to scout conditions in that state and to promote Atlanta Life. When Herndon reached Memphis, he made a point of contacting George Lee. Through Robert Reed Church, Jr., one of Tennessee's most influential black citizens and mentor to Lee, Herndon met the vocal young protest leader and persuaded him to work for Atlanta Life as manager of the new Memphis district. In this new position, Lee employed many of the agents who had joined him in the walkout against Southern Life. To a large number of Mississippi Life policyholders, George Lee's affiliation with the Atlanta firm meant an alternative for their insurance nickels and dimes. Herndon was elated over the possibilities for the company's growth in Tennessee under Lee's leadership and deemed the obtaining of Lee's services "the greatest accomplishment of the tour."[13] Over the next few months the company progressed satisfactorily in Tennessee, and by the end of 1924, in addition to Memphis and Knoxville, where Atlanta Life concentrated its efforts initially, it had set up districts in Nashville, Jackson, and Chattanooga.

Kentucky, on the other hand, never provided as good an opportunity. For several months, Atlanta Life was unable to enter that state because the Kentucky Insurance Department held up its application. During that time, Herndon contacted friends in Kentucky on behalf of the company and visited some areas of the state to study prospects for insurance sales. Returning to Atlanta, he gave an encouraging report of the state's approximately 236,000 blacks. Like Tennessee, Kentucky had suffered from the migration of blacks out of the state during the war, but the African-American population generally appeared progressive and a number of black enterprises operated in the state.[14] Optimistic about the chances of success, Atlanta Life entered Kentucky in November 1923, and by the year's end was operating districts at Lexington, Covington, and Louisville. But the predicted success was not attained, and business in the state lagged for some time to come.[15]

Atlanta Life continued to expand into new states, entering Missouri, Kansas, and Texas between December 1923 and December 1924. Although the great migration swept thousands of blacks into the cities in the North and East, the directors chose not to follow these hordes. Their decision to expand into areas where blacks had converged in the nineteenth century appears to have been tied closely to Herndon's role as company scout and to a combination of historical and contemporary trends that affected African-Americans.

Herndon frequently acted as scout for the company, making trips to various sections of the country to observe the condition of African-Americans and the general state of the economy in various regions. He sought areas where blacks had steady sources of employment, owned their own homes and businesses, and exhibited a cooperative racial and entrepreneurial spirit. Following a visit to St. Louis in 1923, for example, Herndon reported favorably to the board on examples of thriftiness and the savings spirit among blacks as exemplified in their ownership of homes and businesses. On other occasions, he reported that blacks in this region were more prosperous than their counterparts in the South.[16]

Lured by the prospects of free land and an escape from the specter of reenslavement, blacks had been attracted to Missouri and Kansas since Reconstruction. Despite the hardships and frustrations of the frontier, the early migrants established several settlements in the region where they were joined by later hordes from Georgia, Alabama, Tennessee, Louisiana, and the other southern states in the 1870s and 1880s. Affected by preachments on self-help and race solidarity as techniques of uplift, combined with legislative and court efforts to achieve civil and political parity with whites, black settlers in these states had carved out a few prosperous communities by the end of the century. They also enjoyed a measure of economic and political independence generally unavailable in the South, where peonage, violence, and disfranchisement restricted black development. This region had also been affected by the wartime exodus of the twentieth century. Kansas and Missouri were recipients of the second withdrawal of blacks from the South in the great migration of 1916–18, each state showing an increase in its black inhabitants between 1910 and 1920. Unlike those who dispersed into rural sections, however, the new migrants settled in centers like St. Louis and Kansas City, swelling the urban population.[17]

In St. Louis the black population more than doubled between the two wars, with the migrants coming largely from Texas, Mississippi, Oklahoma, and Arkansas. Obtaining expanded opportunities for employment, blacks formed a high percentage of workers in the industrial plants in St. Louis in the period immediately following World War I. In Houston, another city into which Atlanta Life expanded, blacks were also progressive; one report indicated that by the late 1920s blacks had made "heavy investments in fraternal office buildings. . . . Insurance companies, real estate concerns, food enterprises and undertaking establishments represented the major business enterprises."[18]

For these reasons, Herndon was optimistic about the possibilities of success for Atlanta Life in St. Louis and Houston. He also no doubt believed that blacks in these areas had a greater racial consciousness than those in the North. Unable fully to escape discrimination, racism, and violence, blacks in this region were more likely to be motivated to avoid contact with whites when possible and to build and support their own institutions when practical.[19] The promotion of racial enterprises frequently encountered greater difficulties in the North, where blacks sometimes "evinced only an indifferent interest in the success of enterprises owned and operated by their own people," perceiving their encouragement of black entrepreneurial activities as an invitation to segregation. But as migration to the North increased and racial hostilities erupted in urban areas, blacks were brought "face to face with the fact that in crucial moments, North or South, they must rely entirely upon their own resources and efforts."[20] Nevertheless, Atlanta Life's perception of a less than enthusiastic racial and entrepreneurial attitude among northern blacks undoubtedly contributed to its rejection, at least temporarily, of taking its business into the North.

By December 1923, the company had acquired a license to operate in Missouri, and in April of the next year it entered the adjoining state of Kansas. As in Kentucky, business developed slowly, and expected sales in the two states were not immediately realized. Ten years later, the amount of insurance in force in Kansas totaled only $422,000, and it remained stagnant for several years thereafter. In Missouri, sales were only a little better as that state vied with Kentucky for next to last place on the sales charts. The one bright spot in the expansion saga was Texas. Entering the state in December 1924, Atlanta Life struck a bonanza. Company officials reported that Texas was "the most fertile of all insurance fields," and by 1940 that state was challenging Georgia for the largest debit in the system.[21]

Despite its success in Texas, Atlanta Life halted expansion at the end of 1924. The directors were fearful lest the company become a victim of the perils of overexpansion, deeming it undesirable to respond to the appeals received from individuals and groups in other parts of the country requesting that the company enter various states. The directors decided to concentrate on promoting sales within the eight states in which it operated. Atlanta Life now employed nearly seven hundred persons spread over seventy-six branch and subbranch offices.[22] As the excitement of the first major expansion effort subsided, the directors reviewed the progress the company had made throughout the system. In addition to expansion activities, the officers had worked since achieving legal reserve status in 1922 to accomplish three major objectives: a good agency organization, steadily increasing policy sales, and good community relations throughout the system.

Finding capable agents was essential to attaining the first objective. As in Texas, where the assistant agency director and three young men dispatched from the home office set up districts at Beaumont, Houston, Galveston, Dallas, Fort Worth, and Waco and made the initial incursion in sales, new states were generally opened by special teams under the direction of a veteran employee. As a district developed, the company hoped to recruit additional agents in the communities, but finding local manpower proved extremely difficult in many areas. Texas was illustrative of the general barrenness of some areas in prospective agency personnel. Although early sales were satisfactory in Texas, after eighteen months in the field company officials continued to lament that "half of the State has not been touched" because of a lack of acceptable manpower. Agency officials reported, "The business is here in Texas, the people are able and will pay for it, if we can only get the manpower to handle our proposition."[23]

In Texas and elsewhere, because resident agents were not readily available to place in the field retailing Atlanta Life contracts, the special team became an important feature of the developing system. The teams frequently contained a large number of college graduates, who by the 1920s were beginning to find the insurance business an attractive alternative to traditional careers in education and the ministry. As president, Herndon heartily endorsed the idea of employing college graduates, and it was not unusual for him personally to recruit special agents among the students at Atlanta University. Herndon had long demonstrated an interest in the university and its student body. When promising students came to his attention, he frequently invited them to his home near the campus for meals or informal visits, and in a relaxed manner, he urged them to talk about their ambitions and career goals. Not unexpectedly, he encouraged some of them to consider the life insurance business.[24]

As Atlanta University and other black institutions turned out more college-trained men and women, better-trained agents began to swell the ranks of the insurance business. Indeed, as the company grew, the typical Atlanta Life agent had far more formal training than his counterpart in white firms, who usually had only a high school diploma, sometimes less.[25] The employment of college-trained agents, however, did not provide the complete answer to Atlanta Life's need for a strong and effective agency force. Educated black agents had the advantages of a liberal education, but they usually lacked practical experience in insurance or business-related work. Few of the men and women were trained in business management or salesmanship because the black colleges and universities they attended offered few, if any, business courses.[26] Even when courses conveying some business knowledge were available, the lack of practical experience still hampered the agents.

Atlanta Life's ordinary sales were hindered particularly by the new agents' lack of practical experience and specialized training in sales and management. Describing the problem to stockholders, a company official explained that agents usually adapted easily to writing industrial insurance, which required only minimal skills and the solicitor acted as an "order taker" accepting situations as he found them. More training and practical experience were necessary in ordinary insurance for agents frequently encountered enormous difficulty in reaching their sales quotas because they were unable to "create a specialized situation to put men in the market for their contracts."[27]

In 1922 Atlanta Life became the first black company to meet the pressing need to train agents by creating an educational department and "furnishing its workers with a complete course of study in Life Insurance Salesmanship." New agents were assigned for several weeks to the new department and put through a program of training to acquaint them with the fundamentals of life insurance sales techniques. Organized by Cyrus W. Campfield, a graduate of Tuskegee Institute, the department stressed the psychology of retailing insurance and illustrated ways to motivate people to want an Atlanta Life policy. The course, which included instructive texts and pamphlets, also emphasized technical aspects of insurance work, including explanations of contracts, weekly accounting methods, and auditing procedures. Although the program placed its greatest emphasis on producing ordinary business, industrial contracts and their selling points were also included. At the end of the training period, the enrollees were examined on the salient points of the course. Based on examination results and overall showing in the various open forums, enrollees were rated and assigned to districts. In 1922, the first year of operations, 228 salespersons enrolled in the educational department. Upon completing their training in January 1923, these agents received certificates and went into the field selling the company's new ordinary policies.[28]

The educational department did not confine its efforts to the home office. In addition to the initial training sessions, attended largely by special agents, the department organized classes in some of the districts and inaugurated a home study program, sending lessons into the field by special delivery. The district sessions provided training for most of the resident agents. For two or three days of intensive study, the men and women enrolled in these sessions met representatives of the home office and learned about policy contracts and accounting procedures. At the end of the period, they were examined on the course work and provided feedback on their performance.

This was undoubtedly an effective first step toward filling the void in agent training, but the program alone could not mold a perfect agency force, and some districts continued to experience problems of low productivity and high turnover of resident agents. Nevertheless, training was an essential aid, and conferences between the managers and agents took up the process. Along with inspirational talks, the officers usually included instructional subjects in these sessions. At a meeting in January 1924, for example, managers and agents participated in forums covering topics such as "The Agents' Part in Holding Down Mortality and Morbidity among Our People," "Women in Business as Pertains to Life Insurance," "The Child's Educational Policy," and "The Modern Salesman: The Prospects, Approach, Interview, and Close."[29]

Training could help to mold an effective agency force, but competitive salaries were needed to attract and hold competent personnel. Based on commissions, the gross salary of an insurance solicitor was usually subject largely to the agent's personal ambitions and sales ability. Indeed, Herndon and the Atlanta Life workers frequently pointed to the opportunities men and women could create for themselves through personal motivation and attention to the details of Atlanta Life's business. With a fairly liberal salary and commission scale, Atlanta Life offered special agents a base salary in addition to a commission. For sales of industrial policies the commission was equal to two times the business written divided by thirteen, provided the policies remained in force for thirteen weeks. A graded commission was standard for higher-premium-paying ordinary policies. The special agents received a commission during the first year of 35 and 50 percent on whole life and 20 percent on endowment. After the first year they received renewal commissions of 10 percent for the second and third years and 5 percent for the fourth and fifth years. These commissions terminated after five years.[30]

The company approved a different commission plan for resident agents. To induce local men and women, especially well-known persons with long-standing contacts in churches, lodges, and other community groups to become agents, the board meeting in special session in March 1924 voted to pay resident agents a base salary of five times the first weekly premiums on new business, providing the agents collected at least two weekly premiums. In addition, they would receive a commission equal to 75 percent of gross debit collections during the first three months, 50 percent during the second three months, 40 percent for the following six months, and 25 percent after one year.[31] Insurance work clearly offered a greater salary potential for black men and women than most other jobs available in their communities, giving them at the same time greater freedom to engage in race and community activities.

A vital part of Atlanta Life's development strategy involved securing good resident agents wedded to the communities in which they worked. As the company expanded into new states, it generally opened up district offices in the larger cities and more progressive towns, where the lifeblood and vitality of resident blacks could be easily gauged. By 1925, in the six newly served states, district offices could be found at Daytona, Jacksonville, Miami, Tampa, and Tallahassee in Florida; Covington, Bowling Green, Lexington, and Louisville in Kentucky; Beaumont, Dallas, and Fort Worth in Texas; Chattanooga, Jackson, Knoxville, Nashville, and Memphis in Tennessee; St. Louis and Kansas City in Missouri; and Kansas City, Kansas. In these cities, the company tried to open its offices along or near the main black thoroughfare convenient to other enterprises and the clients it hoped to serve. Along Memphis's famed Beale Street or North Jefferson in St. Louis, Atlanta Life stood among the successful home-grown enterprises and institutions, which throbbed with life and vitality in the 1920s. District managers such as George Lee or Pritchett Willard, along with some resident agents, were often important and respected figures along the thoroughfares and in the communities, an important factor if they were to establish the necessary rapport and trust of blacks in these cities to maximize insurance sales.

To maximize sales by other means, Atlanta Life inaugurated a number of sales and promotion campaigns designed to reach the entire agency force. Since June 1917, when the Atlanta district sponsored the first Application Shower honoring President Herndon on his fifty-ninth birthday, special campaigns had been used to stimulate the production of new business. Agents throughout the two-state system participated in the 1917 affair by presenting new applications written during the campaign to the president at a gala shower held on the Roof Garden of the Odd Fellows Building in Atlanta, each district vying for top honors in new business written.[32] Expanding the idea of special campaigns, the company added various incentives for the producers of the largest debit during a campaign.

The Senatorial Campaign of 1924 kicked off a special drive to increase business in the new states. Coming at the end of the year as expansion fever waned, the campaign was aimed both at stimulating ordinary sales and at increasing the industrial debit. The campaign, patterned after the national elections, was planned to create a spirit of competition among districts. The districts were divided into "Republicans" and "Progressives," and each manager became a candidate for "senator," the election to be determined by the amount of new business written in the districts during a nine-week period. When the campaign ended, the winning managers from the Chattanooga, Nashville, Memphis, Atlanta, Macon, Birmingham, Jacksonville, and Rome, Georgia, districts formed an advisory "Senate," which, as a special prize, attended a planning conference in January 1925 at the president's winter retreat in Tavares, Florida.[33]

More than just a campaign perquisite, the Tavares conference was a grand kickoff for Atlanta Life's twentieth anniversary year. Led by the president's son, Norris, an entourage of officers and the eight winning managers formed a motorcade which left Atlanta early on the morning of 12 January to attend the four-day conference. Along the way, a two-day road program occurred, which took the group into Macon, Waycross, Jacksonville, Orlando, and Tampa. At each stop, the officers praised the success of the campaign and the winning "senators" gave short addresses to encourage agents and managers in the towns to increase production. When the motorcade finally reached Tavares, the winning managers were greeted by the president and his wife, and the conference got under way in the relaxed setting of the president's winter home. Highlighted by an address by Herndon, now semiretired, the conference reviewed the achievements of the past twenty years and set forth production plans for the anniversary year.[34]

After the winners returned to their districts, the twentieth anniversary campaign got under way. The *Atlanta Life Bulletin*, which was begun in 1924 and continued publication periodically throughout 1925–26, renewed the spirit of competition among districts as they contended to win a trip to a big anniversary conference scheduled for Atlanta in July. Each issue highlighted the achievements of districts and individuals and prodded or challenged the districts to achieve the campaign's goals. "Augusta has outstripped Macon," "Savannah has completely put Memphis under her feet," "Montgomery is after Mobile," "Tampa has outclassed St. Louis and is now after Waycross. The Fight is on," heralded the special notes in issue after issue of the publication. The *Bulletin* also urged the new districts and agents to get into the spirit of the campaign and to stimulate sales. For the winners, the company offered a trip to the home office, where special activities were planned for them as honored guests. With emphasis on ordinary sales, the agents or managers achieving a million dollars in new business were to be designated victors of the Herndon Honor Drive and given special commendations.[35]

In July, as the campaign neared conclusion, agency officials identified the various categories of winners and made arrangements for them to travel to Atlanta, while the home office staff planned picnics, smokers, and lawn parties for the occasion. Norris Herndon kicked off the conference at the end of the month with a speech highlighting the adversities and achievements of the past twenty years. He spoke of the years of prosperity, mixed with some adversities, that Atlanta Life had experienced, pointing out that "in spite of all foes, and in spite of all misfortunes," the firm had climbed steadily upward and was now "one of the leading insurance companies of the Negro race." Turning to specific evidence of growth, he cited the industrial department with a total of 153,339 policies amounting to $11,653,439. The ordinary department, however, in existence for only seven of the twenty years, had only 3,158 policyholders with $2,839,160 worth of insurance on the books.[36]

Overall, this volume of business was considered low after twenty years but was explained by the various adversities and misfortunes that had hit the company over the years. Norris Herndon's remarks were meant to encourage the agents to work even harder to increase sales and improve the production position of the company. At the campaign's conclusion, the officers declared it a resounding success. But it did not end the year's production efforts. Just as the anniversary campaign closed with the special conference in July, the *Bulletin* hurried to announce plans for the next senatorial campaign to begin in early October with its winners slated to attend a second midwinter conference in Tavares.

Special campaigns became an important aspect of each year's production program. No sooner did one end than plans got under way for another. Each year the company celebrated the president's birthday with a production campaign; later this honor was extended to other members of the president's family and to officials of the firm. Local districts and states also held special campaigns, and the *Bulletin*, along with the *Vision*, the company's official journal, which began publication in early 1926, frequently highlighted efforts in St. Louis, Memphis, and other districts. Agents, too, vied with each other to become "kings of the forest," "$200 debit men," or even "diligent strivers." Whether the prize was a trip to the president's winter retreat in Tavares, a convention of the National Negro Insurance Association, a presidential inauguration in Washington, D.C., a world's fair, or simply a place on the company's production honor roll, a campaign was usually at the heart of each production activity. Herndon very much encouraged production campaigns, and in 1926 he called for "a campaign all the time in order to show progress and a steady growth."[37]

Progress and steady growth were important objectives of the company, and campaigns and other techniques were used to increase business. When all else failed, the managers and agents who remained unproductive were severely chastised, and their names and decreasing debit amounts were published in the *Bulletin* and *Vision*. In 1926 the board instituted penalties of demotion and reduction of commissions for agents and managers failing to meet minimum standards of production. Through these measures the company attempted to meet the objective of increasing sales, to weed out unproductive agents and managers, and to mold an effective team of Atlanta Life workers.[38]

Although working to boost sales consumed the lion's share of the officers' attention, the company did pursue programs in the 1920s designed to improve the health environment of potential policyholders and to promote good public relations. As early as 1921, Cyrus Campfield, director of education and publicity, introduced plans for a social services department within the company and proposed a study of health, housing, and working conditions among African-Americans; the major objective was "to reduce morbidity and mortality among the Atlanta Life policyholders in particular and the people at large."[39]

The poor health environment of large numbers of blacks generally boded ill for insurance companies. In Georgia, as elsewhere, blacks lived in an environment that denied them adequate medical attention. As a group, they earned lower wages, lived in poorer houses, and had less education than whites. These factors, among others, made health problems more acute among the black population. Campfield's social service plans, aimed at combating the poor health situation, were ambitious for a small firm. As part of the proposed program, he anticipated organizing a visiting nurse service to teach ill policyholders about sanitation and hygiene. He hoped eventually to develop an industrial services bureau to cooperate with employers in securing better working and living conditions for workers. The board approved these plans but voted an allowance of only $150 a month to support the department.[40]

This was a very meager sum for so ambitious an endeavor. But Atlanta Life was the first black insurance company to attempt formally to provide such social services. Initially, Campfield launched a health campaign in the public schools of Georgia and Alabama designed to increase community awareness of hygiene practices. He gave lectures to school groups and enrolled children in a school-based program called the Atlanta Life Booster's Club through which the children pledged to work to help reduce mortality and morbidity in their communities. Campfield involved agents in this effort, having them distribute along their routes circulars that stressed good health practices and sanitation methods.

The program also looked into housing conditions among blacks. Campfield undertook a general investigation of the housing stock in several states in which the company operated. As expected, the investigation indicated a need for protective housing laws, and, as a follow-up to the investigation, Campfield mailed copies of protective housing laws to cities in Georgia, Alabama, and Florida in an effort to initiate improvements in housing. Altanta Life's social services effort only scratched the surface of a major problem in the black community, but it had potential for a greater effect. Other black insurance companies expressed interest in the program, and Atlanta Life representatives reported on the pioneer venture at the first annual meeting of the National Negro Insurance Association in Durham in October 1921, highlighting the program's potential for improving hygiene and health in the black community and reducing claims for black companies.[41]

The full impact of Atlanta Life's program is difficult to assess. The records of the social services department in 1923 disclosed the following achievements: three hundred health and social services lectures at public meetings and schools, both public and private, in Georgia, Alabama, and Florida; thirty thousand men and women addressed in public meetings; two hundred thousand pieces of health literature distributed; three hundred conferences held with state, county, and city health officials; sponsorship of the Atlanta Life's Housing Betterment League; organizing of community improvement clubs in Birmingham and other cities; training of four hundred Atlanta Life employees as social services workers; and featuring a "100 Year Old Club" movement to extend the life span of Afro-Americans. Although specific cities were not identified, the report indicated that this investigation into housing conditions had resulted in five cities proposing protective housing codes and in officials of twenty-four counties supporting efforts to improve housing. Beyond these promotional efforts, the extent of the benefits accrued in improved health and housing among black clients and potential clients is unknown. It appears that the company did not venture far beyond these initial measures, and in 1923, the social services department was discontinued, leaving the area of health investigations largely to the medical director. For Atlanta Life, the primary benefit of the two-year program was the favorable publicity gained from Campfield's tours and lectures, which won numerous friends and supporters for the company.[42]

Although retreating from formal social service work, the company continued to manifest a keen interest in the community, particularly in areas where it was also good business. For example, the mortgage loan department was a source of benefit to the community, promoting the company's image and expanding its investment portfolio. This department made loans to individuals and organizations to purchase homes and other real estate. Although the loans were judiciously made from the beginning and the mortgagees were all reputable citizens, including many Atlanta Life employees, the loan program facilitated the purchase of homes, apartments, and businesses by black people. Loans to churches allowed congregations to build religious edifices as well as to extend their charity and community work.[43]

Atlanta Life concluded twenty years of operations in 1925 and moved into the second half of the 1920s as one of the more significant black enterprises in the South. After numerous reversals, the firm seemed at last to be on its way to achieving distinction among black companies and to acquiring the reputation for strength and financial security that characterized it in later years. With over $19 million in insurance in force, the enterprise carried approximately 13 percent of the total $141,274,982 of insurance held by the eight leading black insurance companies in 1925.[44] In the five years since 1920, Atlanta Mutual's assets had increased by nearly $1 million. And though results of the expansion had been uneven and disappointing in many instances, the effort had created a broader business base.

Gross sales were also increased, and in 1924, when expansion activities were halted, the company showed the greatest gain in sales since 1920, and sales figures increased steadily in succeeding years until 1929 (see Table 5.1). Industrial sales, representing fully 90 percent of the in-force insurance, continued to show the greatest growth, although the firm now offered twenty-two contracts, including several classes of ordinary insurance. To keep premium rates competitive,

Table 5.1.　Premium Income by Classes of Insurance, 1916–1932

Year	Life, health, and accident	Industrial life	Ordinary	Total premium income
1916	$ 58,970	$	$	$ 58,970
1917	416,979			416,979
1918	536,188	1,908		538,096
1919	753,592	58,945		812,537
1920	890,288	233,276		1,113,564
1921	698,155	260,637		958,792
1922	590,709	263,455		854,164
1923	619,030	295,929	27,438	942,397
1924	774,986	386,842	69,120	1,230,948
1925	941,262	469,633	106,101	1,516,996
1926	980,287	532,314	142,835	1,655,436
1927	979,274	606,261	153,335	1,738,870
1928	964,652	657,347	165,763	1,787,762
1929	940,862	657,735	168,993	1,767,590
1930	906,299	660,425	167,518	1,734,242
1931	784,921	587,318	159,590	1,531,749
1932	642,866	501,986	140,165	1,285,017

Source: Atlanta Life Insurance Company, Examination Report of Books, Records, and Securities, 1916–32 (mimeographed), in ALCF.

the company offered ordinary policies only on a nonparticipating basis. Unlike participating policies, which included in the premiums a margin to cover expenses and to safeguard against future contingencies, the nonparticipating policies carried lower premiums. Because policyholders shared none of the company's losses, their fixed premiums represented both the initial and final cost. Although the participating policies allowed policyholders to share in company earnings, the higher initial cost was a disadvantage to policyholders, and for firms like Atlanta Life, higher costs might hamper ordinary sales.[45] In 1928, observing the moderate growth, strong reserve basis, ample surplus for contingencies, favorable mortality rate, moderate expenses, and well-selected investments which yielded moderate returns, the Alfred M. Best evaluators gave Atlanta Life the rating of "very good," a designation it never ceased to earn in succeeding years.

Yet even with a favorable rating and the security of an ample and growing financial surplus, Atlanta Life did not create a major stir in the industry or advance readily into new areas. Instead, for the next few years the company dropped any consideration of further expansion of sales territory or the addition of new contracts such as group insurance and pulled inward, especially as the clouds hovering over black insurance reached storm proportions in the 1925–32 period. And as if the ensuing upheaval alone was not reason enough for the company to postpone new ventures, the approaching depression further mandated a general retrenchment.

6

A Great Racial Burden

A dozen white insurance companies might go by the board and
hardly cause a ripple. Such is not the case with us.
—John Hope, Morehouse College

A prominent reason for Atlanta Life's general retreat from expansion activities in the mid-1920s undoubtedly stemmed from several alarming developments in the black insurance industry. The first of these centered around the downfall of Atlanta's Standard Life Insurance Company in 1925. Following closely on the heels of the sale of Mississippi Life, the loss of Standard Life caused a tremendous upheaval in insurance circles and shook the black world in the same way as had the failure of the Freedmen's Bank in 1874. Saddened by the blow to black economic development and actively involved in efforts to rescue the enterprise, John Hope, president of Morehouse College, declared that "the Standard Life Insurance Company is now the great racial burden with many of us."[1]

The second development that focused national attention on black insurance occurred in the midst of the Great Depression. As the impact of the loss of Standard Life receded in the late 1920s, the sensational downfall of National Benefit Life Insurance Company in 1932 again highlighted the weaknesses of black companies. Many leaders of the black entrepreneurial class realized that the disappearance of these long-standing firms was devastating for black business generally, "corroding much of the substance, as well as the spirit of the idea of an independent black economy."[2] They were particularly concerned about the publicity such events generated, believing that unfavorable publicity fueled the negative impact of these failures and sparked rumors of speculation and misrepresentation. For black entrepreneurs, especially the officials of Atlanta Life, the burden of black entrepreneurs was perceived as twofold: to save failing black businesses whenever possible and to pressure newspapers, especially the black press, to keep failures out of the public eye.

Standard Life was an unusually progressive black enterprise. Under the direction of the daring and aggressive Heman Perry, this firm experienced extraordinary success over its eleven-year history. By 1915, after only two years in operation, the company had nearly $2 million in insurance in force and its assets reached $245,170. Seven years later, in 1922, it reported more than $22 million of insurance in force, over $1 million in annual premium income, and assets of more than $2 million.[3] To the general observer, Standard Life seemed to be the most prosperous black business in the country.

Although Standard Life appeared prosperous to outsiders and reports circulated of strong assets and millions in insurance in force, the firm's cash-flow problems became critical by 1924. As the insurance company prospered, Perry had ventured headlong into other phases of a complex business plan. Anxious to increase the business and economic services available in the black community, he established a series of enterprises financed largely by the insurance company. By 1922 Perry had either purchased or organized several firms, including a realty company, a printing company, several pharmacies and laundries, an engineering and construction firm, a farm bureau, a philanthropic unit, and several other enterprises. An umbrella organization known as the Service Company was sole owner of all stocks, and with interlocking directorates, Perry and his closest associates ran all of the businesses.[4]

The expanding and complex system of Service Company enterprises soon depleted the cash resources of Standard Life. The most pressing need was for funds to maintain the necessary insurance reserves and cover operating expenses. As conditions worsened, additional trouble befell Standard Life in early 1924, when the Georgia Insurance Department ruled that the company was impaired. This charge resulted from the large amount of real estate appearing among Standard Life's assets, a result of the increasing number of mortgage foreclosures the firm had experienced as a new cycle of economic depression began in the mid-1920s. When the Georgia Insurance Department examined the company, all real estate, except the home office building, was classified as nonadmitted assets. The omission of this real estate left Standard Life with an impairment which the Insurance Department demanded be corrected through the liquidation of assets.[5]

Faced with continuing cash-flow problems, serious debts resulting from overexpansion, and its impaired status, Perry looked for funds to salvage Standard Life. In financial desperation and unable to obtain a loan from the traditional lending sources, Perry made a deal with Southeastern Trust, a white company, arranging what has been called a pawnbroker's loan. In a contract dated 24 July 1924, he signed a loan agreement which assigned 51 percent of Standard Life stock to Southeastern Trust as security for the loan of approximately $135,000.[6] In return, Southeastern Trust obtained an irrevocable power of attorney to vote the stock of the black company for as long as it was held by the lending agency. In turn, the white firm granted the loan and agreed, with certain provisions, not to foreclose before 15 December 1924.[7]

This arrangement extended the life of Standard Life by only six months. In early January 1925 the company passed from black ownership into the hands of whites. When Standard Life was unable to repay Southeastern Trust, the latter foreclosed on the stock, acquiring fee simple title to 51 percent of the black company, and, as majority stockholder, voted to merge Standard Life with the Tennessee-based Southern Life creating the Southern-Standard Life Insurance Company. The merger agreement required that all assets, including real estate formerly belonging to the Service Company, become assets of the new company.[8]

The failure of Standard Life sent shock waves through black communities across the nation. For years this Atlanta firm had held the attention and admiration of the race, with blacks from all walks of life pointing with pride to the "miracle" that had been created from the small savings of African-Americans. In eulogizing the firm, the *Baltimore Afro-American* pointed out, "Probably no business venture had so stirred the financial ambitions and dreams of the Negro nor given him confidence in his ability to handle commercial affairs than did Standard Life under the direction of Heman Perry, its founder and guiding genius."[9]

From early 1924, as rumors of its troubles began to spread, staving off the calamity facing Standard Life became almost a cause célèbre among black Americans. It seemed that no informed person could calmly face the impending disaster, especially if he or she understood the impact of any failure of a black enterprise on the confidence of the black public in business efforts by the race. For men such as John

Hope, absorbed in race undertakings, this crisis overshadowed Christmas in 1924 as they sought an eleventh-hour reprieve for the firm.[10]

But they were unable to retrieve the insurance company from white interests, and in January, across the country headlines glared: "Standard Merger Forced," or "Biggest Negro Company in South Gobbled up by Smaller White Ins. Co." Among editors as well as the public, reaction to the loss of Standard Life ranged from incredulous shock that this enterprise would, or even could, fail, to angry denunciations of those persons whose actions had brought about the downfall.[11]

Blacks were devastated by Standard Life's downfall, and they viewed it as a racial setback. Commenting on the implications for black business generally, the *Philadelphia Tribune* stated, "The passing of the 'Standard' is more than the failure of a big business institution. It means the shattering of hope and confidence . . . while it is true that crashes will come, let us do our best to prevent them from occurring too frequently. For as the dripping of water wears away a stone so will constant failure break down confidence in our business men."[12]

Several national appeals were made to bail out Standard Life and return it to black control. Although it did not succeed, the most notable of these appeals was made by black educator Robert Russa Moton, president of the National Negro Business League, and Booker Washington's successor at Tuskegee. Moton appealed to white philanthropist Julius Rosenwald and in August 1924 obtained a provisional agreement for a loan to rescue Standard Life from Southeastern's control. A condition of the loan, which was to be made by a group of philanthropists including Rosenwald, John D. Rockefeller, Sr., and Trevor Arnett, called for someone other than Perry to manage the enterprise. Unwilling to relinquish control of the insurance firm, Standard Life's president rejected the loan offer.[13]

Another unsuccessful effort emanated from a meeting of about forty-four of the leading black business and professional men from throughout the country, including representatives of two other black insurance firms. Meeting in the Atlanta headquarters of Standard Life on 18 July 1924, the group, which included prominent black businessmen such as Bert M. Roddy and Thomas H. Hayes of Memphis; John M. Avery and Charles C. Spaulding of North Carolina Mutual Insurance Company of Durham; Emmett J. Scott and several representatives of National Benefit Life Insurance Company in Washington, D.C.; John Hope from Atlanta, and many others, conferred on the problems surrounding Standard Life and the other Standard enterprises and searched for solutions.

Scott, Spaulding, and others were vitally concerned that a group of whites might be "in a position to put a strangle hold on one of our organizations and gain control." For this reason, the black conferees hoped to prevent the merger or, as they perceived it, the takeover. Mustering their resources, they proposed to organize a syndicate to purchase Southeastern Trust's interest in Standard Life. The group selected a board of directors to oversee the syndicate and subscribed to stock in the new organization in an amount totaling $58,000. Despite their genuine concern for rescuing Standard Life, the members of the syndicate were apparently unable to acquire sufficient funds, and their effort failed.[14] With no viable recourse for its recovery left, Standard Life soon passed from existence, merged with two other firms over the ensuing two years.

A block away, on Auburn Avenue, Atlanta Life felt the reverberations of Standard Life's failure and keenly perceived the burdens of a race enterprise. Addressing a meeting of Atlanta Life stockholders a few days after the merger, Herndon acknowledged his sympathy for Perry and the other organizers of the rival Standard Life. He told the gathering, "I do not rejoice at their downfall but I prayed for them and grieved with them."[15] Even more than mere sympathy, the Atlanta Life officials perhaps felt a special empathy for Standard Life, especially as they believed their own firm had only a few years earlier escaped a similar fate largely because of Herndon's personal wealth and commitment to maintaining ownership of the enterprise.

Atlanta Life had experienced similar difficulties at the beginning of the decade. Amid severe problems stemming from the war and migration as well as internal troubles caused by a dual manager system and alleged shortages, the firm had experienced external pressures which some officials believed were exacerbated by racism and greed. These pressures were relieved when Herndon came forward with personal funds to finance a new stock issue, and control of the company had remained in black hands. Nevertheless, this episode made Atlanta Life acutely aware of the particular vulnerability of black firms, and its officals were ever vigilant and aware of opposition to black endeavors, particularly those of a business nature.

Atlanta Life officials reacted to the failure of Standard Life in characteristic fashion. On one hand, they seemed to become more chary or guarded and held fast to Herndon's maxim that the firm should keep its own counsel and not let others know too much about its affairs. Some of the officers reasoned that one of Heman Perry's gravest errors had been an article that appeared in Forbes magazine in February

Atlanta Life Auditing School at Home Office, 1926 (Courtesy of Atlanta Life Insurance Company)

1924. Entitled "The Largest Negro Commercial Enterprise in the World," it gave an impressive account of the life of Perry and the development of Standard Life. The article depicted Perry as a millionaire who earned $75,000 annually, was insured for $1 million, and was worth approximately $8 million. He was described as "a man of humble origin, who by virtue of his uncanny vision, courage, and Napoleon-like leadership, is building up a gigantic commercial institution whose very spirit is already beginning to revolutionize conditions for the Negro in the South." Along with an impressive description of the firm's physical plant, the article highlighted the modern and efficient organization and the unusual employment opportunities the company provided black men and women as clerks, stenographers, bookkeepers, statisticians, accountants, and executives.[16]

It was widely believed among black insurance men that this article caused Perry a great deal of harm, inviting the close scrutiny of the Georgia Insurance Department. Some observers felt that he would have been better off without this publicity, which greatly exaggerated his personal wealth and the true condition of Standard Life. Perry, however, generally welcomed all publicity. He operated on the theory that the more publicity he could acquire the more stock he could sell, and he tended to discount any negative repercussions such publicity might generate.[17]

Atlanta Life officials, on the other hand, were guided largely by Herndon's counsel that "it is often wise to keep our hand hid," and they always avoided sensational and high-powered publicity. Indeed, for a number of years, the company did not publicize even the fact that it was the only black company to receive a rating of "very good" from the Best evaluators.[18] As a rule, the company avoided excessive attention to its affairs and did not flaunt its achievements or provide too much information for public consumption. In a similar manner, the Herndon family avoided public attention to its personal, business, or civic affairs.

For Atlanta Life as well as other black businesses of this era, the case of Standard Life further heightened the belief that blacks' economic success tended to arouse the suspicion and hostility of white groups. Moreover, some black insurance men attributed Standard Life's downfall primarily to the machinations of a small group of white men. They believed that its failure had been deliberately planned as part of a move to take over all black insurance companies and destroy the greatest bastion of black economic strength. Sharing the opinion of Standard Life's minority stockholders, who brought suit on 29 June 1926 in Fulton County Superior Court, some of the city's most respected black business leaders alleged that certain persons had plotted to bring about the black firm's downfall, seeking to appropriate its resources and deprive blacks of this important economic achievement.[19] For others, this blow was seen as part of an economic war waged by the Georgia Ku Klux Klan against the growing achievement and power of urban blacks. Contending that the Klan's "program was not only to intimidate the Negro with the rope and the torch, but also to strike at the foundation of his economic strength," one black insurance official maintained that Heman Perry had been "an unwitting dupe in their scheme to sap the black man's economic strength."[20]

Determined to conserve black economic strength, Atlanta Life reacted to Standard Life's downfall in a practical way. In a period of general upheaval in black business caused by the approaching Great Depression, the company stepped up its practice of reinsuring weaker black companies that were on the brink of failing. In December 1924, as newspapers across the country discussed the possibility of the intervention of white philanthropy in Standard Life's problems and expectations soared regarding that firm's recovery, Atlanta Life quietly reinsured the business of a small Savannah, Georgia, enterprise, a black firm that was also in severe difficulty. Incorporated in March 1919, the enterprise was organized by Paul Edward Perry, a Savannah barber and chairman of the board of directors of one of Savannah's three black banks, the Mechanics Savings Bank, along with other officers of the bank and local business and professional men. After five years of a less than dynamic existence as a small local insurance concern, Liberty Mutual Life and Health Insurance Company made a reinsurance agreement with Atlanta Life consolidating the entire Savannah agency into the larger Atlanta organization.[21]

Atlanta Life saw a twofold opportunity in reinsuring smaller, weaker enterprises. These arrangements not only increased its own income, insurance in force, and agency personnel but could also enhance the confidence in black business and businessmen, stem the flow of black policyholders to white competitors, and save jobs for black men and women. As a concrete example of the deleterious effect on the remaining black companies of the failure or sale of a black firm to a white enterprise, Atlanta Life manager Alonzo F. Herndon II, nephew of Atlanta Life's founder, wrote dolefully from St. Louis in 1925 following the sale of Douglas Life Insurance Company, a small black industrial company, to white-owned Reliable Life that "this [the sale] has brought the greatest blow to Negro business than anything that has happened. We feel the effect of it very keenly, and lots of people are dropping out of the insurance they have with other colored companies." He urged that Atlanta Life do all it could to help blacks retain faith in black companies.[22]

Atlanta Life seemed to feel deeply the burdens of a race enterprise. As the country sank deeper into depression and numerous small enterprises found it impossible to remain solvent, saving black insurance businesses became an even more urgent goal for the Atlanta officials. Between June 1930 and January 1933, Atlanta Life reinsured three Alabama firms that were on the verge of collapse. The first, the Booker T. Washington Life Insurance Company of Birmingham, was the fifteenth company to be reinsured by Atlanta Life in the twenty-five years since its founding. A local organization, the Booker T. Washington Company was operated by a group of black business and professional men which included B. L. Windham and N. B. Smith, both contractors; Dr. Walter Brown, a physician; and John W. Commons, the owner of a coal business. With approximately five thousand policyholders and a debit of $500, the small enterprise could not weather the depression, and its officers negotiated a deal with Atlanta Life in June 1930.[23]

A year later, a second transaction created tremendous goodwill for Atlanta Life in Alabama. In June 1931 the company concluded negotiations with the Union Central Relief Insurance Company in Birmingham, the pioneer black insurance company in Alabama and the parent organization of a number of early insurance companies in Alabama and Georgia. The Union Central, like the Booker T. Washington, could not withstand the depression and looked to a solvent black firm to take over the business. Despite the pressing financial condition of the enterprise, its president reported with pride that his company had rejected a white firm's "tempting proposition for reinsuring Union Central policy contracts [in a manner] consistent with his preachments of Race pride and Race consciousness."[24] For Union Central officials the preservation of black sources of employment was a major consideration in arranging a sale or merger. These men understood clearly that the jobs of key personnel were frequently at stake and were certain to be forfeited in any takeover by a white company.

As its reputation for rescuing black enterprises and preserving black jobs soared, particularly in Alabama, other firms looked to Atlanta Life for redemption. Union Mutual of Mobile, founded in 1898 by C. First Johnson, C. W. Peters, Moses Peters, and James Patterson, also experienced financial crises in 1932. Unable to comply with a newly enacted ruling by Alabama state officials which increased the amount of policy reserves required on business in force, Union Mutual president E. S. Peters initiated negotiations to reinsure its policyholders in Atlanta Life. Writing to Secretary Martin on 15 October 1932, Peters indicated that the hardships worked by the new ruling along with other financial pressures had "caused us to consider seriously the idea of requesting some strong company like Atlanta Life to reinsure our business."[25]

After careful study of the firm's financial situation, Atlanta Life worked out a reinsurance deal that resulted in a net loss to the company. Knowing that a move to place liens on Union Mutual policies as permitted under the mutual aid law would "affect adversely, all other Negro Companies doing business in the State of Alabama" and would "have a tendency to further break down confidence in Negro enterprises and Negro endeavors," Atlanta Life agreed in taking over the business to put up a balance of $18,000 on a required reserve of $22,000.[26] Although reinsurance of these contracts created a financial burden for Atlanta Life, the officials believed that the losses would be offset by increased goodwill and confidence in the strength and stability of Atlanta Life and of black businesses in general. They reasoned that the greater loss would be for another black firm to fail with loss to its policyholders.[27]

In addition to policyholders, the deal also benefited employees and stockholders. In making the agreement, Atlanta Life assured all Union Mutual employees of continued employment provided they were "honest and render good service."[28] And because most stockholders (the firm was mutual in name only) were employed by Union Mutual as well, they too shared in the benefits of reinsurance. The addition of good agents also had benefits for the reinsuring company, and Martin assured all employees that they would be brought in on the same basis as other agents. He instructed his managers to give the new agents "a whole-souled welcome into the Atlanta Life family."[29]

In August 1932, in the last reinsurance deal of this period, Atlanta Life underwrote a good portion of the business of the American Mutual Benefit Association in Houston, Texas. The firm had been in existence for approximately twenty-five years, but a debit of less than $500 caused President James B. Grigsby to work out a reinsurance deal with Atlanta Life. Under the terms of the agreement, Atlanta Life, itself feeling the pressure of the depression economy, reinsured only the so-called healthy risks, limiting the underwriting in this case to policyholders under fifty years of age whose insurability was deemed satisfactory by the inspectors. As it had with the other reinsured enterprises, Atlanta Life absorbed a good portion of the employees and merged them into its operations in Texas.[30]

Solvent and fiscally sound, Atlanta Life attempted to shoulder a great racial burden at the beginning of the Great Depression. In face of weakening confidence in black business, Atlanta Life made a noble effort to lessen the impact of black business failures by underwriting policies and reducing the aggregate loss to policyholders, although the reinsurance transactions were clearly not completely selfless in intent or outcome and important benefits accrued to the company. Through these mergers Atlanta Life obtained new business less expensively than by regular canvassing methods and usually acquired competent and experienced new personnel. Overall, however, the management of Atlanta Life undertook such arrangements primarily to bolster confidence in black enterprises as well as to boost its own image.

The efforts to bolster faith in black enterprises created enormous goodwill for Atlanta Life. In an era when some blacks in insurance circles feared that foes were conspiring to rob them of hard-earned achievements, the company reaped tremendous public relations benefits from actions that appeared to thwart such aims. In some arenas, Atlanta Life began to acquire a reputation as "the strongest Negro insurance company in the world" and "a stalwart champion and protector, not only for her hundreds of thousands of policyholders, but also for any sister companies who may become affiliated."[31] In general, however, Atlanta Life continued to maintain its traditional low public profile and to urge the insuring black public to support black businesses to prove to everyone that black business failures were an exception and that success was the norm.

During the Great Depression, however, another tremendous blow was dealt to black insurance by the failure of the National Benefit Life Insurance Company of Washington, D.C. National Benefit, for a time one of the largest black insurance companies, was chartered on 23 November 1898. Its founder, Georgia native Samuel Wilson Rutherford, had worked for the True Reformers in Virginia before setting up a small insurance association in Washington. Described as "a combination of the old-type Baptist preacher and the shrewd business man," Rutherford dominated the firm for more than a quarter of a century. By all indications, Rutherford was primarily responsible for building up the enterprise, which functioned smoothly for several years.[32]

In 1923 National Benefit began a period of expansion marked by its entrance into new states and into the field of ordinary insurance, reinsurance of other companies, and expansion of the agency force. As part of the expansion drive, the directors authorized an increase in capital stock to $250,000. It was this effort that generated problems for the firm, which soon became insurmountable. As expansion proceeded, prospective buyers were granted loans that were undersecured so as to induce stock sales. Expenses also mounted as new districts were developed, and personnel costs increased, although far too few of the districts actually showed any profit.

In 1927 National Benefit compounded its troubles by reinsuring what remained of the twice-merged Standard Life. Soon after this purchase, large death claims were incurred, and as the Depression set in, policy loans and surrender values pushed up the outflow of funds. In addition, the company was plagued by high lapse rates. To forestall insolvency, the management attempted to whittle down the reserves, changing the basis of the reserve computation to reduce the required amount of reserves.[33]

National Benefit also had a weak investment portfolio, which showed a faulty distribution of resources. With expansion in 1923, the management had begun to invest in real estate and make policy loans and some mortgages, selling its securities to finance these ventures. By 1931 the company held a large amount of real estate, including the Odd Fellows Building in Atlanta and several other "white elephant" holdings. National Benefit's portfolio did not offer a cushion for the Depression, especially as its internal difficulties worsened.[34]

The firm's financial condition became public knowledge in June 1931. A maze of financial transactions and stock manipulations was uncovered, and Rutherford was forced out of the company. Another principal in the firm committed suicide on 21 June 1931, four days after the ouster of the president. In September, John R. Pinkett, manager of agencies and second vice-president, petitioned the D.C. Supreme Court for a bill of receivership and dissolution. For almost a decade, the affairs of this firm remained in turmoil as litigation continued.[35]

The public airing of National Benefit's affairs was extremely disturbing for black firms like Atlanta Life that wished to minimize negative publicity surrounding black enterprises. Black officials knew that, as with Standard Life and earlier failures, this upheaval would mean greater difficulty for black agents soliciting new business and a higher lapse rate for black companies. Few black leaders failed to understand the negative implications of these failures. Hoping to influence the situation for the benefit of black companies, Atlanta Life Secretary Eugene Martin wrote to Pinkett in July 1931, advising that "if it is humanly possible [to] hold it [the company] intact . . . as wide spread Newspaper publicity in the matter of the largest Negro Insurance Company is seriously damaging the confidence of our people in Negro leadership and Negro Insurance." He stressed his personal concern that the scenario played out with Standard Life not be repeated with National Benefit, warning particularly that Pinkett should be wary of the actions of advisers, receivers, and others who would exploit black insurance firms "to enrich themselves at the expense of our race." Martin suggested that the firm's internal problems be handled quietly and out of the public eye.[36]

Despite Martin's advice, National Benefit's problems did become public. In July and August, several states, including Georgia, began receivership proceedings, and the issue remained in the forefront of news. Once again, black business leaders rallied to the support of a troubled black firm. On 18 August 1931, a conference of black insurance executives met in Washington to confer on the problems facing National Benefit and to determine what could be done to "protect and maintain the confidence of our people in the functioning, business ability of the officers of our companies."[37] Unable to find a way to give any substantive help, the representatives of black firms could only try to abate the harmful public effect of another insurance failure.

Again, Atlanta Life's Eugene Martin was vocal in efforts to silence the issue. He was especially critical of black newspapers, some of which he believed were exploiting the issue. He urged black editors to avoid sensational headlines, which did nothing to help black companies. He pointed out, too, that "often when they are playing up some Negro failure in flaring headlines, at that very moment, some white institution has gone under, carrying down many Negroes with it."[38]

These were laudatory preachments, but they had no effect on the eventual fate of National Benefit. Other options for Atlanta Life were unsuccessful as well. In its usual fashion, in April 1932 Atlanta Life explored the possibility of securing National Benefit's Texas agency force and reinsuring the old policyholders in the Atlanta company. But, assured of the eventual reorganization of National Benefit, its officials declined Atlanta Life's offer and the agents remained loyal to the firm for many months.[39]

Despite the loyalty of agents and the chastisement of black editors, National Benefit was not resurrected, and another important example of black economic achievement was lost to black America. Although the Great Depression alone had not caused the failure, it had certainly augmented the troubles of National Benefit, increasing the financial stresses on mortgagees and policyholders. At least two other black firms passed from the scene during this period. Struggling with dwindling resources and high lapse rates, the small Woodmen Union Insurance Company of Hot Springs, Arkansas, capitulated under heavy Depression-related pressures. Like National Benefit and several other black companies, the Woodmen Union had invested its resources heavily in mortgages, especially farm loans, which were of value to farm communities but caused tremendous financial woes for the black company as the Depression hit. In 1931, in a last-ditch effort to stave off failure, this firm merged with Century Life Insurance Company of Little Rock. The combination came too late to save either enterprise, and after about two years, Century Life also collapsed.[40]

In the North, a Chicago firm also suffered from the effects of the Depression. The Victory Life Insurance Company, organized on 3 March 1924 by Anthony Overton, invested its entire paid-in capital of $100,000 in mortgages. The firm quickly expanded beyond Illinois into seven additional states and the District of Columbia. In 1927, achieving a feat theretofore unattained by any other black legal reserve firm, Victory Life qualified to operate in New York. The Chicago enterprise continued to expand and invest in black home development and did well even in the early stages of the Depression. But the lack of diversification in investments and the deflation in property values, along with the failure of the Douglass National Bank, which was also organized by Overton and invested in by Victory Life, caused the firm to fail in 1932.[41]

These failures, especially as they were sensationally aired by the press, could not help but affect the more fragile black business endeavors. Representing the best among black business enterprises, these firms had brought together in their operations the largest amounts of capital and the most skilled management teams available to achieve the greatest advancements in black business history. In short, companies such as Standard Life and National Benefit represented the best examples of economic strength among black institutions. Following periods of high visibility and prosperity, their failures meant the disappearance of perhaps the largest chunk of assets ever amassed by blacks. Their failures caused despair and disillusionment among black leaders, who had seen them as the best hope for an independent black economy that would result in the general economic advancement of African-Americans.[42]

A major consequence of the insurance failures and other economic hardships caused by the Great Depression was a profound change in the spirit of the black business community. With the passing from the scene of men like Heman Perry, it appeared that "the old spirit of daring, the old idea that black businessmen could create and manage billion-dollar enterprises, faded and was replaced by a new spirit of caution and even timidity."[43] Instead, black businessmen adopted a more vigilant stand and became more conscious of the need for greater prudence and sagacity in business operations.

There was much talk about the need for careful, safe management and an adequate financial base for black enterprises. In some quarters, a general wariness of white intercessions in the affairs of black firms continued to be manifested with black leaders cautioning entrepreneurs to remember that "this depression has driven home in sledgehammer fashion the eloquent truth that in our extremity we cannot depend on others."[44] Appeals to race, which had been somewhat dormant in the "fat years" of the 1920s, were renewed in the struggle to combat the high policy lapsations experienced by black firms during the Depression. As in an earlier era, insurance officials attempted to impress upon the general black populace the importance of supporting black enterprises. The representatives of black insurance firms continued to highlight the job opportunities these firms offered, particularly for black youths trained in business, and they argued for support of their enterprises and of young black men and women. They felt that such support constituted the best hope of the race for successful business endeavors in the future.[45]

The difficulties of this era strengthened the commitment of Atlanta Life officials to certain longtime practices and confirmed their beliefs in the importance of financial conservatism and judicious management. No business, particularly a black one, was immune to failure and any enterprise could easily succumb to events or become a pawn in the hands of people who would wreck it. Eschewing credit or overspeculation and urging careful economies, Eugene Martin said, "If our institutions are to survive . . . every step of advance must be thought out with the greatest of care and our general policy must be, for the most part, 'a pay as you go proposition.'"[46] Even as conditions improved for insurance and for the general economy, Atlanta Life remained a strong voice for conservatism and a bulwark for weaker firms against the ill wind of black failure in the industry.

7

The Legacy of Leadership

An old man going a lone highway
Came at the evening cold and gray
To a chasm vast and wide and steep. . . .
But he turned when safe on the other side
And built a bridge to span the tide.
                —Will Allen Dromgoole, *"The Bridge Builder"*

Alonzo Herndon had been at the helm of Atlanta Life for more than two decades. His commitment to the enterprise and its growth and security was instrumental in the company's survival and early successes. More than any other individual, the astute, very conservative founder-president set the enterprise on the way toward accomplishing its goal of becoming one of the safest and most secure black insurance companies in the country. When the company faced financial or other exigencies, Herndon came forward swiftly with his personal funds to see it through crises and lean times. Sensitive to the public obligations of insurance companies to policyholders and stockholders alike, he prudently oversaw the investments and other financial affairs of the enterprise, avoiding speculative and self-serving ends to build up substantial assets and surpluses.

Herndon had recognized the necessity for a competent organization with able and responsible management. During his tenure as head of the company, he developed a corps of dedicated officers and workers who, with few exceptions, devoted their entire careers to the building of Atlanta Life. Among the cadre of longtime officers and workers at Atlanta Life were two fairly distinctive groups, each made up of individuals with unusual abilities and enthusiasm for insurance work.

Both groups served Atlanta Life extremely well. In addition to their

115

important contribution to the survival of the company in its infancy, the older, pioneer workers contributed heartily to building a resolute company spirit and to sparking enthusiasm among sales personnel. It was the younger breed of well-educated individuals, however, who were Atlanta Life's secret weapon. They handled many of the details of administering the growing firm in the period after World War I, propelling it ahead of other enterprises and guiding it cautiously on a steady course through depressions and upswings alike.

One such pioneer worker was Lemuel Harry Haywood, Sr. Haywood made an indelible imprint on the company during his long tenure as the first agency director (1922–55). Beginning in 1907, his early career as an Atlanta Life agent was spent in the small Georgia town of Gainesville, where his talent for dramatics in promotion and sales work proved extremely successful in persuading people to purchase Atlanta Life policies. This success caught the attention of Herndon and the other officers in the home office, and Haywood was given an opportunity to advance in the company. For fifteen years, he served in nearly every capacity in the company, including agent, inspector, special team member, claims adjuster, and district manager. In 1922 he was promoted to the position of director of agency and elected to the board of directors.[1]

As agency director, Haywood engendered much of what came to be known as the "Atlanta Life spirit." It was said that "Supe" Haywood, as he was called by practically everyone, "was the kind of person who could inject excitement into a cadaver," and he used this prodigious talent to promote Atlanta Life. With a bombastic oratorical style, Haywood, described as "tall, dark, slender, with a back that was ramrod straight even throughout middle age," frequently delivered rip-roaring speeches in agents' and managers' conferences throughout the system that electrified his listeners and sent them eagerly off into the field to promote the business. Unlike Herndon, who generally spoke quietly and jovially to the employees, counseling them to punctuality and thriftiness in work and personal habits with illustrations from his own vast experience, Haywood led agency meetings that were likened to pep rallies. Sometimes he excited his audiences to near frenzy with cries of "You're Atlanta Mutual People!" Over and over, his cries punctuated with poundings on the podium for emphasis, he urged the workers to use their positions as managers and salespeople to improve the condition of "mankind in general and Atlanta Mutual in particular."[2]

Another longtime employee was Howard Walter Russell. He had worked as a porter in the Georgia General Assembly and as personal valet to Georgia Governor Joseph M. Terrell before entering insurance work with the Union Mutual Association around 1907. By the time Atlanta Life absorbed Union Mutual, Russell had become vice-president, and Atlanta Life retained him. Similar in temperament and outlook to Haywood, "Dad" Russell also possessed boundless tenacity and enthusiasm for insurance work. He was deeply affected by the failure of Union Mutual and became a passionate advocate of black support of black businesses, a theme he usually emphasized in his promotional talks for Atlanta Life. Spreading his gospel of the virtues of black insurance in general and Atlanta Life in particular, Russell attempted in his speeches to drive home the twin benefits of blacks buying insurance from black companies: protection for oneself and one's family and the creation of job opportunities for African-Americans. On the lighter side, Russell possessed a lively sense of humor and, like Herndon, had a storehouse of jokes that seemed to fit any occasion.

As assistant agency director (1922–45), Russell headed a number of special teams throughout the system and was particularly adept at opening new territory for Atlanta Life. It was said that even into his seventies " 'Dad' Russell could cover as much territory and write as many applications as any of the younger boys of the company."[3] Russell's long-term association with national Baptist organizations facilitated the entry of Atlanta Life into new states, where Russell was welcomed into the churches and homes of some of the most respected citizens. Through these wide associations, he introduced Atlanta Life policies and salesmen into new areas. In 1927 Russell's work earned him election to the board of directors.[4]

Like Haywood, Solomon Johnson was associated with Atlanta Life from the company's early years. A pioneer among black insurance men in Georgia, the Valdosta native had worked as an agent for several small insurance associations and was secretary and general manager of the Royal Benevolent Association, one of the small organizations that had been absorbed when Herndon organized the Atlanta Mutual Insurance Association. Johnson was described as polite and genial with a passion for insurance work. He came to Atlanta Mutual in 1905, working as an agent in the Atlanta district before becoming the district manager.[5] In 1922, he joined with Alonzo Herndon, Lemuel Haywood, Robert Chamblee, Howard Russell, Norris Herndon, James

Officers and Directors of Atlanta Life Insurance Company, 1923 (Courtesy of Atlanta Life Insurance Company)

Harrison, Eugene Martin, Alonzo F. Herndon II, and Charles A. Faison in forming a nine-man board of directors of the newly reorganized Atlanta Life.

Along with Johnson, several of the other early directors made their mark on the company as long-term district managers. Savannah native James Tunno "J.T." Harrison was manager in Birmingham. Alonzo F. Herndon II, a Georgia native and nephew of the founder, managed the St. Louis district. Born in McDonough, Georgia, the younger Herndon was the son of the president's brother Thomas. He came to Atlanta to study at Morehouse College and Atlanta University and worked in the home office for several years. In February 1924, he went to open a branch office at St. Louis, where he remained as district manager until he died in 1944.[6]

Another director, Charles A. Faison, served a lengthy term as director of the company although he had no actual experience in insurance and worked in no active capacity for the company. Born in North Carolina, he migrated to Atlanta at the age of fifteen and obtained work shining shoes in Herndon's Markham House barbershop. Taking Faison under his wing, Herndon offered him an apprenticeship in the barbering trade, and in 1904 the two men became partners in a shop on North Pryor Street in Atlanta. Faison later managed the famed Herndon Barbershop, continuing the tradition of operating the shop for an exclusively white clientele. In 1910 Herndon brought his friend and business partner onto the board of directors of Atlanta Life where he served for nearly three decades (1910–36). After the founder's death, Faison was considered the "senior director"; his role was primarily that of an Atlanta Life booster, offering encouragement to the workers and reminding the younger men of the founder's visions and dreams for the enterprise.[7]

The only female board member in the early years was Jessie Gillespie Herndon, wife of the founder-president. Like Faison, Mrs. Herndon had no prior experience in insurance work, and her participation on the board did not emanate from active employment with the enterprise. Her duties were primarily in the areas of promotion and social relations. Following her husband's death and the elevation of her stepson to the presidency, Mrs. Herndon became first vice-president of the enterprise. Although her new position was largely symbolic (and political), she took a close interest in Atlanta Life affairs, advising company officials primarily in public relations and the maintenance of conservative company ideals.[8]

Beginning as raw novices in insurance work with limited business training, these pioneer workers nevertheless understood the peculiar circumstances of black businesses such as Atlanta Life. They were acutely aware of the numerous barriers to growth and expansion for these firms, especially the hostility of whites and the skepticism frequently encountered among blacks. Through native intelligence and an innate business wisdom, they developed exceptional techniques for selling and promoting the company, emphasizing to agents and other company personnel the necessity for hard work and a resolute spirit. As managers and board members, they devised means for training workers, often without books or literature on life insurance, and for eliminating waste, fraud, and other operational defects. In these areas, their maxim appeared to be simply "Whatever needs to be done for the good of the business, should be done."[9] The pioneer workers and officers were invaluable in igniting the spirit and substance of the infant enterprise.

Herndon was unusually successful in attracting another group of workers to the enterprise. Younger, generally college-trained, these individuals came into the company's ranks with at least some theoretical knowledge of the development and operations of social and business enterprises. This group, building on the substantial foundation established by the pioneer workers, brought about the full flowering of Atlanta Life and achieved economic and social standing in the post-Depression period.

Because the insurance business was relatively new and frequently stigmatized by the unsavory reputation of its early years, college graduates had hesitated at first to forsake the "safe" professions of preaching and teaching to enter the field. Some, like Truman Gibson, a graduate of Atlanta and Harvard universities, were ridiculed by their peers for accepting employment with insurance companies. One of the first college graduates to enter the field, Gibson was once taunted by a friend who remarked, "You are a disgrace to Atlanta University. Why did you come back to Atlanta and enter a fly-by-night five-and-dime company?"[10] Undaunted by his friend's attempt to discourage him, Gibson remained in the profession, and during his nine years at Atlanta Life, he advanced from agent to stockholder, secretary, and a director of the firm. In 1919, however, following a dispute with Herndon over the distribution of stock subscriptions, Gibson left Atlanta Life to begin a new company, the Supreme Life and Casualty Company of Ohio.[11]

Herndon's son Norris was also a graduate of Atlanta and Harvard universities with a master's degree in business administration. The only child of the company's founder and his first wife, Norris Herndon worked in the company while a student at Atlanta University. From boyhood, he spent summer vacations working in the home office under his father's supervision. Although his son's duties were largely clerical, involving the making of policies, filing, and checking reports, Herndon urged the young man to learn all aspects of the insurance business. As Norris grew older, he spent vacations in the field as an agent's apprentice, assisting with canvassing, inspections, and other field activities. While a student at Harvard, he continued to spend summers in Atlanta and to invest time in the company, and he was elected to its board of directors in 1919. After graduation from Harvard in 1921, young Herndon returned to Atlanta and assumed full-time employment with Atlanta Life.

Herndon brought another graduate of Atlanta and Harvard into the company and gave him responsibility in the investment end of the business. Walter S. Smith, a native of Chattanooga, Tennessee, had been a classmate and chum of Norris Herndon at Atlanta University before joining the army during World War I. After completing the officer candidate school at Fort Des Moines, Iowa, Smith was commissioned a first lieutenant of infantry and sent to battle the Germans in the Vosges sector of eastern France. Back in the United States at the war's end, he completed his studies at Atlanta University, enrolled in Harvard, and in 1923 earned a master's degree in business administration. Coming to Atlanta Life in 1924, Smith worked for a time as agent and inspector in Birmingham, acquiring a thorough grounding in the practical aspects of life insurance. A home office assignment soon brought him into the bookkeeping department handling investments and loans to home buyers, businesses, and churches. Smith became an able and efficient investment executive and was named a director in 1936. He remained with the firm until his death in 1972.[12]

One of the company's most valuable employees was Eugene Martin. Born in Atlanta on 17 October 1888 and educated at Atlanta University, Martin came under the influence of President John Hope and other advocates of black business development as a primary key to the economic survival of African-Americans. Like his mentors, Martin came to believe that the greatest need for the black community lay in the areas of business and economic development.[13] As a student, Martin worked as an agent for another company, the Guaranty Mutual of Savannah. There he obtained practical experience in insurance work while earning money to continue his education. In 1912, after graduating from Atlanta University, Martin secured full-time employment with Atlanta Life, entering the agency force.[14]

Insurance became a lifelong career for Martin, and he spent his entire professional life with Atlanta Life. An efficient, likable young man, he showed great aptitude for sales and collections and quickly advanced in the company hierarchy, moving from agent to district manager, branch office inspector, home office auditor, and director of agents in the industrial department. In 1920 he officially became secretary of the company and held the position for nearly fifty years (1920–69). Martin's tenure as secretary began at a particularly difficult time in the life of the enterprise, when the management was under the close surveillance of the Georgia Insurance Department. Martin handled the position with finesse and authority and was elected to the board of directors in 1922. He proved to be a conscientious and capable executive and was made vice-president in May 1947. That promotion made him second in command of the firm with far-reaching responsibilities.[15]

The most dynamic of the Atlanta Life directors was perhaps George

Eugene Marcus Martin, Secretary, 1920–69 (Courtesy of Atlanta Life Insurance Company)

Lee (1924–77). After his early stint with Mississippi Life Lee gained a local and national reputation as a prominent Elk, Republican partisan, novelist, and flamboyant orator. The diminutive Memphis manager had a very successful career with Atlanta Life, becoming a district manager, vice-president, and, in 1939, a director of the firm. Educated at Mississippi's Alcorn College, Lee was among the black men selected for the army's officer candidate school at Fort Des Moines in Iowa and served in France during World War I as a second lieutenant with the 368th Negro Division. When the fighting ended, Lee returned to Memphis to seek Robert R. Church's political intercession in his attempt to remain an officer in the peacetime army but was persuaded by Church to settle in Memphis and "get into the firing line of race progress."[16]

In Memphis, Lee became one of Church's top lieutenants and a prominent figure in Republican politics. Lee acquired "a national forum for race leadership," promoting a number of political and social issues. His position with Atlanta Life proved fortuitous for both the company and George Lee. Atlanta Life benefited by having a manager and director of national prominence with easy access to political, fraternal, and business circles, and Lee's association with the company provided a good underpinning for his social and political activities.[17]

Among the younger and better-educated executives were Fred Armon Toomer and Cyrus Campfield. Toomer was born in Toomerville, a small black section in the middle Georgia town of Byron, near Macon. He studied at Atlanta University and the Chicago School of Embalming. Following a brief stint as an embalmer, Toomer abandoned the funeral business and, in 1919, embarked upon an insurance career as a member of an Atlanta Life special team. From the special team, Toomer was sent to manage the Selma, Alabama, district. A later assignment brought him to the home office, where he served as general auditor and a director of the company (1948–62).[18]

Campfield, a graduate of Tuskegee Institute, had worked as executive secretary of the Atlanta Urban League before becoming the first director of Atlanta Life's social services department. In 1923, following the demise of that program, Campfield became director of publicity and education (1923–55), working with agency officials to develop and implement training programs. As editor of the *Vision* and other internal publications, Campfield kept the field forces well informed about company affairs and generated external publicity for the enterprise. Traveling throughout the system, he also kept eyes and ears open to general insurance trends, gathering information on new business or other companies that Atlanta Life might reinsure. In Atlanta, as the company's main contact man with the public, the outgoing Campfield sat on the boards of a number of social agencies. This role enabled him to keep Atlanta Life before the public and freed the president of some of the demanding civic and social obligations associated with his position.[19]

Atlanta Life's close relationship with Atlanta University and the large number of graduates of Atlanta and other universities who were employed explain much of the social and philosophical bent of the enterprise. Founded on 16 October 1867 by the American Missionary Association, Atlanta University grew out of the need to prepare black leaders and to inculcate in them liberal thinking and high ideals. With Yale University graduate Edmund Asa Ware, described as "one of the major prophets of higher education for Negroes," as the first president, the university launched a broad program of higher training

Departmental Heads of Atlanta Life Insurance Company, 1923 (Courtesy of Atlanta Life Insurance Company)

dedicated to providing "social leadership for a seriously disadvantaged group."[20] Along with Ware, Horace Bumstead (the source of Norris Herndon's middle name) and Cyrus W. Francis, two other graduates of the Yale Class of 1863, took up the crusade of training freedmen in Atlanta, using their class motto, "I will find a way or make one," as the guiding precept for the new university. According to Clarence Bacote, chronicler of the university's history, "This Yale spirit, transplanted to Atlanta University, was to become for Negro men and women in the South the Atlanta University spirit."[21]

The "Atlanta University spirit" was reflected in the curricular offerings and in the alumni. Students at Atlanta received a classical education meant to prepare them for personal and social uplift. The university emphasized the economic and utilitarian value of a college education and sought to instill in its graduates the ideals of honest and conscientious work with the highest aim being service to one's fellow man. Atlanta University graduates were urged to seek work in areas that promoted the progressive and enlightened development of the race, particularly teaching and the ministry. The training also involved the inculcation of a sense of the importance of enterprises that attempted to remove racial and economic barriers against blacks and encouraged individual and group cooperation, stimulation of racial consciousness, and promotion of racial solidarity.[22] According to Du Bois, Atlanta University's "great cultural mission as a school of liberal arts involved leading the American Negro into a new economic era where his political power can be soundly placed upon economic security and his function in a new democracy made clear."[23]

Atlanta University took up the issues of economic cooperation and business enterprise through its annual investigations into the status and progress of blacks in 1907 and 1917. The conferees commended black business progress and extolled the growing number and variety of such enterprises. At the same time, however, they deplored "the too prevalent haphazard method of conducting business" and called for improvement. In 1917, specifically considering Atlanta, the investigators noted that except in banking, insurance, and secret and benevolent societies, economic cooperation among blacks remained rudimentary largely because of the residual effects of slavery, which had stifled cooperation. In conclusion, they noted that "business of any appreciable proportions calls for individuals with liberal intellectual culture, efficient business training, and keen business sense."[24]

Atlanta University provided a cadre of leaders for Atlanta Life. These liberally trained individuals eagerly accepted the positions assigned them in the company. Although college-educated, they were expected to learn the basics of insurance and to acquire practical experience at nearly every level of the company. Serving as solicitors, special agents, supervisors, auditors, and managers, they attained a thorough grounding in the work of the enterprise. The blending of practical knowledge with liberal training and a desire to serve resulted in a new breed of stable leaders who by the 1920s were prepared to assume leadership of the company.

Indeed, by 1924, Herndon had shifted many responsibilities of his office onto the shoulders of younger men. Now in his sixties, he enjoyed semiretirement. He spent many afternoons playing checkers with cronies at the YMCA or exchanging jokes and spinning tall tales in the company of street-corner friends along Auburn Avenue. He and his wife traveled frequently to Tavares for extended stays. When in the home office, he usually rejected the formality of the office setting, preferring to mingle with the employees and to "ramble casually around the various departments, chewing the fat and discussing the business of the company . . . informally in a relaxed, familial atmosphere."[25] Yet Herndon remained a conscientious president; he seldom missed an important stockholders' or directors' meeting. When his health deteriorated, he arranged for meetings to be held at his home and remained the most dynamic generator of company spirit, counseling the officers and workers to greater industry, efficiency, thriftiness, square dealing, and unstinting support of Atlanta Life.

With an eye to the future, Herndon carefully groomed the younger officers to carry on the firm's activities. Norris Herndon, as first vice-president, took on day-to-day leadership during his father's absences. At these times, he was expected to give the same exacting attention to the business of Atlanta Life as his father had. The senior Herndon once wrote from Tavares advising his son to "keep an eye on the business. . . . You are me when I am away."[26]

The elder Herndon put considerable trust in his son. Satisfied that Norris possessed both theoretical knowledge and practical training in the business, his father gave him important responsibilities in the company. Norris entered the executive circle as first vice-president and served as cashier, controlling the disbursement of all company funds.[27] Demonstrating his ultimate trust in his son, Herndon shared a good deal of fiscal authority with him, assuring managers and workers at Atlanta Life that "the assets of the company are just as safe with him [Norris] as with me."[28]

The elder Herndon was concerned that Atlanta Life not fail at the death of the founder or major benefactor, as so many black enterprises did. An astute observer of black business life, he was undoubtedly aware that the cause of this endemic weakness was that a black entrepreneur would seldom "train his son to carry on after him, or instruct enough of his associates so that they could manage successfully without the founder."[29] Hoping to avoid this pitfall, Herndon not only prepared his son to step into the presidency but also secured a cadre of capable and loyal associates to carry the enterprise forward after his death.

Herndon died on Thursday, 21 July 1927, a few weeks following his sixty-ninth birthday, after several months of feeble health. His funeral was held several days later at the First Congregational Church. Hundreds attended the rites at which blacks and whites alike eulogized Herndon as a humble man as well as a great philanthropist and capitalist. Among the several dozen participants and pallbearers, both active and honorary, were persons of eminence in religion, medicine, and the other professions as well as longtime friends and associates in barbering and insurance. The tributes, interspersed with a few of his favorite hymns, recalled his tremendous achievements in business and his civic contributions.

Among those paying tribute to the life of the former slave were Dr. George Cleveland Hall, cofounder (with Dr. Daniel Hale Williams) and chief surgeon of Chicago's Providence Hospital; Myron W. Adams, president of Atlanta University, who had the previous spring nominated Herndon for the prestigious Harmon Award for achievement in business; Alfred Lawless, superintendent of southern Congregational churches; Ernest Davidson Washington, the younger son of Booker T. Washington, who represented Tuskegee Institute; Judge J. H. Hutcheson, Stone Mountain Circuit (Georgia); George Brown, a former Georgia legislator; the Reverends Peter James Bryant and James Arthur Hopkins, promoters of the old Atlanta Benevolent and Protective Association; J. C. Chapman and Charles Faison of the Herndon Barbershop; and Amy Chadwick, director of the Leonard Street Orphanage of which Herndon was chairman of the board of trustees and a loyal contributor. The insurance field was represented by Dr. Joseph E. Walker of Universal Life; John R. Pinkett of National Benefit; C. N. Walker of Guaranty Life; and Charles Clinton Spaulding of North Carolina Mutual. Speaking for the fraternity of black insurance men, Spaulding gave high praise to Herndon's "life, character and integrity [which] speak so loud among Negro business men of the country that what we might say would not be necessary. The Negro business men of America regarded Mr. Herndon as one of the sanest and most successful men of the Race."[30]

From Atlanta Life, George Lee was chosen to make remarks on behalf of the company. With impassioned eloquence, he used the metaphors of battle to expound upon the life and death of Alonzo Herndon, describing the "Captain of our army" as falling "on the battlefield of economic conquest with his boots on. His sword was unsheathed and held high and dying he flung back to his hosts 'Fight on, Fight on until the cause has been made secure.' "[31] Some Atlanta Life districts responded to Herndon's death in a more practical, businesslike manner, restating their commitment to the growth and stability of the enterprise. Resolutions poured in from throughout the system. Following the lead of the Florida special team and the Jacksonville agency force, which resolved to set aside every fourth Sunday in July as a day of memorial to the founder and to dedicate the fourth week in July as an annual Herndon Memorial Week marked by increased production and collections, the other districts followed suit and reaffirmed their commitment to increasing business.[32] Even at the saddest time in the firm's history, the managers remembered Herndon's maxim "to make good the opportunity" and used the occasion to build the enterprise.

The grief at Herndon's passing undoubtedly reached beyond Atlanta Life into the larger Atlanta community, where he had supported a number of social and commercial activities. In addition to his involvement in the Southview Cemetery Association and the Atlanta Loan and Trust Company, he had served on the board of directors of the Atlanta State Savings Bank, which opened on 6 January 1909 under the leadership of John Oliver Ross, a merchant and real estate broker. After a difficult beginning, the bank was officially chartered as a state bank with $25,000 capital on 23 July 1913. Located in the Odd Fellows Building on Auburn Avenue, Atlanta's first black-owned bank enjoyed some stability until a second black bank, the Citizens Trust, opened in August 1921. Several large withdrawals, especially the removal of the Standard Life accounts, undermined the bank, and it closed on 15 February 1922, relinquishing all assets to a liquidating agent appointed by the state banking department.[33]

Herndon had also been a vice-president and director of the Gate City Drug Store, a firm that grew out of the first black-owned drugstore in Georgia. Founded in 1898 by Moses Amos, the original business was initiated with less than $10 of investment capital. Amos, the first licensed black pharmacist in Georgia, had begun an apprenticeship in 1876 when a white druggist, Dr. J. C. Huss, hired him to do odd jobs. Amos used this opportunity to learn the pharmacy business, and when Huss died, he purchased the business and started his own drugstore in partnership with a group of local black doctors. On the basis of his years as an apprentice under Dr. Huss, Amos passed the state's pharmacy examination. The first black to sit for this exam, Amos scored the highest of all individuals taking the test and was widely acclaimed in the city. Therefore, when the original drugstore succumbed to heavy debts, Amos had little difficulty reorganizing the business with a group of new investors, which included Alonzo Herndon. By 1914 the Gate City Drug Store was one of the largest enterprises on Auburn Avenue.[34]

Herndon's financial investment in the Atlanta State Savings Bank and the Gate City Drug Store was probably very small, and by the time of his death, both had passed out of existence. But in addition to Atlanta Life, another visible reminder of his entrepreneurial interests dominated Auburn Avenue. In 1924 Herndon built a three-store office building at 251 Auburn Avenue across from the Odd Fellows Building and Auditorium Complex. The Herndon Building, as it was named, housed a number of black businesses, professional offices, and organizations. The building also contained one of the earliest hotel complexes catering to a black clientele. Like the older Odd Fellows Building, the Herndon Building helped facilitate the settlement and growth of black businesses and professionals in the community.

Because of his interests and long-standing involvements in the Auburn Avenue community, the residents and businessmen along the thoroughfare held Herndon in great respect. At the conclusion of the services at the First Congregational Church on the corner of Courtland and Houston streets, Herndon's funeral procession moved slowly down Auburn Avenue on the way to Southview Cemetery. As the cortege passed Atlanta Life and the Herndon Building, hundreds lined the street where he had made a mark as businessman and liberal contributor to social and charitable efforts. Many in the crowd undoubtedly recalled the afternoons of playing checkers with Herndon, or his street-corner lore, or the jobs they had obtained in the various Herndon enterprises, or some other personal benefit they had experienced from his civic and educational philanthropy.

His admirers, both black and white, saw Herndon as a builder, working to free his race from the "tyranny of poverty." Indeed, his support of the insurance company was described by the editor of the *Atlanta Independent* as extending well beyond concern for his financial investment in the company. He was praised as a man who "was as great in the uses of his wealth as he was in accumulating it . . . who [used] his good office, business or opportunities to provide ways and means for those he lives among to make meat and bread, provide a home, and save a dollar."[35]

Herndon was buried in Atlanta's first black-controlled cemetery, which he had helped organize in 1885. With shares of stock in the Southview Cemetery Association and the Atlanta Loan and Trust Company, three barbershops with a total of fifty chairs, a great deal of valuable real estate, and approximately 91 percent of Atlanta Life stock, Herndon was the wealthiest black man in Atlanta when he died.[36] He had risen from slavery to become the wealthy head of a growing black enterprise, overcoming poverty and illiteracy. Du Bois, in eulogizing Herndon in the *Crisis*, stressed his limitations and achievements as a black man in America. He wrote, "This representative of Negro America lies dead today and buried in a separate Negro cemetery which he helped found; but if ever an American 'burst his birth's invidious bar' that man was Alonzo Herndon."[37]

Herndon was proud of Atlanta Life and of its standing among black Americans. He often spoke of the number of companies it had taken over to salvage the confidence of blacks in race enterprises. He never failed to emphasize the firm's ability to provide employment to black men and women. He believed that the commitments he had made in time and money had not been in vain. His vision for the future of the company was simple. He often expressed to the younger men his desire "to live to see the Atlanta Life Insurance Company the largest Negro company in the world."[38]

The younger officers shared Herndon's vision and accepted as their own the goal of developing a large, financially secure company. Even in the founder's absence, they looked to the future with optimism. Although they would greatly miss his wit and counsel, he had left a legacy in the form of a strong and reputable enterprise. Their immediate goal, however, was to show that Atlanta Life was capable of escaping the endemic weakness of black enterprises, which too often failed after the death of their founders. Therefore, in the next years, they put their experience and knowledge to work in building upon the foundation Herndon had laid.

8

Depression and War Years

People have no money and unemployment is prevalent . . . the
only folk doing any business are bootleggers, undertakers and
doctors.
—Minutes, Board of Directors Meeting, 1 July 1929

Norris Herndon officially assumed the reins of Atlanta Life after being elected as the second president in January 1928. Besides the vacancy created by Alonzo Herndon's death, several other changes occurred in the firm's management in 1927. Robert Chamblee, vice-president and longtime general manager, resigned to go to Century Life in Little Rock, Arkansas, and Solomon Johnson died a short time later. The three vacant board positions were filled by Fred Toomer, Howard Russell, and Jessie Gillespie Herndon.[1]

Along with Norris, Herndon's widow, Jessie, assumed a major position in the company. Following her husband's death, Mrs. Herndon became first vice-president of the enterprise. This appointment gave her status in Atlanta Life commensurate with her new standing as a major stockholder. As the heirs to Alonzo Herndon's large estate, which included approximately 91 percent of the company's stock, Jessie Herndon and her stepson jointly controlled the enterprise. Mrs. Herndon continued to stay in the background of the operation, and Norris Herndon was assisted by Eugene Martin, Walter Smith, Lemuel Haywood, and the other men his father had brought into the company.

Alonzo Herndon's successors looked forward to a new era of growth and expansion. Believing that Atlanta Life could not rest on past achievements, they immediately began plans for expansion into additional states. This decision was influenced by a survey of the major black insurance firms which showed that the saturation point in state debit-building was approximately $16,000. The survey findings also noted that no matter how hard agents worked an area or how much money was expended this point was seldom passed in any state. The officers therefore concluded in 1928 that the original territory of Georgia and Alabama was nearly saturated, and they began focusing on newer territory, sending special teams into Texas, Florida, Kentucky, and other states to increase sales. They also began anticipating additional expansion, and in March, Ohio was chosen as the next state to be penetrated.[2]

The move toward expansion ended suddenly, however. Within the next few months, the directors decided not to enter Ohio, and, fearful of the approaching Depression, they began a program of retrenchment. Indeed, rising expenditures and decreasing collections necessitated reductions throughout the system. As the Great Depression took its toll in unemployment and hard times, the effects were reflected in debits that decreased from $34,406 on 30 June 1927 to a low of $21,630 on 16 January 1933. In this same period, total insurance in force was reduced from an all-time high of $26,253,717 in 1929 to $20,841,806 in 1932.[3] Many longtime policyholders, having become destitute, allowed their contracts to lapse. Indeed, the pace at which lapsations occurred caused a director to report that "it looked as if the men [agents] were going to lapse 'hell off the hinges.'" Because money was tight for most families, the company encountered increasing difficulty collecting from policyholders who were unable to pay their premiums each week. From all parts of the system came reports that "people have no money and unemployment is prevalent." In some cities, the agents reported that "the only folk doing any business are bootleggers, undertakers and doctors."[4] Throughout the peak Depression years, as conditions worsened, the company experienced decreasing amounts of insurance in force in both the ordinary and industrial categories. This held true until 1933, when the business experienced an approximately 40 percent increase over the previous year.[5]

Other problems aggravated this situation. An influenza epidemic in 1928–29 contributed to spiraling sick and death claims with death payments alone reaching $371,072 in 1930.[6] As privation increased, some policyholders claimed illness to get a few dollars to purchase food or other necessities. In addition to these attempts to defraud the company, which contributed to rising expenditures, the problem of arrears in agents' remittances to the home office increased, making it necessary for agents to work harder to make collections.

Retrenchment brought some terminations and salary cuts. Throughout the system, steps were ordered to eliminate all unnecessary expenses, cutting spending to the bare bones. The Atlanta district, which had for some years operated two branch offices in the city, was reconsolidated. Atlanta Life pared approximately 255 persons from its payroll. These conservation measures extended to both agency and home office operations, and for a time, even the vital special teams were threatened by cutbacks.[7]

Yet even in the worst of the Depression, Atlanta Life continued to promote a vigorous building program. Each year, the firm did well enough to enable it to meet all obligations to staff and policyholders. The officers established specific goals for sales and collections and pressed all agents and managers to reduce rising claims. Hoping to avoid the doldrums affecting many companies, they made a special effort to maintain new business campaigns and continued to put special teams into the field canvassing for new business and revivals. In areas where debits operated at a loss for too long or agents and managers remained unproductive, they were dismissed and supplanted by special workers. In August 1930, the agency director reported that "the Special Teams had thus far done excellent work . . . in spite of many people being out of work."[8]

In an era of grave business crises and uncertainties, Atlanta Life augmented its financial strength. As a result of the intense austerity efforts, emphasizing prudent conservation and economy, income exceeded expenditures in each year, and the firm showed modest operating gains in each year except 1929, when an all-time drop occurred (see Table 8.1). As a result, the stockholders received modest dividends each year from the company's earnings. A special achievement took place in June 1929, a few months before the stock market crash, when Atlanta Life increased its capital stock to $250,000 and voted a 150 percent stock dividend from the surplus.[9]

The *Vision*, the company's primary organ, highlighted this event as part of a Forward Atlanta Life Movement. The editor urged the field forces to "enthusiastically broadcast this valuable information to the buying public." Alert as ever to the value of economic strength within black companies, the article continued, "Their [the black insurance buying public] confidence will be greatly strengthened, not only in Atlanta Life, but in Negro business in general." The article encouraged

Table 8.1.   Total Income and Disbursements, 1924–1932

Year	Total income	Total disbursements	Operating gains
1924	$1,291,665.71	$1,180,654.71	$111,011.00
1925	1,543,644.67	1,427,228.48	116,416.19
1926	1,725,301.92	1,541,501.29	183,800.63
1927	1,794,091.63	1,605,816.00	188,275.63
1928	1,847,975.73	1,672,874.35	175,101.38
1929	1,867,474.14	1,842,976.74	24,497.40
1930	1,833,442.46	1,691,942.58	141,499.88
1931	1,628,262.83	1,507,386.48	120,876.35
1932	1,385,693.63	1,297,755.98	87,937.65

Source: Examination Report of Books, Records, and Securities, 1924–32, in ALCF.

agents to remain optimistic despite rumors of approaching depression and business failures. Cautioning the agents against a "failure mentality," the author warned, "We must not talk Negro business failures. Keep everlastingly before the public mind such accomplishments as just released concerning Atlanta Life's increase in capital stock."[10]

This move advertised Atlanta Life's vitality and financial strength. From another perspective, the officers viewed the increase in capital stock, which now was the second largest among black firms, as a bulwark against failure, calling it the "bullet proof breastwork" in the scientific defense the company had constructed to protect its resources.[11]

The firm's financial strength was built upon conservatism and prudence in investment matters. A three-member committee, including Norris Herndon, Walter Smith, and Eugene Martin, kept abreast of all regulations relating to investments by insurance companies and invested company funds prudently. They heeded the old stock market axiom that one should "never try to buy at rock bottom or top, but [should] take a reasonable profit and be satisfied."[12] They invested primarily in municipal, county, and United States bonds, and when it was impossible to get both quality and high yields in the market, they invariably chose quality.

In Georgia, as in most states, insurance companies' investments were strictly regulated. Following the Armstrong Investigation, most legislatures instituted more stringent rules for such enterprises. In August 1929, Georgia approved a new regulation specifying the securities and property in which Georgia companies were permitted to invest their funds and assets. The list of approved investments included bonds or securities issued by the federal, state, county, or city government or by township or school districts; loans secured by any of the specified securities; loans secured by first liens on improved real estate not exceeding 50 percent of the value of the real estate; policy loans not exceeding the reserve on such policies; a building for home office purposes providing the company's assets exceeded $100,000 and the investment was limited to not more than 25 percent of total company assets; federal reserve notes and other marketable bonds; bonds, debentures, or common stock of solvent railroads, street railways, and other public utilities as well as industrial corporations; and promissory notes secured by pledges of securities. Furthermore, the regulations held that no insurance company could own more than 10 percent of the securities of a single corporation, nor was an enterprise permitted to invest more than 10 percent of its assets in any single company.[13]

Atlanta Life's investments went overwhelmingly into bonds. Avoiding risks that were too speculative, the directors put most of the company's surplus in secure, although lower-yielding, bonds. The portfolio contained bonds of the states of Georgia, Alabama, and Texas; cities of Houston, Galveston, Bessemer (Alabama), Greensboro (Georgia), and others; Monticello, Georgia, District School bonds, and U.S. Liberty bonds. They liberalized the portfolio somewhat after the 1929 legislation broadened the kinds of securities permitted and invested a small percentage of funds in stocks. As a rule of thumb, however, the committee generally purchased only stocks with a record of unbroken dividend payments for not less than three years before the date of purchase and included in the portfolio after 1930 stocks in Georgia Power Company, the Consolidated Gas Company of New York, American Telephone and Telegraph, Allied Chemical and Dye Corporation, and similar companies.[14]

The primary drawback in the posture of financial defense developed by Atlanta Life was that at a time when some black companies were putting much of their investment capital into the black community through mortgage loans, the firm cut back drastically on the percentage of its surplus invested in this area (see Table 8.2). Indeed, a 1935 study showed that Atlanta Life had invested only 6 percent in mortgages in contrast to other black companies, which invested in mortgages in the following proportions: Southern Mutual Aid, 12 percent; Domestic Life, 14 percent; Supreme Liberty Life, 22 percent; Univer-

Table 8.2. Major Investment Data of Atlanta Life for Selected Years, 1927–1954

Year	Bonds	Percent earned	Percent assets	Mortgage loans	Percent earned	Percent assets	Stocks	Percent earned	Percent assets
1927	$ 779,149	4.6	67	$ 162,155	8.2	14			
1928	911,659	4.6	69	160,033	8.2	12			
1930	1,113,305	11.4	66	205,169	10.2	12	$ 100,000	1.5	6
1934	1,511,057	4.2	75	129,405	8.2	6	119,050	9.6	6
1936	1,833,039	4.5	70	74,422	6.5	3	375,588	6.6	15
1939	2,622,618	4.3	70	45,632	11.8	1	572,954	5.6	16
1942	4,433,444	3.7	72	289,392	4.1	5	603,888	5.4	10
1944*	5,334,009	3.8	55	229,264	4.1	2	720,244	4.9	7
1946	11,501,939	3.3	80	135,059	4.1	1	1,203,394	4.7	9
1947	14,027,074	2.4	85	108,763	3.9	1	1,188,377	5.0	7
1949	18,083,562	2.5	86	86,283	3.8	1	1,249,940	5.4	6
1952	24,576,746	2.6	83	1,276,859	4.5	4	1,639,520	5.0	6
1954	28,410,880	2.7	79	2,801,129	5.0	8	1,907,631	4.8	5

Source: Best's Life Insurance Reports, 1927–54.

*In 1944 31 percent of assets reported in cash—a total of $3,022,881.

sal Life, 35 percent; and North Carolina Mutual, 32 percent. The author of this study expressed the opinion that Atlanta Life had "overshot a desirable proportion [of bonds], neglecting mortgages almost completely."[15]

The firm had not always been so neglectful of black homeownership. Between 1923 and 1928, Atlanta Life had put a greater portion of its investments into home mortgages. Its investment had enabled a large number of black families to finance home purchases; many of the purchasers were associated with Atlanta Life as officials and employees. With the Great Depression, however, the investment managers retreated from this practice because of the risks involved despite the appealing idea of helping black families obtain homes. The reasons for the reversal in investment policy stemmed from the Depression experience when the company nearly phased out its mortgage program. In a four-year period, between 1931 and 1935, the company foreclosed on more than $100,000 worth of real estate which it carried on the books into the 1970s. Troubled by this experience and aware of the role of defaulting mortgages in the downfall of Standard Life, Atlanta Life did not aggressively reenter the home mortgage business until the 1950s.[16]

The investment committee undoubtedly felt that mortgages were not profitable for the company in abnormal economic times. Nevertheless, the well-being of the firm was never in jeopardy because Atlanta Life experienced a relatively good return overall on its investments. Indeed, the net yield from investments approached that of the leading firms in the industry, both white and black, and generally exceeded the rate of interest, usually 3 or 3.5 percent, needed to maintain policy reserves and existing premium levels. For example, in 1933, the net yield earned on all assets was 4.2 percent, a showing equal to that of Aetna (4.2 percent), Metropolitan Life (4.4 percent), New York Life (4.3 percent), North Carolina Mutual (4.2 percent), Pilgrim Life (4.3 percent), and Prudential (4.2 percent).[17]

Although the majority of black firms experienced a decline in net yields during the Great Depression, some falling to dangerous levels in 1933 (Supreme Liberty, .9 percent, and Universal Life, 2.6 percent), Atlanta Life consistently maintained a good return. Guided by a policy of financial conservatism, the investment committee kept the firm on a par with leading insurance companies. Vigilant in their stewardship of the firm, they husbanded the surplus so it would earn a respectable, although modest, return. As a result, between 1931 and 1936, company assets increased by more than $1 million.

For Atlanta Life, the Depression years confirmed long-held beliefs in the importance of financial safety and judicious management. Company officials knew that no business, particularly a black one, was immune to failure, and without careful, safe management and an adequate financial base any firm could succumb to events or become a pawn in the hands of people who would wreck it. With safety and strength always in the forefront of planning, the company's strategy for survival, including prudent investments, sensible management, and careful economies permitting no frills, proved a satisfactory bulwark against the Depression.

Atlanta Life's survival during the Great Depression was another significant milestone in its history. It was certainly not unscathed; like other black businesses, it experienced severe blows during this period in the form of high lapsations, decreasing collections, natural epidemics, and other woes. Recovery occurred swiftly, however. As economic conditions improved, the black industrial policyholders were quick to renew contracts, thereby building a basis for recovery. Indeed, the entire sagging black insurance industry was able to sustain itself in the post-Depression era through increased industrial sales, combined with a more prudent investment policy and better-trained and more efficient managers. By 1940, 81 percent of all insurance in the industry was in industrial contracts, a level that was maintained until the end of World War II.[18]

As the country began to recover, Atlanta Life positioned itself to begin "to reap the harvest of good business." Even during the hard years, the officials had spent hours mapping strategies for recovery and future growth. Now, feeling all the stronger for having survived such an economic crisis, they entered the post–Great Depression era with a renewed determination to make Atlanta Life a splendid example of black capitalism.

A necessary first step involved garnering a larger share of the available market. Therefore, in early 1933 Atlanta Life reorganized its agency force, dividing the entire sales territory among four agency officials. Lemuel Haywood, Howard Russell, Cyrus Campfield, and Charles W. Greene, all of whom except Greene were longtime employees of the firm, were designated as the first "generals" of the Atlanta Life sales force. Always cautious, the officials hoped to avoid the mistakes made by too many other companies that tried to cover too much territory as they expanded. The "generals" were expected to concentrate their efforts in larger urban areas where greater sales were

Atlanta Life Board of Directors, c. 1937. *Left to right:* Howard W. Russell, James T. Harrison, Lemuel H. Haywood, Norris B. Herndon, Mrs. Jessie Gillespie Herndon, Eugene M. Martin, Fred A. Toomer, and Walter H. Smith (Courtesy of Atlanta Life Insurance Company)

expected. To augment these more experienced agency generals, Atlanta Life looked for college-trained men and women to serve as agents in the urban districts. The firm experienced some success in this effort as Campfield reported in July 1935 that "30 men coming from 14 colleges were at work boosting Atlanta Life" in Birmingham, Alabama.[19]

A growing new market for black insurance existed in the post-Depression North. As the economy recovered, migration into northern centers was renewed with African-Americans continuing their flight in search of better opportunities and fuller enjoyment of fundamental human rights. The market they created held a great potential for black firms that were daring enough to venture into new territory.

Atlanta Life officials were well aware of the potential of northern markets. Even before the economy had stabilized, they had begun to study insurance possibilities in the North. But they were slow to make the decision to expand northward. Earlier plans for expansion had been canceled with the onset of the Great Depression, and preliminary investigations into the possibility for renewed activity in 1933, when the economy seemed to be reviving, were not immediately developed.[20] Many of the policyholders who migrated to northern cities held onto their old policies and mailed premiums to the home office or to relatives to be paid to agents in their home areas. But the migration clearly affected new sales, especially to younger men and women, and by 1936, Atlanta Life prepared to move northward. In that year, the company entered Ohio, the first new state added since 1924.

Ohio initially proved to be a productive state for insurance. As a result of postwar migration, the population in the state had increased each decade since 1919 by a number greater than the total population in 1900. Blacks were a significant factor in some production industries, and in some of Ohio's larger cities they could boast of expanding economic opportunities. In general, the growing population of black migrants experienced an increased standard of living. Now receiving unprecedentedly high wages in their new jobs, this group, by virtue of its size, income, and psychology, constituted a fertile market for rapidly growing black businesses.[21]

The Ohio market presented no insurmountable difficulties for Atlanta Life. Sales approaches and techniques used in the South were easily adapted to this market. Howard Russell's connection with national Baptist organizations helped facilitate the firm's entry into the churches and homes of potential customers in the larger cities, where branches were soon established. At home among Baptists in cities such as Cleveland and Cincinnati, Russell went to nearly every church telling the congregations about the Atlanta company that provided jobs and policy contracts for blacks. Therefore, when Atlanta Life agents knocked on doors in these cities, "there was a common-base of introduction from Russell's church attendance."[22]

Ohioans apparently reacted favorably to Atlanta Life's presence in the state. Following the failure of National Benefit, for which residents of Cleveland in particular had evinced support during its crisis, Ohioans seemed willing to support another black enterprise, and business grew rapidly. Once established in Ohio, however, the Atlanta firm made no further expansion before World War II despite direct requests from citizens in several states asking that agencies be set up in their cities.[23]

Additional expansion would wait for a later period as other issues claimed the company's attention. The era following the Great Depression held many bewildering changes. The government gradually began to regulate businesses that once had operated largely under the principles of laissez-faire. Increasingly stricter regulations were imposed and new rules set regarding the roles of both capital and labor. The operating expenses of insurance companies increased drastically as a result of income taxes, social security and unemployment payments, and the minimum wage.[24] Faced with the certainty of higher expenses, Atlanta Life considered revamping premium rates to meet increasing costs of operation. It is not clear that premiums actually went up, but the firm faced a number of problems that were attributed to the "tightening process of Government on business throughout the country."[25]

Labor unions were an anticipated source of trouble for Atlanta Life, particularly the Congress of Industrial Organizations (CIO), which began organizing activity in the South. Several of Atlanta Life's officers, meeting in the office or informally with other Atlanta businessmen at the YMCA, spent long hours discussing the possible repercussions of labor unions. As far back as the 1920s, Alonzo Herndon had expressed concern about labor unions, which he felt limited an insurance worker's possibilities by demanding shorter working hours. In a similar vein, the officers now viewed union organizers as potential troublemakers. And, though the home office did not attempt to formulate rules to prevent collective bargaining on the part of employees, the officials argued that the salaries and commissions paid by Atlanta Life were competitive within the industry. "The insurance business is a commission business and not a sweat shop proposition," Eugene Martin reasoned. "The Atlanta Life agent is his own boss . . . and he has in his hands the right to make his pay check whatever he makes himself fit to receive."[26] Throughout the 1940s, the union made sporadic efforts to organize Atlanta Life employees. The efforts were generally unsuccessful, apparently because the company instituted a noncontributory welfare plan in 1945 and improved the system of internal promotions.[27]

Potential problems of unionization subsided temporarily as war appeared on the horizon. For management, the major concern became the manpower shortage resulting from the military draft, which went into effect some fifteen months before the Japanese attack on Pearl Harbor. Even before the draft began, Atlanta Life had experienced a relatively high rate of terminations in the agency force. Records indicate that 456 agents were terminated in 1939, the majority for inefficiency and financial irregularities. More than two-thirds of these agents had been in the company's employ for less than two years.[28]

World War II intensified Atlanta Life's personnel problems, espe-

Jacksonville, Florida, Managers' Conference, c. 1940 (Courtesy of Atlanta Life Insurance Company)

cially as the company began losing agents to the draft. The inductions, however, represented only a fraction of those leaving the company. Many employees found jobs in the federal government in bomber plants or other war production industries that offered higher salaries than insurance. In 1944 the number of terminations reached 658, but by then more people were leaving for better positions than were being let go because of incompetency and dishonesty. Opportunities to work in war-related industries were opening up not only because of the desperate labor shortage, but also as a result of the protests of A. Philip Randolph and others as well as the efforts of the Fair Employment Practices Committee, which enacted revisions in the rigid antiblack employment policies of the public and private sectors.[29]

Company officials viewed the problem of personnel shortages with alarm but moved swiftly to deal with it. To meet competition, the company approved a 15 percent salary increase for office workers, amending the salary schedules upward to a range of $16 weekly for an apprentice clerk to $50 for an executive secretary or supervisor.[30] Women were hired in greater numbers, taking over the job of making weekly collections from drafted men. As more and more men left the company for work in war-related industries or were drafted into the armed services, women assumed greater responsibility for retailing policies in the company. In a report to the directors in 1942, Agency Director Haywood stated, "The hope of our work in many places depends upon women." Projecting a growing need for women to replace drafted men in the districts, he urged managers to "look ahead and prepare before the Army takes their men."[31] Two years later, Haywood indicated in a follow-up report that women made up approximately 70 percent of the Atlanta Life organization.

Women proved extremely capable of maintaining large debits and made a significant contribution to debit-building during the war era. Many of the districts with the best records were those in which women with longtime associations in local churches, clubs, and civic associations worked as agents. Women agents used social and community affiliations to their advantage in selling life insurance, especially in gaining entry into homes, where most sales were made. The employment of women agents was not altogether a new phenomenon of the war era. Alonzo Herndon had earlier recognized the abilities of women agents and had given them opportunities with the company.[32]

Although dominated by males, the insurance business had long benefited from the involvement of women at high levels. In addition to Jessie Herndon, who held a central place in Atlanta Life as director and chief stockholder, Mary McLeod Bethume and Minnie Cox were active in the early years of the founding of the Afro-American Life Insurance Company (Florida) and Mississippi Life Insurance Company (Mississippi), respectively. It was not unheard of for women to serve as directors of insurance companies, although frequently they were widows and family members of the male founders. Some of the more progressive firms, however, attempted to provide opportunities for younger black women, who, like their male counterparts, had become educated for careers in business. One such example was Mamie C. Hickerson, a skilled statistician for the Supreme Liberty Life Company of Chicago, who in 1938 was elected general statistician of the National Negro Insurance Association.[33]

Women had long played an integral role in the operation of Atlanta Life, especially in the Atlanta home office, where they dominated the clerical force. Two longtime female employees, Jessie Eugenia Reid and Marie Sims, are illustrative of the managerial ability of women at Atlanta Life. Reid, who began with the company in 1912, served as head of the clerical department and later as supervisor of the industrial department. Sims joined the firm a decade later as a clerk in the book-

Home Office Clerical Force, Atlanta Life Insurance Company, 1923 (Courtesy of Atlanta Life Insurance Company)

keeping department, becoming head bookkeeper and remaining with Atlanta Life throughout her career. By the mid-1930s a "coalition of women supervisors" in the home office provided effective management in all clerical areas.[34]

Women were also found at all levels among the field staff. The 1927 listing of Atlanta Life district managers showed seven women among the growing list of managers. According to the report, women were managers of districts in Rome, Athens, Cartersville, Cuthbert, Carlton, and Toccoa, Georgia, and Tallahassee, Florida. In addition, even in the early years, there were always a number of women agents throughout the system, although Atlanta Life's practice of listing agents by initials rather than first names makes gender identification difficult.[35]

Along with the increase in the number of women agents following the Depression, the company continued to look to colleges for new personnel as the war progressed. Increased use was made of the so-called new business teams; some were made up largely of agents selected from colleges in the localities where they were to serve. College graduates had long constituted a significant portion of the agency personnel, but they were sometimes a mixed blessing because their tenure was uncertain. As better-paying jobs opened in other areas, many moved into new occupations, leaving company officials to lament that "these New Business Teams did well for a while and then failed."[36]

Staffing concerns remained troubling for some time. The company officials became extremely alarmed in 1942 when it appeared that the president might be drafted. Because Norris Herndon controlled all but a small portion of the stock, as well as serving as executive head of the firm, his prolonged absence could have a negative effect. The board petitioned the local selective service board for a deferment for him, arguing the significance of his presence in the firm and the contributions the firm was already making to the war effort by distributing war-related literature and purchasing millions in war bonds.[37] The request for deferment was granted because Norris Herndon, now in his forties, was beyond the draft age.

In spite of this scare and other staffing concerns, the company nearly tripled its debit from what it had been at the start of the Depression. By 1942, the debit stood at $73,106.72, an increase of $46,640.82 over 1933. All agents, men and women, apparently took advantage of the prosperity the country enjoyed as a result of the war to increase sales. Blacks were accepted in larger numbers into skilled jobs with higher pay, thereby improving their economic status. As incomes improved, black families became better prospects for insurance sales, although they purchased primarily industrial policies. In 1933 the company's total premium income had been only slightly higher than in 1924. Within a decade, it had more than tripled, and it continued to increase in every category (see Table 8.3). Increasing from slightly over $.5 million in 1933 to over $3.3 million by 1950, industrial growth was impressive.

The reinsurance of Western Mutual Insurance Company, a small Dallas-based firm, in April 1941 added another $1 million of insurance in force. This takeover, the twenty-sixth for Atlanta Life since its founding, helped to expand operations throughout the nine branch and four subbranch offices in Texas.[38] Unlike many of the companies that Atlanta Life reinsured, this deal did not result from the firm's near bankruptcy. Although the company had not made a large amount of money, it was not in severe financial difficulty when reinsured by Atlanta Life. In this case, it was reported that President L. G. Pinkston and the other officers invited Atlanta Life to bid on the business to divest themselves of the responsibility.[39]

Table 8.3. Premium Income by Classes of Insurance, 1933–1950

Year	Life, health and accident	Industrial	Ordinary	Total
1933	$ 606,788	$ 525,988	$ 131,427	$1,264,205
1934	686,672	697,916	143,705	1,528,294
1935	715,084	769,653	164,003	1,648,740
1936	787,670	888,453	183,658	1,859,781
1937	898,675	983,036	208,433	2,090,144
1938	966,505	1,052,398	235,985	2,254,888
1939	1,083,692	1,150,668	262,441	2,496,801
1940	1,194,731	1,244,389	297,067	2,736,187
1941	1,410,456	1,376,143	335,253	3,121,852
1942	1,734,574	1,602,985	391,533	3,729,092
1943	2,199,646	1,877,047	466,458	4,543,151
1944	2,706,114	2,140,580	523,501	5,370,195
1945	3,120,726	2,421,062	615,545	6,157,333
1946	3,338,977	2,639,527	681,180	6,659,684
1947	3,405,447	2,830,062	751,695	6,987,204
1948	3,347,591	3,065,544	825,998	7,239,133
1949	3,199,752	3,193,451	938,522	7,331,725
1950	3,021,716	3,321,259	1,036,668	7,373,643

Source: Examination Report of Books, Records, and Securities, 1933–50, in ALCF.

The Texas deal was another tangible indication of Atlanta Life's full recovery from the Depression. Along with the addition of the ninth state and the expansion of insurance in force, the company prided itself on its ability to pay regular dividends to stockholders. Since 1924 the company had annually paid cash dividends ranging from 8 to 12.5 percent to the small and closely knit group making up its stockholders. This action was viewed as a good omen for the firm, especially during the Depression years when many enterprises had failed or were barely holding on, unable to pay any dividends. The ability of Atlanta Life to expand its sphere of operation, increase dollars coming into the company in premium income, meet obligations to the policyholders, keep an outflow of dividend checks going to stockholders, and still maintain a large surplus to ensure safety was concrete evidence that the firm was in good shape.[40] Although the directors and officials remained circumspect and cautious in their public utterances regarding the company's success, one official boasted in private correspondence that "Atlanta Life is undoubtedly the strongest Negro business organization in America today."[41]

Perhaps a more objective indication of the company's post-Depression standing occurred at the end of the decade. In 1939, ten years after increasing the capital stock to $250,000, the board of directors approved a 100 percent stock dividend, augmenting the capital stock to $500,000. Within five years this amount had again been increased by another 100 percent and Atlanta Life's capital stock stood at $1 million.[42]

The Great Depression spared Atlanta Life few of its ills. This enterprise, like others in the industry, experienced many fears and suffered numerous reverses. Nevertheless, it appears that the Depression also had a constructive impact on the firm. Occurring soon after the death of Alonzo Herndon and a shift in company management, it tested the mettle of Herndon's successors, who proved themselves capable of guiding the firm through this perilous period. Indeed, the growth and strength of the company in the Depression era fulfilled the founder's belief that the company would be as safe under the son's leadership as the father's. Norris Herndon followed closely the business teachings of his father, advocating "square dealing" and counseling moderation in public utterances about the company's successes or relative standing in the industry. Indeed, the new leadership demonstrated its commitment to safety and financial strength as the hallmarks of the enterprise and, in the decades that followed, adhered closely to a strategy for survival that included prudent investments, skillful and sensible management, and careful economies which permitted few frills.

9

An Anxious New Era

---

*We are [a] ripe plum hanging on a shaky limb with all the
power, wealth and finance at the finger tips of those who might
come to reap without sowing.*
—George W. Lee, Atlanta Life manager

Norris Herndon's years as president of Atlanta Life are frequently described as a period of solid growth for the enterprise. Stretching over more than four and a half decades, Herndon's administration pursued solid financial growth and development; the firm became the largest stockholder insurance corporation owned by African-Americans. Under his leadership, the territory covered by Atlanta Life increased from nine to eleven states as the sales forces entered several northern states. Expansion also occurred in the variety of policy contracts offered as the firm joined other black companies in the group insurance market. Perhaps the hallmark of this period involved efforts to perpetuate the enterprise as a black-owned corporation and to ensure the continuation of Alonzo Herndon's philanthropic and humanitarian ideals.

As the company grew and prospered, fears increased about its future as a black enterprise. Although Atlanta Life had passed fully intact into the hands of capable and constant successors, the presence of the founder and chief benefactor was sorely missed. Without Alonzo Herndon to propel the company on its course, even the most loyal worker and supporter experienced some uneasiness about the ability of the enterprise to meet the new challenges and to keep pace with changing trends and markets in the industry. The greatest area of concern for most workers was the ability of the new leadership to protect the enterprise against interlopers. Unable to forget the experiences of Standard Life and National Benefit, this group understood that even in postwar America, black businesses remained vulnerable to the adversities of a segregated society.

Since childhood, Norris Herndon had been associated with Atlanta Life, working as a boy at his father's side and under his watchful tutelage. Upon completion of his formal education, Norris assumed the important responsibilities of cashier and first vice-president. Following his father's death in 1927, the young heir had dutifully, if not enthusiastically, stepped into the presidency, pledging to carry on the business as his father had done before him.[1]

In the months after Alonzo Herndon's death, a sense of anxiety pervaded the company, especially among the field forces. Although the son had been carefully groomed for the role of president to ensure the perpetuation of the institution, he was nevertheless an unknown quantity to most Atlanta Life workers. Employees everywhere sent messages to the home office in Atlanta expressing sympathy at the loss of the founder and pledging loyal support for his successor, but they felt a vague uneasiness. It was an uneasiness that stemmed primarily from fear of the unknown. Few Atlanta Life workers actually knew the new president. They knew that he had grown up in the company, working in the field during school vacations. They had heard, of course, about his formal training at Atlanta and Harvard universities and about his experience with the company. For most employees, however, "these things were like a litany they had heard chanted over and over in the company's weekly bulletins and other official organs. But they didn't really know the man behind these chanted litanies."[2]

The anxiety appears to have subsided as Norris Herndon kept the enterprise on a firm course, especially in the difficult Depression period, but many of the workers would never really get to know him. Indeed, a good many of the employees would never have an opportunity to see him in person. Unlike the elder Herndon, the son was reticent and introverted and, as president, was content to remain largely behind the scenes. He left details of the operations to a team of longtime officers who maintained much of the responsibility for the public affairs of the enterprise, although he by no means fully relinquished responsibility for major decisions. Reserved and retiring, he did not relish the public role of president or enjoy the day-to-day encounters involved in operating an insurance business. Soon despairing alto-

Norris Bumstead Herndon, President, 1927–73; Board Chairman, 1973–77 (Courtesy of Atlanta Life Insurance Company)

gether of what he called "conspicurarity," he adopted an almost "invisible presidency."

Unlike his gregarious father, who had mixed with employees as a matter of course, the younger man seldom came into direct contact with most workers. Agents and branch office personnel were unlikely to meet him, and it was not unusual, especially in later years, to hear accounts of home office personnel who had never directly encountered the president. Indeed, an amusing story is related of an occasion on which Norris Herndon paid a rare visit to a branch location about a block away on Auburn Avenue, where a fun-loving longtime cashier greeted the tall mulatto president, whom she had not seen before, with the statement: "Good morning, I'm Mrs. Norris Herndon. What may I do for you?" The visitor, undoubtedly surprised, stammered, "W-e-l-l, since I am Norris Herndon, I'm having a little trouble understanding why I haven't met my wife before."[3]

The incident demonstrated the president's sense of humor. The employee was not fired for her gaucherie, and the president is said to have laughed heartily at the episode. Nevertheless, the president's general invisibility and inaccessibility continued and increased as he reached middle age. He appeared to become more reclusive and spent his time traveling, enjoying the arts, and hosting small whist parties attended by a small coterie of longtime friends. From time to time, he relented, at least temporarily, in his passion for privacy to attend a managers' conference or to participate in special celebrations. At these times he seemed to revert to an earlier period when he too had canvassed the field along with other agents, inspectors, and managers. These occasions served to give him some visibility, and the *Weekly Report*, a company newsletter, usually highlighted such events with photographs of the president interacting with the other participants. Commenting on the photographs, the editors once noted, "These likenesses should give every worker a realistic idea of how the president looks."[4] It was, therefore, primarily through photographs and reports that most workers were acquainted with the president.

Herndon had few contacts outside of the company, especially with contemporaries in the insurance industry. He appeared at none of the conventions and accepted no speaking engagements. Few, if any, among the other insurance executives knew him well. After participating in the early organizational meetings of the National Negro Insurance Association in 1921, he ceased attending convention sessions. In short, he clung tenaciously to a very private existence and, even as head of a growing firm, avoided taking a public role in the firm or the profession. In 1955 *Ebony* magazine featured an article on Norris Herndon, calling him "the millionaire nobody knows." It described the stately home in which he lived, the immense wealth he had inherited, the quiet lifestyle he enjoyed, and his general inaccessibility to the public. Perhaps exaggerating the facts, the article stated, "It is a good deal easier to see President Eisenhower than it is to see this millionaire. A number of executives and servants stand between him and the public."[5]

Chief among the executives who helped the president maintain his privacy was Eugene Martin. A close confidant and adviser to the president, Martin oversaw many of the matters typically handled by the chief executive officer in other firms. With far-reaching duties, he served as the chief operational officer and frequently acted publicly in the president's stead. As a young employee of the firm, Martin had been described by Alonzo Herndon as "conservative and trustworthy . . . [with the] ability to see straight through things,"[6] and over his career with Atlanta Life as secretary and, after May 1947, first vice-president, he fulfilled that prophecy. Entrusted with a great deal of responsibility, Martin was very visible and powerful in the day-to-day operations of the company.

Along with Eugene Martin, the administrative team in this era was headed by Walter Smith, Lemuel Haywood, and Fred Toomer. Smith's purview included the extremely important area of investments, Haywood continued to direct agency and sales operations, and Toomer served as company auditor with the responsibility of policing the system. Surrounding and supporting the president, this team provided continuity of leadership for more than two decades and was largely responsible for the growth occurring in the post–World War II period.

Initially, the team tackled the general problems facing businesses following the war. Reconversion was one concern that claimed the attention of Atlanta Life. The company experienced a surplus of personnel as veterans returned from the armed services, many expecting to resume the managerial and supervisory positions they had held before serving in the military. For Atlanta Life, reconversion meant finding positions for a large number of the 215 men and women returning from the war.[7] As the returnees reported to the company, many were reassigned to their old positions. This effort was complex and unsettling, however, because few of the veterans had kept up with changes in the insurance profession and it frequently took months to get them fully into the spirit of work. One officer lamented the complications caused by the returnees in a report to the board, noting, "It has been

Atlanta Life Board of Directors, c. 1953. *Left to right:* Charles W. Greene, George W. Lee, Lemuel H. Haywood, Norris B. Herndon, Gilbert E. DeLorme, Walter H. Smith, Dr. Henry L. Lang, and Eugene Martin (Courtesy of Atlanta Life Insurance Company)

a lot of work to try to switch these men around and give these veterans their former positions and at the same time, instruct them in the business of Insurance." Unlike returnees desiring their old positions, other veterans requested new assignments elsewhere.[8] For the Atlanta Life management this problem seemed "as great, if not greater than war."[9]

In addition to having to deal with returning veterans seeking their old jobs, businesses felt the impact of wartime migration and growing postwar inflation. Dissatisfied with the conditions they found at home, many workers left for other parts of the country seeking better jobs and futures for their families. Atlanta Life was not unaffected by this problem as workers in every district were described as "upset and undecided—moving from one section to another."[10] Dissatisfaction and defections increased within the firm, with some district managers complaining of inadequate compensation and agents already trained in sales leaving for employment in higher-paying industries and professions.[11] At the same time, Atlanta Life officers were concerned that the threat of postwar inflation would create serious problems. These and other difficulties of postwar conversion kept the officers occupied and were the focus of many of the sessions in which they attempted to map strategy and plan for the firm's future security and development.

A significant aspect of the postwar strategy involved further expansion into new states. In 1945, at the war's end, Atlanta Life operated in nine states, having entered only one new state since the death of the founder. The postwar era seemed to offer opportunities for expansion. Additional growth could help solve the problem of reassigning surplus personnel and at the same time allow the company to tap the growing market in the North, which had been made more attractive by wartime prosperity. By 1948 Atlanta Life was carefully watching the burgeoning exodus of blacks into sections of the North and West and looking into further expansion of the company.[12]

The expansion strategy was closely tied to wartime migrations, which brought another large influx of workers into certain states. Drawn to the centers of war production in the North and West, more than 5.5 million people from farms and other depressed areas in the South flocked to these centers during the war to locate better-paying employment. In time families followed the heads of household and made the move permanent. Although whites and blacks alike joined the migration, the percentage of black migrants surpassed that of whites in some places. California, Michigan, Oregon, Washington, Utah, Colorado, Wisconsin, Illinois, and New York experienced large percentage gains in black population, whereas Oklahoma, Arkansas, Mississippi, Alabama, and Georgia suffered a decline.[13]

Reacting to the migratory trends and increasing concentrations of blacks in these regions, Atlanta Life projected expansion into Illinois, Michigan, Pennsylvania, and New York. In 1948 the firm seemed anxious to begin work in the new territory, applying initially to the insurance departments in Illinois and Michigan. The officers resolved to apply immediately to the Pennsylvania Insurance Department should any delays be encountered in gaining admission into Michigan and Illinois. But Atlanta Life did not enter Pennsylvania or New York, principally because of prohibitive labor costs and the large deposits required by regulatory agencies in many northern states.[14]

Instead of expanding into states in the Northeast, Atlanta Life concentrated its efforts in the industrial Midwest. By late 1950 the company had entered Michigan and Illinois. Charles W. Greene, one of the individuals designated as an "agency general," spearheaded the opening of Michigan, issuing the first policy in Detroit on 25 July 1949.[15] Recognizing the importance of well-placed publicity, Atlanta Life hired John Wesley Dobbs, the noted Masonic leader who had popularized Atlanta's "Sweet Auburn" Avenue throughout the country, to assist with publicity in Michigan. He joined Greene for a twelve-day tour through the state, speaking in churches, lodges, schools, the YMCA, the YWCA, and on radio in an effort to introduce Atlanta Life and its products to Michigan residents. In September 1950, Gilbert DeLorme entered Illinois with similar fanfare, opening an office in the Chicago area and launching the official kickoff. Following the official openings and the initial publicity blitz in each state, a corps of agents who had been trained for several months under Agency Director Haywood were placed in the field to canvass the communities and sell policy contracts.[16]

The addition of Michigan and Illinois brought the number of states in which Atlanta Life now operated to eleven. As it had in previous times of expansion fever, however, the company decided not to enter any more new states. Despite market conditions favorable for growth, sales in these states did not immediately skyrocket. The Illinois debit remained below $1,000 through 1956, and in Michigan the debit dropped from $1,139 to $918 in 1955–56.[17] Increasing competition from larger white firms, which were invading the middle-class black market with new intensity, provides much of the explanation for sagging sales. In the 1950s, as the black market became more attractive because of improved mortality rates and higher incomes, an increasing number of white firms began wooing this group, offering contracts at standard rates. Many white firms concentrated their efforts in larger urban centers and made heavy incursions into the new market. Indeed, Robert Puth indicates that between "1950 and 1959, five of these white firms increased their insurance on Negro lives by two and one-half times the increase in insurance recorded in the entire Negro industry."[18]

Along with the growing encroachment of white competitors, another factor appeared to hamper sales among segments of the black population. With the erosion of war-related prosperity, and as labor unions continued to exclude blacks, they fell victim to poverty and chronically high unemployment. For many urban black families, prosperity occurred in painfully small doses and was difficult to sustain. Therefore, insurance salesmen were hampered in their efforts to sell

Table 9.1.   Comparison of Industrial Debits by States, 1943–1956

States	1943	1948	1954	1955	1956
Alabama	$16,353	$19,930	$21,136	$21,608	$22,019
Florida	11,553	17,967	21,396	21,608	21,581
Georgia	21,331	28,849	31,881	32,334	33,410
Illinois			771	908	928
Kansas	633	1,629	2,269	2,129	2,330
Kentucky	2,281	2,953	3,367	3,255	3,270
Michigan			1,208	1,139	918
Missouri	3,621	6,009	6,995	6,973	6,967
Ohio	3,939	7,435	9,915	10,419	10,449
Tennessee	8,681	12,563	14,265	15,059	15,418
Texas	21,914	32,336	42,390	43,927	45,637

Source: Examination Report of Books, Records, and Securities, 1955 and 1956, in ALCF.

policies among families for whom the burdens of living were imme-diate and paramount. Some of the urban newcomers, especially those who considered insurance a valuable commodity, continued to send their insurance premiums to relatives in the South to keep in force long-held policies.[19]

Atlanta Life's incursion into the northern market was tentative at best. Beyond the initial blitz, fewer resources were invested in this area, as is reflected in a comparison of debits by states (see Table 9.1). The company made a poor showing in Illinois and Michigan, where the debit reached barely $1,000. Atlanta Life remained committed to the South, concentrating its greatest efforts in the older states, which showed a rise in insurance in force throughout this period. By the 1940s, Texas had assumed the lead with the largest industrial debit in the system, followed by Georgia, Alabama, Florida, Tennessee, and Ohio. Three of the older states, Missouri, Kentucky, and Kansas, re-mained near the bottom of the debit chart.

Several other factors appeared to belie the growth orientation in this era, at least on the surface. The slow development of ordinary insur-ance sales seemed to confirm the company's commitment to its tra-ditional market. Ordinary sales, initiated in 1922, reached only $1 million by 1950. Although these policies were promoted increasingly among the better-salaried professionals and workers and ordinary sales methods were emphasized in both training and retraining efforts, greater results were netted in industrial, life and sickness insurance, which accounted for approximately 79 percent of the insurance carried on the books.[20] In characteristic fashion, Atlanta Life did not rush headlong into group insurance. Although the directors kept keen eyes on developing trends and innovations in the insurance industry at large, they avoided joining the rush by larger firms to add group insurance sales to their portfolios, preferring to follow a slower course until they gained a firmer grasp of the situation.

In the United States, group insurance dates back to the last half of the nineteenth century, when groups of workers in industrial, public utility, and railroad companies began to band together in mutual benefit organizations. With the issuance of the first group life policy about 1912, the life insurance industry slowly took over the group idea, although "very few in those days thought [it] would grow very much."[21] Group insurance developed slowly until the 1930s, but as the Depression crisis subsided, more and more insurance administrators came to see group insurance as a way of providing coverage to larger segments of the population. By 1938 the industry was showing substantial sales in this area with a reported $12 billion in group insurance in force.[22]

The clamor for group insurance grew out of conditions associated with the New Deal and postwar period. Although economic conditions improved and incomes rose, memory remained of the acute traumas of the Depression years, and employees, showing an increasing desire for more financial protection, began pressuring employers to provide additional security. Labor unions began demanding so-called fringe benefits for workers. In addition to life insurance coverage, such packages usually included a disability plan, payments for loss of limb or sight owing to accident, and hospital and medical benefits for workers and their dependents. More than any other single factor, it appears that "the labor union movement was responsible for the great development of group insurance after the war."[23]

Employers found that group insurance attracted people to their corporations. Forced to seek new personnel in an increasingly competitive market, they looked for opportunities to organize appealing benefit packages. By 1954 indications were that group insurance had become the most popular benefit offered by employers.[24] Owing to these trends, the major firms rapidly expanded their policy portfolios to include broad new avenues of group coverage. Considered to be "the fastest growing and most exciting innovation since John F. Dryden launched industrial insurance in America in 1875," such coverage ranged from creditors' life insurance to "association" group insurance for workers in small industrial and business enterprises.[25]

The group market proved very difficult for minority-owned companies to penetrate. These firms competed only in the segregated market, where few, if any, black enterprises employed a hundred or more workers. For this reason, companies like Atlanta Life generally remained outside the group arena until the 1970s, when affirmative action and joint-venture arrangements opened participation on a broader basis. Atlanta Life entered the group market experimentally around 1958, although once again, few resources or staff were committed to this area. Little publicity was given to this work as the officials talked about getting a nucleus of about $250,000 in premium income before "making any noise" about its group prospects. Even as the industry projected group sales as the area of greatest expected growth in the future, Atlanta Life remained unwilling to commit too fully. The immediate prospects in this area were handled only by home office executives while regular agents continued to give full attention to individual protection.[26]

Despite its slow development in the northern market and in ordinary and group insurance sales, Atlanta Life maintained a course of steady, healthy growth in both sales and assets. As one indication of growth, income from premiums, which totaled $7.3 million in 1950, climbed to over $10 million by the end of the decade. The admitted assets of the firm, which stood at $23.9 million in 1950, more than doubled by 1959, reaching $51.3 million.[27] This level of financial growth was more than adequate for a black firm considered small by industry standards.

With increases in 1929 and 1939, the company acquired $1 million in capital stock in 1943 and doubled that figure again in 1948. In 1955 another stock increase pushed the amount to $4 million. Committed to continuing growth in this area, the company took another major step forward in 1962, when the board authorized increasing the capital stock by stages up to a maximum of $20 million. In every case, the increases occurred through the declaration of a stock dividend with no public subscriptions to Atlanta Life stock.[28]

Along with periodic increases in capital stock, the company kept a large surplus on hand. Its management thought this gave added credence to Atlanta Life's fiscal watchwords, "Safety, Strength, Security." The surplus referred to the amount of reserve a company maintained on its policies. Never disposed to paying excessively high dividends to stockholders, the company held on to a large portion of its earnings, keeping on hand an amount that varied from between $50 and $43 per $1,000 of insurance in force by the 1960s. Although this amount was nearly five times greater than the ratio for the total industry, Atlanta Life officials perceived a large surplus as a necessary offset against business reverses.[29]

In the three decades between 1930 and 1960, Atlanta Life maintained its standing among black-owned firms in the industry. Until 1950, the Atlanta enterprise showed a greater amount of insurance in force than most of its major black competitors. Only the Chicago-based Supreme Liberty Life ran ahead of Atlanta Life in several years until North Carolina Mutual outdistanced all other black firms in sales after 1950 (see Table 9.2). In the categories of total income and assets, Atlanta Life compared favorably with the Durham-based company, holding firmly to second place when compared with five of the leading black firms (see Tables 9.3 and 9.4). In its own category as a stockholder corporation, Atlanta Life was distinguished in the industry as the largest among black-owned enterprises.

The distinction of being the largest stockholder corporation caused anxiety among some of the directors and stockholders in the postwar period. The reason for their concern lay in the distribution and control of Atlanta Life's stock. With the death of Mrs. Jessie Herndon in 1946, all but a minute portion of the stock, approximately 92 percent, came under the control of one man, Norris Herndon. The remaining shares were held by a few pioneer workers or their descendants. Unmarried and childless, Herndon had no close relatives to inherit his shares and to continue the tradition of a family-owned enterprise. Moreover, sufficient financial resources did not exist in the black community to purchase this large block of stock.

The company's vulnerability was clear. Atlanta Life workers came to fear that control of this substantial business, one of the largest among black Americans, might pass out of their control. Addressing this issue in the May 1948 meeting of the stockholders, Director George Lee compared Atlanta Life to North Carolina Mutual, emphasizing that the latter "is protected by its plan of organization—mutual plan. We are [a] ripe plum hanging on a shaky limb with all the power, wealth and finance at the finger tips of those who might come to reap without sowing." In his usual image-filled and flowery manner, Lee spoke of the company's future as bound up in the existence of the president, calling Herndon "our greatest strength. . . .

Table 9.2.   Total Insurance in Force of Atlanta Life Compared with Five Black Insurance Firms, 1930–1960

Company	1930	1935	1940	1945	1950	1960
Atlanta Life	$24,975	$37,373	$56,971	$112,642	$143,397	$176,193
North Carolina Mutual	36,613	36,683	51,227	100,546	152,948	277,187
Supreme Liberty Life	26,555	27,739	57,161	89,770	118,662	164,512
Universal Life	3,341	15,031	19,247	42,863	69,581	116,220
Golden State*				23,601	58,293	146,845
Chicago Metropolitan†					60,200	112,551

Source: Best's Life Insurance Reports, 1930–60.

*Incorporated as a legal reserve company in 1942.
†Incorporated as a legal reserve company in 1946.

Table 9.3. Total Income of Atlanta Life Compared with Five Black Insurance Firms, 1930–1960

Company	1930	1935	1940	1945	1950	1960
Atlanta Life	$1,833	$1,782	$2,934	$6,698	$ 8,012	$11,376
North Carolina Mutual	2,094	2,045	3,065	7,073	10,553	16,971
Supreme Liberty Life	1,235	1,203	1,416	2,769	3,988	6,408
Universal Life	914	886	1,308	2,515	3,732	6,216
Golden State				1,582	3,884	7,696
Chicago Metropolitan					*	4,739

Source: Best's Life Insurance Reports, 1930–60.

*Report for 1950 not available.

Table 9.4. Total Assets of Atlanta Life Compared with Five Black Insurance Firms, 1930–1960

Company	1930	1935	1940	1945	1950	1960
Atlanta Life	$1,692	$2,440	$4,559	$12,287	$23,954	$53,634
North Carolina Mutual	3,784	4,345	6,416	14,430	29,541	67,601
Supreme Liberty Life	1,825	1,743	2,595	5,542	10,631	25,705
Universal Life	540	597	1,130	3,796	8,233	18,749
Golden State				2,044	4,815	17,645
Chicago Metropolitan					9,189	14,485

Source: Best's Life Insurance Reports, 1930–60.

Norris Herndon addressing Alabama-Florida Managers' Conference, 1954 (Courtesy of Atlanta Life Insurance Company)

Without him with his sword in hand leading this great aggregation of men and women no man or woman in this organization can foretell our future."[30]

This concern had gnawed at some of the stockholders for some time, but the 1948 stockholders' meeting was the first time the issue was aired formally in a business meeting. Despite the unrealistic imagery of the solitary and mild-mannered Herndon at the head of a battalion of Atlanta Life stalwarts with sword lifted high, the very real concern for the company's future after Herndon's death was clear in Lee's remarks. How Atlanta Life could be perpetuated as a black-owned enterprise, with jobs and other services assured for African-Americans, was a matter of great importance to Lee and others associated with the company.

A good deal of the anxiety came from the older stockholders and directors, who had worked closely with Alonzo Herndon. They had seen him in battle with hostile external forces to save the enterprise and knew that his victories came only because of the personal resources he had committed to the struggle. Some officials feared that similar forces were waiting and watching for an opportunity to strike again. A few even suggested that the directors should consider moving the company's headquarters to a northern state, where, it was presumed, friendlier forces existed, or at least the company might more easily defend its rights.[31]

Like the other stockholders, Norris Herndon shared the concern about the vulnerability of Atlanta Life. In attendance at the 1948 meeting, the usually silent president spoke forcefully about finding a solution to this problem. He explained that several avenues were already being explored by which Atlanta Life could continue intact after his death under the same organizational form. Affirming his personal commitment to efforts to secure the company perpetually, he announced, "You can rest assured that I am going to see to it that Atlanta Life lives as long as I live and it is going to be perpetuated when I am gone."[32]

By 1950 a plan had materialized for securing Atlanta Life and for perpetuating the humanitarian endeavors of the Herndon family. On 22 November 1950, Norris Herndon created the Alonzo F. and Norris B. Herndon Foundation, Inc., as a memorial to his parents, Alonzo and Adrienne Herndon, and as a nonprofit corporation to which the huge block of Atlanta Life stock which he owned would be bequeathed at his death. He also agreed to contribute shares of his stock to the foundation every year until his death. All earnings of the foundation were to be returned to the black community for religious, educational, scientific, and literary purposes. In this manner, Herndon demonstrated his aim to continue the humanitarian and charitable giving long associated with the family. A will and trust were later executed to complete the transaction. Dated 25 November 1955, the will specified that the family's magnificent home on University Place become the property of the foundation at Herndon's death. The will expressed Herndon's desire that the "home be kept in a good state of repair and appearance and that it be used by the Foundation in such a manner as to appropriately memorialize the good work of my mother, Adrienne Elizabeth Herndon."[33]

Herndon's action proved him to be an angel for Atlanta Life in much the same way his father had been before him. His will and the establishment of the Herndon Foundation showed his dedication to the perpetuation of the enterprise, which was now nearly fifty years old. Even though Herndon became even more of a recluse in his declining years, the Atlanta Life people knew that the aloof personality in no way masked an uncaring and insensitive attitude about the firm and its workers. Although he continued to shun publicity, "he zealously guarded his authority to make all final decisions, abrogat[ing] that power to no one else."[34] He attended all meetings of the directors and stockholders, although he made very few speeches before these assemblies. People who knew the situation understood that his silence merely reflected his disdain for public speaking. Indeed, company publicity explained his taciturn manner this way, noting that "N. B. Herndon will not use a gallon of words to express a spoonful of thought. His guiding motto is: 'Not words—But Deeds.' "[35]

Along with the settlement of the issue of future ownership of Atlanta Life, there were positive indications that the future management of the firm was secure. During the 1930s and 1940s, several of the pioneer workers, now well past their prime, were removed from the scene by death, beginning with Charles Faison in 1936; James "J.T." Harrison in 1938; Alonzo Herndon II and Dr. Charles Cater, the company medical director, in 1944; Howard Russell in 1945; and Jessie Herndon in 1946. There was also the recognition, in the 1950s, that some of the active leaders were fast approaching old age. It was important that as men such as Norris Herndon, Eugene Martin, Fred Toomer, and Walter Smith reached the age of retirement the management of the firm would pass smoothly to younger, well-trained individuals of proven ability.

Several appointments in the late 1940s confirmed the company's intention of forestalling a crisis of leadership as the aging officers retired or died. The appointment of William Charles Thomas as company actuary in 1942 was the first significant step in this direction. For fifteen years, Thomas had worked closely with Samuel Barnett, the white actuary who served the company on a consulting basis. Through initiative and hard work, he became proficient in actuarial skills, and when Barnett became ill and was unable to handle the duties, Thomas quietly took over the work alone. His appointment as actuary of the company made him the first black person to hold the position in Atlanta Life's history.

By the end of the decade, Thomas was joined by Jesse Hill, Jr., a young actuary trained at the University of Michigan.[36] In bringing Hill into the company, Atlanta Life became one of the first black firms to acquire the services of a limited number of black professional actuaries. In assigning Hill to work with Thomas, however, the company continued the practice of training its newer employees under the tutelage of conservative, more experienced workers.

Edward Lloyd Simon, Board Chairman, 1977–84 (Courtesy of Atlanta Life Insurance Company)

In addition to Thomas and Hill, several other younger men became associated with the company in various capacities. They too worked closely with the senior executives in the home office to gain practical firsthand knowledge of Atlanta Life and the insurance business generally. Henry N. Brown, who joined the firm when Atlanta Life absorbed Western Mutual in 1941, proved to be an extremely capable assistant to the executive group. After earning a degree in business administration at Harvard University, he returned to the home office to work closely with Eugene Martin as assistant secretary and with Walter Smith in investments. Edward Lloyd Simon, a graduate of Clark College employed by the firm since June 1934, was brought into the home office and tutored by Haywood and Toomer in agency management and auditing techniques.[37]

These younger men represented the pool of future executives for the firm. With degrees earned at some of the most prestigious universities in the country and practical knowledge gained from work with the older leaders, they were well qualified to assume management of the enterprise at the appropriate time. Therefore, as vacancies occurred with the deaths of pioneer workers, they were filled swiftly from within the system. As an indication of the movement of the younger leadership within the company, by 1949 William C. Thomas, Gilbert Earl DeLorme, Dr. Henry Lang, and George Lee sat on the board of directors along with Herndon, Martin, Smith, Toomer, and Haywood.[38]

For the time being, however, the reins of the enterprise were firmly in the hands of men who had guided its destiny for several decades. All had come up through the ranks before attaining important management positions in the firm. As part of their leadership training, they were thoroughly imbued with an understanding of the importance of the firm's commitment to securing economic and social dignity for the race. Secure in the knowledge that, at least for the foreseeable future, appropriate measures were in place to protect the enterprise and to perpetuate its place in the community, the leaders remained actively involved in many of the social issues that faced the communities they served. In the 1950s, as the nation witnessed the beginning of a frontal attack by blacks to secure full citizenship rights, Atlanta Life's leaders, both old and new, were front-line participants.

10

Civil Rights and Social Responsibility

Supporting the struggle for economic dignity, civil rights and general uplift of Black America and the struggle against racism and bigotry has been a way of life for Atlanta Life over the years.
—Jesse Hill, Jr.

In the fight to secure full civil rights as guaranteed all Americans under the Constitution, Atlanta Life people were "a core of men [and women] of competence and organizational discipline who constitute a talented leadership reserve" in the community.[1] By economic position as well as civic and social affiliations, the major officers and directors were respected members of the black leadership in Atlanta. A largely homogeneous group, the majority of the directors in almost any period were graduates of Atlanta University or one of the affiliated colleges in the Atlanta University Center, held membership in the prominent 27 Club, the local Boule of Sigma Pi Phi, or both, and belonged to the First Congregational Church.[2] As businesspeople and influential citizens, they could not watch quietly from the sidelines as blacks waged a desperate struggle for freedom and equality in America. Instead, these individuals frequently attempted to use their positions in business and in their communities to inspire economic, political, and cultural development among African-Americans.

Atlanta Life had never forsaken important race issues and causes. It had long been the philosophy of the founder that the company should stress its service motive along with its profit motive. The company's leaders, while perceiving themselves primarily as guardians of black economic dignity, had always been active participants in the long struggle of African-Americans to achieve equality. From a strong record of personal philanthropy to membership and participation in local and national groups and associations that worked to remove the color bar in America to efforts and activities to promote enfranchisement and race pride, the involvement of Atlanta Life people in the civil rights arena represented a continuous link with the broad social activism of Alonzo Herndon, reflecting the social consciousness of both the enterprise and its leadership.

The influence of Atlanta University was reflected in the social efforts of the leadership of Atlanta Life. In addition to its central mission of providing higher education, the university adopted the ideal of racial equality as a major tenet of its philosophy. Even during the nadir in race relations in the South, the university generally took a firm stand for racial and social equality, seeking to demonstrate its full commitment to the achievement of this goal. For example, white professors at the university held firmly to the practice of eating in the dining hall alongside their black students despite persistent criticisms from whites who objected to this breach of southern racial etiquette. Perhaps of greater significance, the university refused to succumb to the prevailing educational policies, which sought to restrict blacks to industrial training or to deny admission to white applicants (generally children of white professors at the university) despite the taboo against coeducation of the races. Indeed, in the summer of 1887, following an almost unanimous vote by the Georgia General Assembly, the university forfeited an annual appropriation of $8,000 from the state rather than violate the principle of providing education to youth of Georgia on a nonsegregated basis.[3]

The growing cadre on Atlanta University graduates contained a large number of distinguished individuals, many of whom made significant contributions in various fields of endeavor including education, law, religion, government, civil service, social services, business, and the arts. The fundamental lessons learned and inspirations gained during their tenure at the university provided fodder for their activism in the black community. They understood that the dynamics of the American social order meant that they could not remain aloof from social and racial involvement. In addition to the Atlanta University ideals, these individuals could not help but be galvanized to work toward the achievement of greater respect for human brotherhood by the brutal lynchings and other chilling examples of inhumanity to blacks in the country.

Through their various capacities and in their various ways, many graduates of Atlanta University were instrumental in efforts to abate the "injustices suffered by African Americans in the nation, especially in the southern region." Whether through efforts to establish institutions, secure antilynching and civil rights legislation, advance human rights, or improve living conditions generally, these men and women were dedicated to the task of uplifting their people and improving their communities.[4] The cadre of leaders at Atlanta Life, including Norris Herndon, Eugene Martin, Fred Toomer, Walter Smith, and others, were not exceptions to the general influence of the Atlanta University ideals. An active alumnus and supporter of the institution, Martin once commented on its significance for him personally, noting, "I have lived all of my life within the shadow and influence of Atlanta University."[5]

A distinctive humanitarian and philanthropic influence emanated from Norris Herndon. Unlike the men around him, the younger Herndon did not elect to have a direct involvement in social and community affairs. His intense predilection for privacy and overwhelming desire to preserve anonymity prevented active participation in most causes or movements. He remained generally detached from community activities and shunned the active leadership role ordained by his position as president of the company. He sat on none of the boards of civil rights organizations and did not write letters expressing indignation at the evils of lynching and segregation.

Yet Herndon did not abdicate a social role in Atlanta or the country. He merely chose to make his participation quiet and unobtrusive. He continued his father's custom of giving financial support to local and national organizations which he deemed worthwhile. His personal philanthropy benefited groups such as the NAACP, National Urban League, and United Negro College Fund (UNCF). On a local level, his philanthropic support went largely to benefit the United Way, Butler Street YMCA, First Congregational Church, Atlanta University, Carrie Steele Pitts Home for Orphans, and Morris Brown College, among others.[6]

As with everything else, Herndon spurned publicity about his philanthropy. The extent of his giving was usually unknown by the public. His contributions were made without fanfare, often almost apologetically or impulsively in an out-of-pocket fashion. For example, several contemporaries remembered a Sunday morning when he approached the pastor of the First Congregational Church and quietly conveyed his wish to donate an air-conditioning system because he had "seen the ladies fanning in church this morning." In another situation, he observed the need for a new gymnasium floor at the Butler Street YMCA and suggested that the director have it replaced and send the bill to him.[7]

Contemporaries generally described Herndon's personal philanthropy as generous. They found his financial commitment to First Congregational Church, his family church, and to Atlanta University, his alma mater, particularly praiseworthy. They were, however, sometimes quietly critical of his failure to give himself fully to any cause or to provide leadership commensurate with his background, talent, and training. Nevertheless, his close friends and associates forgave this omission and cited the Herndon Foundation as a satisfactory symbol of his commitment to the larger cause of black economic and social development. They also praised Atlanta Life's role in providing jobs, home mortgages, and business loans to blacks. Important, too, was the social consciousness exemplified by the firm through the active leadership of some of its officers and personnel. Observers reasoned that though Herndon himself may not have been an overtly active community man, the more socially involved Atlanta Life people could not have maintained their positions in the company had their social ideas been radically different from that of their more introverted chieftain.[8]

Eugene Martin perhaps best symbolized the activist role assumed by Atlanta Life's leadership. Although insurance and economic issues were his major interests, Martin described the race problem as "my greatest hobby."[9] He frequently broke with the routine of work at Atlanta Life to assist in the efforts of the NAACP or to write a letter protesting some aspect of segregation or racial inequality in the city, state, or nation. Even before World War II, Martin's work with local and national interracial groups had characterized him as a race man of great conviction and energy. And in the wake of the brewing battle for civil rights in the 1950s and 1960s, he remained a steadfast supporter of efforts to extirpate racism and provided much of the leadership that propelled Atlanta Life to the forefront of the movement in Atlanta.

Like others within the company leadership, Martin knew well the system of injustice and racial oppression in the South. In 1931 an incident in his own family demonstrated firsthand the bestial nature of the system as well as the grievous and inhumane absurdness of the color line in Atlanta. George A. White, Sr., a retired postal employee and father of Helen White, whom Martin married in 1926, and of NAACP Executive Secretary Walter Francis White, was struck by an automobile as he stepped from the curb at Houston Street and Piedmont Avenue near his home. The white driver of the car, a doctor at the Henry W. Grady City Hospital, took White immediately into his car and drove him to nearby Grady Hospital. A segregated facility, Grady had set aside a "Negro ward" in a deteriorating building across the street from the larger, more modern, sanitary, and beautifully equipped hospital for white patients. Although a black man, the light-skinned, unconscious White was taken into the white side of the hospital at Grady, "where the best doctors in the hospital worked fever-ishly to save his life." Upon Martin's arrival at the hospital inquiring about his father-in-law, officials were aghast at the discovery that they had put a black man in the white ward. According to Walter White's account, his father "was snatched from the examination table . . . and taken hurriedly across the street in a driving downpour of rain to the 'Negro' ward," where he remained for seventeen days until he died.[10]

This was by no means Martin's first encounter with the horrors of racism, but the incident undoubtedly left a strong impression on him and propelled him to work harder to improve conditions for blacks in Atlanta and the South. A few years later, in 1937, he was elected to the Georgia Interracial Commission, where he worked with a number of prominent white southerners in pressing for the abolition of discrim-ination in various areas. Martin also sat on the executive committee of the Fulton-DeKalb Committee on Interracial Cooperation, working with blacks such as Rufus Clement, president of Atlanta University, Asa T. Walden, and Forrester Washington. Martin's copious files in-dicate his involvement in the committee's efforts to initiate change in such areas as the legal system, voting, welfare programs, and social accommodations.

Martin's work with the interracial committees gave him a forum in which he could attack social ills. It also helped to make more evident the dimensions of racial bigotry and the circumscribed existence of blacks in the state. Even in areas like Atlanta, where the state or local interracial committee functioned most effectively, racial proscription and prejudice prevailed. For example, municipal and county authori-ties in Atlanta took every precaution to keep "an understanding be-tween the two races here as to the correct place in our local society of each." This meant, of course, as Mayor Roy Lecraw responded to a complaint by a white member of the interracial commission about the general situation for blacks in the city, that "the white race should have priority."[11]

Martin complained about the priority given to white citizens in Atlanta for service on jury panels. In a letter to the editor of the *Saturday Evening Post* in 1940, Martin said that because of race prejudice and hatred, businessmen like himself had never been called to jury duty. Although Martin had been for over twenty years secretary of a life insurance company that had "invested in state, county, and municipal bonds in the state of Georgia more than a million dollars, and . . . cleared through the city of Atlanta during the past twenty years more than 33 million dollars," neither he nor his associates had been called upon for jury service. Expressing his irritation at the situation, Martin lamented, "I sometimes wonder if I can truthfully say that this is my country, too."[12]

Martin's ire was also aroused by the blatantly discriminatory service provided by many of the nation's railroads, especially southern companies, which denied first-class accommodations to blacks as a class. As an Atlanta Life official, Martin traveled frequently by rail and knew firsthand the horrible facilities coped with by the black traveler in the South. He was also dismayed by the degrading treatment blacks usually received at the hands of ticket agents and other railway employees. Writing to the board chairman of the Southern Pacific Railroad Company in 1939, Martin described his own experiences with rail travel over the past twenty years. He referred to the filthy waiting rooms and toilets reserved for blacks and to bigoted ticket agents who invariably served whites first and generally treated black travelers with contempt.[13]

Martin's grievance with the railroads also included the refusal of some carriers to provide first-class pullman accommodations to black passengers. In 1939 eighteen Atlanta Life managers and agents in Texas qualifying for a company-sponsored trip to the National Negro Insurance Association's meeting in California were denied first-class accommodations, prompting Martin to address this issue. In the letter to the Southern Pacific official, Martin lashed out at the overall issue of racial discrimination by rail carriers, referring to the railroads' "colossal blindness" in refusing to understand that the difference in color among passengers in no way implied a "difference in love of travel and the need for the fundamentals of food, shelter, and sleep." In protesting the railroads' discriminatory practices, Martin mentioned that Atlanta life was a bondholder in several railroad companies, including Southern Pacific. Couching the protest in economic terms, he castigated the carrier for its "unprogressive business methods" in refusing to "cultivate a market representing twenty-four per cent of the population of the South and that should supply a large percentage of the revenue of the roads."[14]

Martin suggested that the company's policy was not in the best interest of Atlanta Life or its policyholders. He threatened to sell all railroad bonds owned by Atlanta Life. As a further criticism of the carrier's policy toward blacks, he added, "With such an ignorant attitude manifested toward millions of Negroes on the part of your road, the question arises in my mind that possibly the same unenlightened thought and lack of vision may be exemplified in other matters pertaining to the best interests of the Bondholders."[15] Although Martin's threat did little to influence the carrier's attitude or policy, it does demonstrate his clear thinking on this issue as well as his understanding of the possibilities of economic pressure by companies like Atlanta Life in effecting social change. Martin directed similar complaints to other individuals and institutions that supported or practiced discrimination and segregation. For example, he protested numerous instances of segregation in Atlanta. In 1935, when a noted evangelist preached in the city, Martin conveyed his displeasure with the segregated arrangements. Writing to Gypsy Smith, Sr., Martin reproached the evangelist, indicating his desire to hear the noted speaker and his disappointment upon learning that blacks "were welcome only in the gallery or in a final 'Jim Crow' meeting to be held at the end, after other Christians and Sinners had been served." Martin wondered "if there was much Christianity in such a meeting."[16]

In the letter, Martin also discussed the role of the Christian minister in effecting social change. He called upon Smith to demonstrate moral courage by conducting "one great meeting in Atlanta, in which all will be welcome, regardless of race, class or creed; a meeting in which there will be no segregation in thought or action." Nevertheless, Atlanta continued to require separation of the races in seating at all public gatherings, and Eugene Martin, like other opponents of segregation, continued to press for its abolition. On one occasion, however, in an effort to persuade the black performer Paul Robeson to come to Atlanta, Martin sanctioned the idea of a recital before a segregated audience, contending that "as much as I hate segregation, I sometimes feel that . . . it is good strategy to sing to segregated audiences and make money . . . and then use as much of the profits as possible to fight segregation."[17]

Despite this concession, Martin was greatly offended and frustrated by the indignities of southern society. It was humiliating that he, as well as the president, other officers, employees, and stockholders of a company that invested heavily in the city and state, could not perform jury duty, a civic responsibility for most citizens, and were relegated to Jim Crow galleries when attending lectures, concerts, and other public gatherings. The company invested millions in railroads, yet Atlanta Life delegates to a national convention could not travel by train unencumbered by race restrictions. More profoundly repulsive were the horrors associated with the tensions of southern living. Increasingly, fear, frustration, and hopelessness seized black Americans in many parts of the South as lynch mobs terrorized black communities, boldly parading their victims without any retaliation. In addition to his moral indignation at such dramatic examples of man's inhumanity to man, Martin was frustrated by the pragmatic issue of the impact of racism and violence on the future of Atlanta Life in the South. In the late 1930s, district managers in Bainbridge, Georgia, and Tallahassee, Florida, begged for reassignments after lynchings occurred in their towns.[18]

Martin felt that national exposure of the evils and inequalities and national pressure to reform conditions in the South represented the best strategy for blacks, especially before the decision in *Smith v. Allright* (1944), which ruled that the exclusion of blacks from the Democratic primary was a clear violation of the Fifteenth Amendment. "As the Negro is practically disfranchised in Georgia, there is very little that can be done at this time through and by use of the ballot," he wrote in 1941. "I believe that if we could expose, in a national way, the littleness, the bigotry, and the hatred . . . and make the country realize that the Negro, as a group here in Georgia, is circumscribed and limited . . . such an exposure would have a tendency to create more friends for the oppressed Negro."[19] Through work with the NAACP and other organizations, both local and national, as well as through his job as Atlanta Life's secretary and its most visible head, Martin contributed to the exposure of racial inequalities in America. When provoked, he seldom hesitated to lash out at lynchings and other violations of civil rights or at instances of discrimination and segregation in economic or social areas, in education or housing, political restrictions, or law enforcement problems.

Walter White was probably largely responsible for Martin's involvement in the NAACP, especially at the national level. Martin admired and respected his brother-in-law; his correspondence indicates that the two men maintained a close, mutually supportive association. Born in Atlanta in 1893, Walter White grew to manhood in the segregated atmosphere of a southern city and knew well the racial enmity that existed in the South. White was light-skinned, with blond hair and blue eyes, and his features were indistinguishable from those of a Caucasian. His youth in Atlanta, however, especially his observations during the Atlanta race riot of 1906, confirmed for him his identity as an African-American.

White graduated from Atlanta University in 1916 and worked as an agent and cashier for Standard Life Insurance Company before accepting the invitation of NAACP field secretary James Weldon Johnson, also a graduate of Atlanta University, to become assistant secretary of that organization in 1918. In White's work with the NAACP, his ability to pass for white became a useful asset as he investigated lynchings and went on fact-finding missions throughout the South. The information he obtained as a "white man" was invaluable in the organization's campaign for federal antilynching legislation. In 1929 White succeeded Johnson as executive secretary of the NAACP and remained in the position until his death in 1955. Under White's leadership, the organization achieved a number of important legal victories in the fight for civil and social equality.[20]

No doubt with White's support and backing, Martin was elected in 1939 to the national board of directors of the NAACP, replacing Atlantan Asa T. Walden, who became a member of the organization's legal committee. Few southern cities were represented on the national board, and Martin's views were eagerly sought on issues pertaining to the "southern problem." He became a valuable man-on-the-scene in Atlanta, who could advise the organization. For example, he was queried on matters relating to the safety of the Scottsboro boys in Atlanta and in other places in the South. When Olen Montgomery, one of the Scottsboro nine, moved to Atlanta to live with his mother, Martin was advanced a sum of money by the NAACP to provide funds to the young man should circumstances in the city become such that Montgomery should leave.[21] Another inquiry requested information about feelings in the South toward Jews. The board also sought Martin's opinion on the advisability of the NAACP becoming involved in the Georgia State Colored Teachers Association's fight for equalization of teachers' salaries and other matters. When Walter White required a poll tax receipt or needed data on the treatment of black servicemen at Fort Benning in Georgia, Martin usually supplied such information to the New York–based group.[22]

It was with his pen, however, that Martin was at his best in abetting the NAACP and protesting inequalities in society. In 1938, as the

NAACP campaigned in Congress for passage of an antilynching bill, Martin wrote an open letter to the United States president and Senate denouncing lynching. He particularly blasted the southerners responsible for the filibuster that caused the bill's defeat, castigating "the spirit of this group of reactionary southern senators who throughout the years, as former governors and officials of their respective states, have never had sufficient political or Christian influence or ability to apprehend or cause to be punished a single murderer in upward of 5,000 lynchings."[23] It is unclear whether the letter, which Walter White described as "superb," was printed and read by Congress or anyone else. From White's perspective, however, such letters would serve "to arouse . . . a wave of indignation which will let the Senate know that they had better not adjourn without doing something on lynching."[24]

Martin participated in various efforts to arouse feeling against racial injustice. He closely embraced the NAACP's philosophy and supported its leadership, especially in antilynching efforts. His correspondence shows a particular disdain for leaders who advised blacks "to stay out of politics and stop turning the spot light on Lynch law socially, politically, and economically." He was full of praise for the efforts of individuals such as Walter White and others who spoke out forcefully on lynching, enfranchisement, school desegregation, equal pay for black teachers, legal justice, and other issues. He declared, "I thrill inwardly when one has the nerve (it is so rare) to speak out." He offered particular encouragement to White, urging him to "keep up the good work and you will go down in history as one of the greatest men that America has produced." Stressing his own role and personal identification with the struggle, he added, "Give these damnable scoundrels, in high places, who consign Negroes . . . to merely menials and serfs, barring opportunities higher up, hell, and then let's be happy, realizing that we have done a great and noble task."[25]

Martin brought Atlanta Life more fully into the civil rights struggle around 1941. In this instance, the fight centered around the legal battle of black teachers to end the school board's policy of paying lower salaries to black teachers than to white teachers. It was estimated that the pay of the 360 black teachers in the Atlanta school system ranged from 62 to 70 percent that of white teachers in the various classifications. Similar discrepancies existed across the state because the Georgia school law fixed the salary of white teachers on a scale from $40 to $80 per month while black teachers earned between $25 and $60 per month. In February 1942, when William Hunter Reeves, a black teacher at Atlanta's David T. Howard Junior High School, filed a petition in the federal district court asking that black teachers employed by the Atlanta Board of Education be paid the same salary as white teachers, it was estimated that it would cost the city about $400,000 a year to equalize the salaries. To equalize pay throughout Georgia, the differential was projected at more than $1 million.[26]

The NAACP commenced the fight against unequal teacher salaries in 1939 in the case of Melvin O. Alston against the school board in Norfolk, Virginia. In the next few years, affirming Thurgood Marshall's assertion that "we are aiming at hitting every state in the South," an onslaught of cases followed in practically every southern and border state where such gross differentials existed.[27] In Atlanta, Reeves's suit on 18 February 1942 followed two earlier petitions in which black teachers had requested redress of this grievance. The first petition, filed by the Gate City Teachers Association on 30 January 1941, was followed by a second on 26 November of the same year identifying Reeves as primary petitioner. Both petitions urged the board of education to discontinue discriminating in teachers' pay. The school board ignored both petitions.[28]

Reeves, a former employee of Atlanta Life, had taught in the Atlanta school system since 1934. Described as a mathematical whiz, he had mastered several languages including German, Spanish, and Latin, played the violin expertly, organized a school band at Atlanta's David T. Howard school, and managed the school's cafeteria. Reeves put his teaching career on the line when he offered himself as plaintiff in the equal pay case. Reeves had the backing and support of Atlanta Life and several other Atlanta groups, including the local branch of the NAACP and the Atlanta Citizens' Committee for the Equalization of Teacher Pay. Atlanta Life became a party in the fight by agreeing to employ any teacher fired as a result of bringing suit against the school board. In this instance as in others, the company offered the use of its facilities as well. Any number of strategy meetings were held in Atlanta Life's "Little House," a refurbished carriage house on the back lot of the company's home office on Auburn Avenue which usually served as a recreation and meeting room for employees.[29]

Reeves's suit received the expected reaction from the Atlanta school board and other segments of white Georgia. For its part, the school board argued that the federal courts had no jurisdiction in the matter and requested dismissal of the suit. The general tenor of the response from the state was that if the federal government imposed such a dastardly ruling it would have to pay the costly differential.

The reactions and arguments in Atlanta and Georgia ran parallel to those in other places where all manner of justifications were offered and ruses attempted in an effort to block equal treatment of black teachers.[30]

For the next decade, the situation in Atlanta remained unchanged as the school board refused to adopt the principle of equal pay. On 28 October 1942, the Atlanta school superintendent suspended Reeves from his job, alleging that an adverse report following an examination for the army showed Reeves to be "incapacitated" physically and "unfit" morally for his work as a teacher. Despite the testimony of Eugene Martin and others who appeared as character witnesses for Reeves, the board unanimously approved the superintendent's recommendation, and Reeves was discharged on 24 November 1942.[31]

The dismissal of Reeves served as an effective ruse for the school board. Although board members admitted that no complaint had ever been made against Reeves and the charge that he was morally unfit to continue in the school system was stricken from the formal accusation, the decision regarding his removal remained in effect. Therefore, when the case opened in federal court six days after Reeves's dismissal, attorneys for the school board asked for dismissal of the case on the ground that the plaintiff was no longer a teacher in the Atlanta system. This argument was successful, and the federal judge granted a continuation in the case while the NAACP searched for another teacher to substitute for Reeves in the suit.[32]

Reeves was banished from the school system and rehired by Atlanta Life. He worked for several years as an agent before taking a position in the Atlanta headquarters as director of the printing department. Maintaining its commitment to provide employment to any teacher who suffered reprisals as a result of participation in the equal pay suit, Atlanta Life offered the same arrangement to Reeves's successor as plaintiff in the case. A teacher at Booker T. Washington High School, the substitute plaintiff had worked for thirteen years in the Atlanta system. When the case won support in the federal court, the new plaintiff retained his job in the school system. Upon appeal to the Fifth District Court, however, the decision was reversed, and the case was finally dismissed in 1951, leaving the plaintiff, Samuel L. Davis, to pursue "administrative remedy" through the school board. As an obvious reprisal for his part in the suit, Davis was never able to obtain a salary increase, his efforts blocked by a complicated track-step system instituted by the board. For the remainder of his tenure in the system, he earned the same salary as in 1943. Davis, however, refused to leave the school system for employment with Atlanta Life lest he lose his pension accumulated over more than twenty years.[33]

The equal pay case demonstrates Atlanta Life's efforts at social action in the 1940s. Through the participation of its leaders, the firm did what it could to promote social action in the black community, proving in this instance that "individuals can do a lot that institutions cannot do."[34] Norris Herndon's philanthropy, like his father's, became an important source of support for several local and national social action agencies and organizations, and the personal involvement and leadership of executives such as Eugene Martin demonstrated the social consciousness that existed within the enterprise.

Atlanta Life people also played major roles when black Atlanta stepped up the fight for full citizenship in the 1950s. Jesse Hill, Jr., described as a powerful recruit in the civil rights struggle, gave strong leadership to a variety of social movements in the city. A native of St. Louis, Missouri, Hill arrived in Atlanta in July 1949 expecting to be assigned work on an Atlanta Life special team. Instead, he was assigned temporarily to the firm's actuarial department, where he remained for several years, becoming a valued employee and earning a promotion to chief actuary.

Although a newcomer to Atlanta, Hill quickly settled into the city, becoming what Atlanta school board president Benjamin E. Mays described as a "total community character."[35] Believing the franchise to be the most effective weapon in the battle for civil rights, Hill initially projected his leadership into voter registration activities, serving as chairman of the All-Citizens Registration Committee and working to add more than fifty thousand black voters to the list of registered citizens. Hill was also a member of the Atlanta Committee for Cooperative Action (ACCA), a group of young professionals who met regularly to address the broader issues affecting blacks in the city. Through this affiliation, he assisted in the planning and coordinating of major strategies in the school desegregation battles at the secondary and university levels. As an astute organizer, he was also involved in managing aspects of the movement in Atlanta to end segregation in restaurants, lunch counters, and other public facilities.[36]

One of the earliest areas of civil rights activity was the push to desegregate the state's colleges and universities. Occurring in the late 1950s, this effort struck at one of the greatest bastions of institutional segregation in the South. Since the beginning of the decade, Atlanta University political science professor and president of the Georgia NAACP William Boyd had led a fight to gain Horace Ward's admission to the School of Law at the University of Georgia. This effort failed because the courts were unwilling to uphold the plaintiff's request for equal access to the state-supported institution, and Ward enrolled in the Law School at Northwestern University in September of 1956.[37]

Beginning in 1959, a second attack was leveled at university segregation as the ACCA spearheaded an effort to open Georgia's colleges and universities to black students. Along with Atlanta Life's Hill, ACCA members M. Carl Holman, a Clark College English professor; Clarence D. Coleman, assistant director of the Atlanta Urban League; Leroy Johnson, a young attorney; Dr. Clinton Warner, a prominent black physician; Whitney Young, dean of the School of Social Work at Atlanta University; Herman Russell, a businessman; Q. V. Williamson, a businessman; and several others took on the tasks of organizing for the assault on school segregation. The group's tasks involved planning and mapping strategies, finding potential applicants, providing transportation to meetings, and accompanying students to the college admissions offices. Hill and the other members of ACCA acted as troubleshooters in the overall desegregation effort.

Through work with the ACCA and NAACP, Hill played an active role in routing Jim Crow from Georgia's university system. For its initial effort, the organization selected Georgia State College, a small institution located only a few blocks from the Atlanta Life home office building near downtown Atlanta. But because several admission regulations appeared to loom as effective roadblocks barring black applicants to this college, the ACCA changed the target to the University of Georgia in Athens. When the university denied admission to Charlayne Hunter and Hamilton Holmes, two highly qualified black students recruited by the committee, a legal battle ensued to gain their admission to the school. It was only after an eighteen-month fight led by attorneys Donald L. Hollowell and Constance Baker Motley of the NAACP that Hunter and Holmes were finally admitted to the University of Georgia and permitted to register for classes in early January 1961.[38]

In addition to his role in the school desegregation movement, Hill worked energetically with other groups to destroy the color line and to improve the social, political, and economic situation for blacks. For example, when students at the Atlanta University Center colleges took up the sit-in movement in March 1960 and began protesting the inability of blacks to obtain service at lunch counters in public buildings, bus and train stations, and major department and five- and-ten-cent stores, Hill was among the new black leadership that supported the student-initiated efforts. From the beginning, he advised the black students and in July 1960, along with several other members of the ACCA, began publishing the *Atlanta Inquirer* as a mouthpiece for the movement.[39]

Hill was dynamic, articulate, and a skillful negotiator, and he aided in bringing about the compromise agreement that ended the sit-ins and opened the way for the inauguration of a new era in race relations in Atlanta. Over the next decade, he moved to the forefront of black leadership in the city, becoming perhaps the race's top ombudsman. He was elected to the boards of numerous local and national organizations and became a prominent figure in the organizational echelon of black America. By the 1970s, Hill had penetrated the downtown power structure in Atlanta, becoming the first black man to sit on a number of boards and committees responsible for policy making in the areas of employment, transportation, crime, law enforcement, and other vital issues. By the end of the decade, he had served a term as president of the traditionally lily-white Atlanta Chamber of Commerce—the first black elected to that post in its history.[40]

In 1973 Georgia Governor Jimmy Carter appointed Hill to the Georgia Board of Regents, thereby making him one of the makers of policies for the state's entire university system. From the role of sympathetic adviser and compromise negotiator during the student sit-ins at Rich's, a leading department store, which had refused stubbornly to modify its policy of segregated facilities, Hill became a member of that company's board of directors in 1973. A short time later, he was elected to the board of directors of Delta Air Lines. From membership in the ACCA, a loosely formed organization that had undertaken the publication in January 1960 of a pamphlet, *Atlanta: A Second Look*, which detailed the conditions of blacks in health, housing, education, jobs, and other areas, Hill moved to membership in the important Atlanta Crime Commission and the board of the Metropolitan Atlanta Rapid Transit Authority (MARTA). These involvements put Hill squarely in the midst of the power brokers in Atlanta, and he did whatever he could to influence them to improve race relations and to solve some of the problems affecting blacks.[41] Hill seemed to believe in the power structure theory that social and political changes are most effectively achieved when the top business leaders are confronted with problems or issues and persuaded to grapple with them.

Jesse Hill, Jr., President, 1973–Present (Courtesy of Atlanta Life Insurance Company)

Atlanta Life people in areas outside of the state's capital city did not "sit quietly on the sidelines without firing a musket" in the post–World War II social revolution.[42] The idea that the economic success of the company was closely intertwined with the progress of the race prevailed on all fronts, and Atlanta Life men and women contributed in various ways in their communities.

George Lee, longtime manager at Memphis, was in the earliest generation of black activists among Atlanta Life's leadership. In the early 1920s, before joining the company, he had promoted racial pride and economic solidarity among black Americans. As a writer and orator, Lee spoke forcefully about the importance of black pride. "For Negroes to protect themselves against the barrage of white insults," he argued, "black pride was absolutely essential." With similar fervor, Lee called for the establishment of black businesses, urging African-Americans to promote enterprises that would advance the group economically. His appeals for black pride and black business were published in leading race journals such as the *Messenger* and *Opportunity*, black newspapers including the *Chicago Defender* and *Pittsburgh Courier*, and his own books *Beale Street* and *River George*. Lee was prominent among the businessmen in Memphis who served as "the real cutting edge of Negro protest."[43] In organizations and groups, Lee challenged the ideas of accommodation and racial inferiority whenever he could and provided, for that era at least, a militant and aggressive philosophy of black pride.

George Lee found in politics an important forum for racial leadership. His connection with Robert Church, a wealthy black Memphian, and with the Republican party enabled him to become involved in some of the leading issues of the race problem. Prominent among the groups to which Lee belonged was the Lincoln League of America, an organization begun locally by Church in 1916 to deal with race awareness and the registration of black voters. A few years later, it became a national organization to which nearly every important black politician in the country belonged. The league's efforts were directed primarily at guarding the rights allegedly bequeathed to blacks by Abraham Lincoln, including the right "to register and vote whenever the free ballot box is found, to present themselves as candidates for office whenever opportunity permits, to buy land, to build homes, strike out in trade and commerce, support the public press, and keep the lamp of faith trimmed and filled with oil."[44]

As an active Republican, Lee held various positions in the party, both at the local and national levels. Through these affiliations, he worked to promote increased voting participation among blacks and enhanced their influence in the party and in the country generally. Lee was an effective communicator and was usually willing to appear in a variety of forums to articulate his belief in racial equality and to condemn segregation publicly. As Lee's biographer contended, "Republican politics held a constant and understandable fascination for George Lee because it perpetually involved defending the race."[45]

Lee's voice in national Republican politics ended with the defeat of the party in 1932. He remained active in local politics, continuing in a major role for many years until he was displaced in the 1950s by a new group of leaders who talked of pressure, power, force, and a "politics of liberation" to which Lee refused to adjust.[46]

Lee did not abandon race work; he merely directed his efforts into another arena. In the Improved Benevolent and Protective Order of Elks of the World, one of the largest black fraternal organizations, Lee found a medium through which he could continue to work for race advancement. He was elected grand commissioner of education by the Elks in 1951. In this position, he initiated a number of adult education programs in an effort to stamp out illiteracy as a major racial blight in the country. As the civil rights movement emerged, Lee adopted as a slogan for his department: "You Integrate Them—The Elks Will Educate Them," announcing the availability of scholarships for students who sought to integrate formerly all-white educational institutions.[47]

Lee's work in securing freedom for African-Americans was independent of his job at Atlanta Life, emanating primarily from his affiliations in politics or fraternal life, but his aims were closely attuned to the philosophical ideals that had long guided the company. Like Eugene Martin, Lee sought to advance black Americans in areas broader than business and economics, to expose social disparities, and to provide a moral voice in issues that affected the race. These men believed that the national arena, whether through politics or uplift organizations, offered an important forum for leadership, and they attempted to be heard at that level even in the decades before the full flowering of the civil rights movement.

Similar roles were played by other Atlanta Life personnel in other communities. In 1945 Atlanta Life's district manager, Alonzo C. Touchstone, spearheaded a registration campaign in rural Spaulding County, Georgia, which added more than 338 black voters to the lists. In Griffin, the county seat of Spaulding, the NAACP organized in the Atlanta Life office. As early as 1942, at the initiative of Touchstone, the Griffin Civic Improvement League came into being. In addition to getting blacks on voting lists, the league was instrumental in adding black men and women to the jury rosters, finding employment in federally supported projects, in city and county government, and in industry, and in assisting in the election of blacks to city and county governments. This action was repeated in other sections of the state and country where progressive community leadership groups were often spearheaded by Atlanta Life people.[48]

In Montgomery, Alabama, Johnnie R. Carr, an Atlanta Life staff manager, worked with Martin Luther King, Jr., and Ralph David Abernathy in the Montgomery bus boycott, which generated the nonviolent social revolution of the midcentury. In Montgomery, as in many other cities in the South, public transportation was a constant source of humiliation for blacks. Carr was among the persons representing various organizations and associations which called on the city commissioners and bus company officials with petitions requesting action to relieve the unpleasant and demeaning situation for black commuters. The group's efforts were largely unsuccessful, and the situation remained unchanged until the arrest of Rosa Parks in December 1955 for failing to move to the rear of the city bus when ordered to do so by the driver.

Carr was among the groups that formed the Montgomery Improvement Association (MIA) in response to the arrest of Mrs. Parks. During the bus boycott that followed, Carr served as secretary of the Transportation Committee, which purchased a number of station wagons to transport boycotting citizens about the city, set up schedules, routes, the signals for hailing a driver or for indicating that transportation was not needed, and even the kind of gasoline to be used in the vehicles to get maximum mileage. Because of the effectiveness of the MIA in handling the transportation problem and the determination of Montgomery's black citizens to stay off the buses, the boycott was successful.[49]

With the transportation problem resolved, Carr moved up in the hierarchy of the MIA. She eventually became president of the organization as well as a board member of the Southern Christian Leadership Conference (SCLC) organized by King in Atlanta in 1957 to give leadership to the nonviolent movement of blacks to achieve equality and civil rights. In Montgomery, the activities of the MIA widened to include voter registration drives, job development programs, and the spearheading of desegregation of the city's public schools.[50]

Charles W. Greene presenting contribution to Dr. Martin Luther King, Jr., at Chicago Conference (Courtesy of Atlanta Life Insurance Company)

Commenting on the social consciousness of Atlanta Life, a long-time observer noted, "An individual cannot advance in an organization if political and social philosophies do not coincide with those of the enterprise."[51] And though it is undoubtedly true that individuals can do much that institutions cannot, the civil rights efforts of Atlanta Life employees were supported and emboldened by their positions at the firm. For example, people knew that Eugene Martin's actions carried the force of the largest black-owned shareholder life insurance company. Perhaps even more important, they believed that he had the personal endorsement of Norris Herndon, the largest shareholder. With Herndon's backing, Martin was in a position to undergird civil rights and protest activities economically by promising employment to a fired teacher or posting bail for jailed students or providing meeting space and printing and communications facilities to causes he supported.

In a similar vein, Jesse Hill's association with the respected enterprise provided a thrust into the community. It served also as a base from which his ideas and social concerns could be put into action. Indeed, the same observer contended that "in Atlanta, Jesse Hill has had no thrust in the city that was not made possible by Atlanta Life." Recognizing the mutual benefits of such an association, another longtime observer perceived the situation differently, noting that "Jesse Hill . . . has given it [Atlanta Life] a larger thrust in the community by his business contacts. . . . Hill is a total community character—more so than his predecessors in the company have been. [He] has given clout to Atlanta Life in the larger community of politics and business in a way that has not been true with others."[52]

In districts and communities outside of Atlanta, workers such as Lee, Touchstone, and Carr frequently acted in a manner consistent with the spirit of community involvement exemplified by the officials in the home office. Over the years, they could always point to men and women who, in their respective communities, offered inspiration and leadership in the planning and execution of various social movements.

Over the years, observers of Atlanta Life have generally assessed the company's involvement in race and community affairs in degrees varying from "committed" to a total "involvement in everything of social significance for blacks in Atlanta and the South." Clearly, since the early phase of its development, Atlanta Life has been an important benefactor of social action.[53] As founder, Alonzo Herndon left a record of social service to the community in the form of philanthropic and charitable support of various organizations and institutions. After his death, a number of Atlanta Life people, both in the home office and throughout the districts, perpetuated this social interest and, in most cases, broadened their activities to assume activist roles in their communities. Church and social affiliations notwithstanding, their positions with a growing and progressive black enterprise gave Atlanta Life workers greater stability and respectability in the community. It also gave them freedom from the economic constraints that often prohibited other groups and individuals from overt involvement in activities and movements that challenged the status quo.

11

Challenges of a New Era

---

*Black firms cannot offer many of the benefits offered by the
large white firms; . . . several firms have had to merge to pool
their resources to remain viable and competitive; and most
important, the black masses have not overcome their prejudice
about the quality of black-operated businesses.*
—Edward Jones, *Blacks in Business*

With the important exception of the creation of the Herndon Foundation, the 1950s were quiet years for Atlanta Life. Buttressed by solid
assets and large surpluses, the firm had successfully weathered the
fluctuating market conditions caused by depression and war. In spurts
of expansion fever, Atlanta Life grew until its territory included eleven
states in the South and Midwest. But a lethargy characterized some
aspects of company operations in the 1950s. In contrast to the expansion in the years immediately following the war, the growth fervor
seemed to subside and no new states were entered. Similarly, no new
companies were purchased, although by the end of the decade negotiations were under way to reinsure new businesses.[1] Another note-
worthy move came at mid-decade, when the directors once again
declared a 100 percent stock dividend, increasing the company's capital stock to $4 million.

This was not an unusual pattern for Atlanta Life. Following earlier
spurts of activity, the company generally had retrenched to devote
time and effort to developmental operations. In a similar manner, officials now decided that before expanding further or buying additional
businesses, unless these could be purchased at minimal cost, the firm
would direct its energies to the development of existing territory. In
the early part of the decade, in an effort to spur the field forces forward,

the agency officers adopted catchy slogans such as "Be Thrifty in '50," "Atlanta Life Is #1 in '51," or "Earn More in '54" to enhance the company's promotion effort.[2]

Conditions dictated a realignment of the administrative agency staff, which by 1955 had been depleted by illness and death. Lemuel Haywood, the agency director, died in August 1954 after nearly fifty years with the firm. Within a year, Cyrus Campfield, the assistant agency director, also succumbed to death. Illness prevented Charles Greene, the remaining member of the old agency "generals" from carrying out his responsibilities on a full-time basis. It was imperative that changes be made in administrative personnel. To this end, the directors named Edward Simon to the position of agency director in May 1956 and placed assistant agency directors in different territories with responsibility for the development of a state or a group of states. To strengthen the northern territory, consisting of the states of Kansas, Kentucky, Missouri, Ohio, Illinois, and Michigan, where sales were lowest, the company established two divisions and put two assistant directors in charge.[3]

Slogans and administrative realignments were not enough as the company encountered demands and challenges of a new era in black insurance development. Like other black companies, Atlanta Life faced several pressing issues with the onset of the 1960s. Among these were the problems of a changing black market and the slower growth rate of black insurance firms.

At the core of the new trends were the positive factors of rising black incomes and declining black mortality. Since World War II, the insurance market among blacks had become increasingly more attractive and significant increases both in size and income had occurred. A wider range of occupations opened up to young educated blacks, especially in urban areas, bringing about higher levels of income for the group. Life expectancy also increased for this group to about 40 percent above the rate for 1940.[4]

Despite the positive changes occurring in the portion of the market traditionally served by black companies, these firms failed to show comparable growth in sales and premiums. This situation was largely because of the incursion of larger national market firms into the black market. Robert Puth, the biographer of Chicago's Supreme Liberty Life Insurance Company, noted: "Before 1940 competition from national firms was restricted almost entirely to policies with weekly or monthly premiums. . . . But in the next two decades competition increased rapidly. More and more firms began actively to solicit applications from Negroes, to broaden the range of coverage offered, and to reduce or eliminate premium differentials."[5]

With their considerably greater resources and manpower, national market companies solicited selectively among the more insurance-conscious black consumers. Indeed, one firm reported a twelvefold increase in ordinary life insurance sales among this group between 1949 and 1962. Increasingly, too, raids on the personnel of black firms augmented the number of black agents in white companies. Once employed in white firms, black agents made strong solicitors for the business of the rising black middle class. This trend also effectively destroyed one of the salient selling points of black firms, which had always offered white-collar employment to black Americans.[6]

Although the incomes of blacks rose and the demand for larger policies increased among the growing middle class, the overall growth rate of black insurance companies showed a decline after 1960. Indeed, among some black firms, "the only areas of superior performance" were identified as being group and industrial insurance. Puth noted that "the 1960–70 growth rate of the Negro industry did not match that of all U.S. firms—though before 1950 the Negro industry had a faster overall growth rate, a differential which continued until 1955."[7]

Along with the growing competition from national firms, other disparities acted to produce constraints on the black industry. With comparatively smaller face values (the average estimated at $282 by Puth) and higher premium rates, most black firms, including Atlanta Life, maintained industrial policies as the major part of their business; these contracts accounted for two-thirds of the industry's insurance in force in 1960. But because such policies induced higher operating costs, black firms operated at a disadvantage in that premiums charged were of necessity higher than those charged by the national industry, thereby giving a cost incentive to more savings-conscious black families to purchase insurance from white firms. The inability of black companies to discriminate selectively within the black market meant a disadvantage in the mortality experience, which was usually offset by slightly higher premiums. In the area of group sales, although at least two black firms showed substantial gains, the overall prospects for black companies seemed dim. This situation would hold at least until social and economic barriers no longer hindered the competitive position of black firms or until black business activity increased more widely in the country. As the market changed in the 1960s, these differentials worked to place black enterprises at a keen disadvantage in a rapidly changing industry.[8]

The era saw some changes in Atlanta Life's relative standing in the black industry. Among the six leading black firms in 1950, Atlanta Life had the second largest amount of insurance in force. Only North Carolina Mutual exceeded the Atlanta company in this category, although within two decades, Golden State Mutual of Los Angeles would step boldly into second place. The difference in the rate of growth in insurance in force between the three companies involved primarily group sales. Organized in 1925 by William Nickerson, Jr., Norman O. Houston, and George A. Beavers, Jr., Golden State Mutual had remained fairly small for several decades (becoming a legal reserve company in 1942) with operations in only six states until the mid-1950s, when it vigorously entered the group insurance market. Between 1968 and 1970, its group business jumped tremendously, expanding from $59 million to more than $202 million, an increase of 209.4 percent, which made the group category the largest percentage of the company's total insurance in force. Ordinary insurance represented the second largest percentage of the total, and by 1970 this area had increased to over $249 million.[9]

North Carolina Mutual also recorded dramatic growth through group sales in this period and in 1971 became the first black company to attain $1 billion in insurance in force.[10] In most areas that are usually compared, particularly assets, income, disbursements, and payments to policyholders, the Durham enterprise generally outdistanced Atlanta Life. The Atlanta company, however, maintained its position relative to all other black insurance companies, surpassing Golden State in all categories except insurance in force.

The management of Atlanta Life was not unaware of the changes taking place among black consumers, within the insurance industry, or in its own relative standing among black companies. The administrative staff team composed of Eugene Martin, Walter Smith, Charles Greene, Dr. Henry Lang, Gilbert DeLorme, Jesse Hill, Edward Simon, and Henry Brown frequently discussed the demands of the new era. They carefully set out ways of enhancing the overall condition of the enterprise, although the group never opted to move too swiftly from the firm's traditional course. The decision was made to offer larger contracts to attract the new black customer. Throughout the decade, new business campaigns also stressed the selling of ordinary policies. A variety of term and endowment contracts became available for customers, allowing applicants to obtain coverage in excess of $100,000. Group contracts were also extended, although on a limited scale.[11]

Atlanta Life developed fairly modest goals for the new era. Still, the company maintained a consistent rate of growth throughout the decade of the 1960s and continuing into the 1970s. In this period, company assets increased by more than $30 million, insurance in force by $170 million, and total income by approximately $1 million annually (see Table 11.1). Although the modest projections in group sales were not met in this period, other areas showed satisfactory increases. Ordinary insurance grew sluggishly and by 1973 had reached just under $2 million. The company stayed close to its natural market, exhibiting its greatest growth in small-policy industrial sales (see Table 11.2).

At least two factors dictated this outcome. On one hand, although the officials appeared to accept enthusiastically the idea of advancing into the growing middle-class market as both a challenge and an obligation, they seemed unwilling to forsake the clients of more moderate to poorer means. They pointed frequently to the long-held special mission of Atlanta Life and other black companies to lift the

Table 11.1. Growth of Atlanta Life Insurance Company, 1951–1973 (in millions)

Year	Total income	Total paid to policyholders	Admitted assets	Insurance in force
1951	$ 8,417	$2,112	$26,623	$145,722
1952	8,976	2,117	29,653	152,642
1953	9,540	2,311	32,628	156,941
1954	9,906	2,465	36,013	159,225
1956	10,689	2,843	42,526	164,419
1957	10,906	3,227	45,334	165,947
1959	11,663	3,579	51,332	172,296
1960	11,376	3,942	53,634	176,193
1962	12,307	4,463	58,778	182,126
1964	13,325	5,001	63,686	189,575
1967	14,387	5,310	69,952	204,731
1968	15,298	5,458	72,583	218,887
1969	16,189	5,663	74,158	279,207
1970	17,440	6,186	75,888	303,007
1971	18,462	5,323	78,162	308,723
1972	19,263	6,616	80,804	317,097
1973	20,854	7,187	84,494	346,226

Source: Best's Life Insurance Reports, 1951–73.

Table 11.2. Premium Income by Classes of Insurance, 1951–1973 (in millions)

Year	Life, health and accident	Industrial	Ordinary	Life/group health and accident		Miscellaneous	Total
1951	$2,516	$4,168	$1,119	$	$	$5	$ 7,809
1952	2,784	4,272	1,221			7	8,284
1953	2,998	4,456	1,276			7	8,738
1954	3,091	4,550	1,331			8	8,980
1956	3,319	4,774	1,415			9	9,517
1957	3,463	4,750	1,377			9	9,599
1959	3,867	4,727	1,520	–1		17	10,131
1960	3,426	4,741	1,554	1		24	9,744
1962	4,018	4,859	1,547	2	7	27	10,459
1964	4,649	4,993	1,548	2	6	30	11,228
1967	4,890	5,235	1,707	3	12	39	11,883
1968	5,215	5,631	1,764	3	28	45	12,686
1969	5,558	5,935	1,841	5	51	49	13,439
1970	6,317	6,332	1,788	9	73	53	14,573
1971	6,717	6,681	1,864	8	72	58	15,400
1972	7,050	7,085	1,775	8	69	62	16,049
1973	7,722	7,471	1,972	63	63	–	17,290

Source: Best's Life Insurance Reports, 1951–73.

masses from "the quagmire of economic serfdom." The company, on the other hand, was restrained in making large-scale or persistent inroads into the growing middle class by the lack of a reserve supply of agents and by dwindling field personnel as agents moved to other occupations and institutions.[12] For these reasons, at least, Atlanta Life continued to find the traditional insurance market its strongest area. As late as 1973, the firm showed over three-fourths of its total contracts in the industrial coverage category.[13]

Moreover, Atlanta Life continued to follow other traditional managerial practices. For example, the officials continued to keep a large financial surplus on hand. In 1959 the president's report clarified this position before the stockholders, emphasizing the concerns of the company for safety and superiority in its contracts. The report stated that although blacks were "more and more taking on larger and larger policies, the big business is bound to go to the companies who offer superior contracts, and with something back of them more than contracts on paper." The company's official position was to continue to husband its surplus so as to secure its public standing and image. The president's report to the stockholders added, "You can say to the public, Atlanta Life is not an empty shell, but a great fortress of strength for policyholders and the general public."[14]

In 1973 the company's surplus funds amounted to about 17 percent of the total assets. Each year, the officials continued to plow the bulk of the earnings into the company, increasing the amount of surplus or raising the capital reserves. By 1975, $8 million of the authorized $20 million had been paid into the latter category. Dividends to stockholders were kept relatively modest as a more substantial portion of profits went into surplus.[15]

Atlanta Life approached the new era cautiously, holding to the principles of race and business which had served well in the past. When initial overtures into the national market fared poorly, the management seemed to accept the premise that for some time to come the major share of the market would rest in the black community and resolutely continued to wrap its appeals for business in race pride. Whereas black firms such as North Carolina Mutual seemed to deemphasize race, "soft-pedal[ing] the old slogans of solidarity and model[ing] its advertisements after the industry," Atlanta Life continued to put heavy emphasis on its traditional role as the "citadel of black capitalism" or the "guardian of the economic dignity" of black Americans.[16] By investing its surplus funds in solidifying policy contracts and capital reserves, the company avoided more imaginative investments that might have netted higher return. It also failed to invest substantively in real estate, such as a modern headquarters building, which would have provided much needed space as well as boosted its image as the largest stockholder life insurance company owned by blacks. It can be argued that such an investment by Atlanta Life could have aided Atlanta in recapturing the title of "capital of black business"—a title the city is said to have lost to Durham in 1966, when North Carolina Mutual occupied its gleaming new home office building.[17]

Another vital issue arose at the end of the decade. Although the officials had considered the matter settled for many years, the question of black control of Atlanta Life once again claimed their attention. As stipulated in the agreement creating the Alonzo F. and Norris B. Herndon Foundation, each year the president, as major stockholder, donated shares of stock from his personal holdings. By 1969, 21 percent of the total stock of Atlanta Life was held by the Herndon Foundation, with Norris Herndon retaining approximately 71 percent.

The 1969 Tax Reform Act, however, created a problem for Atlanta Life. Designed to eliminate the use of private foundations to maintain control of businesses and to guarantee spending by these organizations for charitable purposes, the act seriously threatened to undermine the central purpose of the Herndon Foundation. Of particular concern to officials were the provision that barred a foundation from owning more than 20 percent of a company's voting stock and the payout provision, which required a foundation to distribute its annual income or 5 percent of the fair market value of investment assets within twelve months. To reinforce the first provision, the act provided for "a second-level sanction" in the form of a tax of 200 percent of the value of excess holdings. These provisions were initiated primarily as a means of eliminating certain abuses of the tax relief allowed foundations and to prevent unreasonable accumulations of funds.[18]

The new tax act would have wrecked Atlanta Life's plan for future ownership and control. As proposed, the act would not allow the Herndon Foundation to become a repository for Atlanta Life stock. Without the Herndon Foundation, Atlanta Life risked serious impairment and even destruction as a black firm when its chief stockholder died. The payment of federal taxes, estimated at close to two-thirds of the entire value of the stock, would necessitate the sale of stock. The company's concern was augmented by the knowledge that purchasers for the company were unlikely to be found within the black community.

To combat the impact of the Tax Reform Act on Atlanta Life, Jesse Hill, Henry Brown, and George Lee, accompanied by counsel, lobbied the issue on Capitol Hill. Specifically, the officials petitioned the Ways and Means Committees of the House and Senate for a special amendment that would permit the Herndon Foundation to hold 51 percent of Atlanta Life stock and to receive all stock that might be donated as gifts or bequests. "Should this not be possible," the petition stated, "we believe that as a minimum the Foundation should be permitted to hold fifty per cent of the stock of the company."[19]

Fortunately, the act occurred at a time when the federal government was advocating support for minority economic development. The basis of Atlanta Life officials' arguments was that without special relief for the Herndon Foundation a substantial block of black capital already in existence would be effectively destroyed. To illustrate the disastrous effect this loss would have on minority enterprises, they explained that the net worth of Atlanta Life in capital and surplus represented approximately 30 percent of the value of all black insurance companies. To destroy Atlanta Life at a time of major efforts to encourage ownership and operation of black businesses would be untenable, they argued.[20]

Atlanta Life won the first round when Congress approved an exemption from the 20 percent provision for the Herndon Foundation. When the Tax Reform Act was passed in 1969, it contained a special amendment permitting the Herndon Foundation to retain permanently up to 51 percent of the stock of Atlanta Life without being taxed on the excess business holdings. It also stipulated that at Herndon's death, or whenever the shares of donated stock reached 90 percent, the foundation would be given fifteen years to reduce its holdings to 51 percent.[21]

Although this was a major concession, the victory was not yet won. The officials knew that this exemption, by itself, was not sufficient to secure Atlanta Life. Without additional relief, the intent of the amended section would be frustrated by the payout provision of the tax act, which required a private foundation to distribute annually its adjusted net income or a stated percentage of its investment assets, whichever was greater.

By 1973, the Atlanta Life officers had persuaded Congressmen Wilbur Mills and Phil Landrum to introduce H.R. 13289, a measure that would amend the tax act to allow the Herndon Foundation to determine minimum investment and adjusted net income without regard for the foundation's stock holdings in Atlanta Life. They proposed instead that income derived from such stock holdings would determine the annual amount that the foundation must pay out to public charities. Hill testified before the House Ways and Means Committee in March 1973, contending that though foundations with high-yield stocks could meet the minimum payout provision easily by drawing on dividend income, the Herndon Foundation, with assets consisting almost entirely of Atlanta Life stock, which paid relatively low dividends, would be forced to sell some of its stock to meet the required distribution level of 5 percent. He stressed that the sale of stock would thwart the purpose of the special amendment that had been won earlier permitting the foundation to retain permanent controlling interest in Atlanta Life.[22]

By 1974, the issue had been settled. In October, after several setbacks and many delays, Congress approved another amendment to the 1969 act exempting the Herndon Foundation from the payout provision. In lieu of the minimum payout of investment assets, the Herndon Foundation was required to contribute up to 100 percent of its earnings to charity. The company's victory in this second round meant that once again Atlanta Life's future seemed secure and that the officers and stockholders could now rest easy about black control of the company.[23]

On the home front, however, the years after 1969 saw a decline of the old order. The men who had led the company since the 1920s passed gradually from the scene. Fred Toomer died in 1962, Dr. Henry Lang in 1967, Eugene Martin in 1969, and Walter Smith in 1972. Norris Herndon formally retired as president in 1973 and died four years later in 1977. George Lee, the writer, master speechmaker, politician, and editor of the *Vision*, retired as an active manager although he remained on the company's board of directors.

Moving into the position vacated by the old order were well-trained individuals with experience and leadership ability. Hill and Brown had provided impressive leadership in the efforts to obtain legislative protection from the baneful effects of the Tax Reform Act. In many respects, their leadership symbolized the changing of the guard at Atlanta Life. At Martin's death, Brown was elected company secretary, and within a few years he also assumed Walter Smith's duties as chief investment officer. In 1973, when Herndon retired, Hill was elected president and chief executive officer. Several years before, with Fred

Atlanta Life Board of Directors, 1973. *Left to right:* Leonard J. Gunn, Henry N. Brown, Pritchett W. Willard, Gilbert E. DeLorme, George W. Lee, Jesse Hill, Jr., Johnnie M. Lowe, Charles W. Greene, and Edward L. Simon (Courtesy of Atlanta Life Insurance Company)

Toomer's death, Edward Simon became chief auditor, and in 1968 Leonard Gunn was made agency director after working for nearly thirty years as manager of Atlanta Life's Nashville district. Norris Herndon, now well into his seventies, assumed the chairmanship of the board when he retired in 1973. In addition to the chairman and executive team, George Lee, Charles Greene, Gilbert DeLorme, Pritchett Willard, manager of the Beaumont, Texas, district, and Johnnie Lowe, the first woman to sit on the board of directors since the death of Mrs. Alonzo Herndon, made up the enterprise's new board.

Formation of the new executive team of Hill, Brown, Simon, and Gunn constituted the first major reorganization in the company's administration since the 1920s. They succeeded men of definite achievements, enduring optimism, tremendous vision, and firm faith in the possibilities of Atlanta Life and other black business concerns. As founder, Alonzo Herndon had transformed a group of small, nearly failing mutual aid societies into a sturdy insurance organization. His tenure was highlighted by the achievement of legal reserve status, expansion of operations into eight states in the South and Midwest, and acquisition of over $1 million in assets and nearly $25 million of insurance in force. Under his son's leadership, the company survived the Great Depression and emerged to make significant strides in sales and financial growth. At Norris Herndon's retirement in 1973, the record showed $84.5 million in admitted assets and more than $346 million in insurance in force.

In addition to a strong financial foundation, the early presidents left a solid reputation among the insuring public. They had also secured a loyal force of workers in the home office and at the managerial and supervisory levels. The legacy also included an enduring tradition as a race enterprise that, in face of unrelenting racial hostility and economic deprivation, had provided a source of savings for the nickels, dimes, quarters, and dollars of thousands of African-Americans. The company had provided an important economic service in the form of employment for hundreds of blacks. In addition, the policy and mortgage loans available from the company had benefited numerous black policyholders.

The newest executives faced the ageless challenge of matching the records of their successors in a changing market environment. Like other black businesses, they were faced with the dilemma of forsaking the traditions of a race enterprise or running the risk of losing ground already achieved by being too complacent in a changing cultural setting. The new leaders hoped to avoid both pitfalls and talked often of making the company more attractive to the new black market. They also wanted Atlanta Life's costs and services to become more efficient while at the same time finding ways to capture a larger share of the total market.[24] They seemed clearly to reject the forces that compelled some companies to spend heavily on what they perceived as overly optimistic attempts to pursue white policyholders. Instead, they opted to preserve and bolster the traditional ethnic identity in a way that permitted Atlanta Life to direct its own integration.

The continued involvement of Atlanta Life in race issues and problems was vital, especially those growing out of the economic conditions of the times. After a decade of advancements in civil rights, the 1970s saw blacks move from the streets into the political and social arenas to continue their quest for full recognition as citizens. As mayors of some of the largest cities, members of Congress as well as state and local legislatures, superintendents of major school districts, and heads of important civil rights organizations, blacks now worked to eliminate the remaining problems in housing, education, politics, and employment.

In his first annual message, the new president made clear the company's continuing commitment to race advancement: "We have been involved in social action and black America's struggle against racism, bigotry, and discrimination. . . . Our continued involvement is a responsibility, is needed and crucial if the large masses of black families caught up in a cycle of poverty . . . are to enjoy an improved quality of life."[25] From the standpoint of overall economic benefit, one of the company's most significant involvements was in efforts to halt eroding business gains in the black insurance industry. In 1974 thirty-nine black firms operated in thirty-four states and in the District of Columbia, representing a decline of twenty-one companies since 1957, when sixty firms—the largest number ever—operated in the United States. Although the failure of black businesses or their absorption by nonminority companies caused less sensation in the media or among the general populace than in earlier eras, the impact on black economic development was very real nevertheless. Keeping its early commitment to save black companies in difficulty whenever possible, Atlanta Life continued to purchase smaller firms, eventually merging them with its own assets and business in force. The June 1977 issue of *Black Enterprise* quoted Hill as stating, "For us, it's become a matter of corporate resolution to help assure black control whenever possible."[26]

Several absorptions in this era indicate the reality of Hill's statement. In 1962, more than ten years before the changing of the guard at Atlanta Life, the company reinsured Guaranty Mutual, a small insurance company based in Savannah, Georgia. Following the purchase, the company operated as a separate enterprise until 1972, when Atlanta Life officially merged the principally industrial business, adding about $8 million in insurance in force and nearly $2 million in assets to its holdings.[27]

After absorbing Guaranty Life, the officials turned to Louisiana. Since 1930, a larger number of the sixteen firms then in existence had been either merged or purchased by other companies, three of them acquired by white firms. In 1974, hoping to reverse the trend, Atlanta Life obtained control of two of the remaining enterprises. The first, the Keystone Life Insurance Company of New Orleans, was a relatively small company with assets of $1.2 million and less than spectacular earnings and insurance in force. The second, acquired a few months later, was also in imminent danger of passing into nonblack hands when Atlanta Life stepped in and purchased the People's Life Insurance Company. The largest black company in Louisiana, it had over $4 million in assets and ranked fifteenth among the thirty-nine black companies, representing both entrepreneurial effort and economic significance in the state. Atlanta Life acquired 90 percent of Keystone stock and approximately 99 percent of that of People's, operating both firms as separate companies until January 1977, when they were merged with Atlanta Life. As business acquisitions, these firms contributed to the company's growth and expansion. They also smoothed the way for its entrance into a new state.[28]

During 1975, Atlanta Life ventured into Virginia, where the Southern Mutual Aid Society had operated since February 1893. The oldest black company then in existence, it had from its beginning been conducted as a fully chartered insurance enterprise operated along the lines of an industrial company. By 1975, when Atlanta Life acquired 67 percent of the stock of Southern Mutual, it had assets of about $4.4 million. Purchased at a cost of $3 million, the three acquisitions augmented Atlanta Life's assets and earnings by more than $10 million. Although these acquisitions were obviously very good business deals for the company, they were also important efforts toward saving black assets that had been accumulated through years of toil and struggle.[29]

Among other economic benefits, Atlanta Life and other black insurance companies emphasized their role as producers of employment for blacks. In a fluctuating job market, these firms provided useful training and employment as agents, supervisors, and in other clerical and managerial categories; Atlanta Life's annual payroll of commissions and wages exceeded $9 million in 1980. With significant investment assets, these companies also remained a source of mortgage loans for families, businesses, and churches.

Perhaps the most significant challenge of the new era for Atlanta Life has come since 1977. Norris Herndon's death in June of that year brought about the long-anticipated changes in the ownership of the business. Following his death, controlling stock in the enterprise shifted to the Herndon Foundation and to the control of the foundation trustees. The trustees, Jesse Hill, Jr., Henry Brown, Norris Connally, Helen Collins, Dr. James Palmer, and Edward Simon, were also officers and directors of Atlanta Life. For the first time in its history, the company was not controlled directly by a member of the Herndon family.

Under this arrangement, the firm made a smooth transition. It remained firmly in black control as the company approached seventy-five years of corporate existence. The leaders continued to make sub-

Atlanta Life Board of Directors, 1980. *Left to right:* Edward L. Simon, Norris Connally, Charles F. Cooke, Jesse Hill, Jr., Helen J. Collins, Henry N. Brown, and Dr. James Palmer (Courtesy of Atlanta Life Insurance Company)

stantial and significant progress. In the 1970s, as in other decades, the firm recorded gains in every category, including assets in 1979 of more than $107 million and insurance in force reaching $980.5 million. In the 1980s the company has continued to demonstrate financial growth, remaining the largest shareholder life insurance company controlled by black Americans in the nation.

In addition to financial progress, the company demonstrated other outward examples of its growth and maturation as a major black corporation. In early 1979 Atlanta Life began construction of a new corporate headquarters on Auburn Avenue in Atlanta. The building's dedication in September 1980 was part of a gala seventy-fifth anniversary celebration, which drew hundreds of local and national dignitaries, including President Jimmy Carter, to witness the capstone of the era. The magnificent new six-story, rose-hued marble and glass structure cost $10 million to construct and was paid for in full on opening day.[30]

The new headquarters building offered more than just an architectural face-lift. It provided greatly needed space for the firm's expanding operations as well as relief from the "Spartan, out-of-fashion" surroundings of the old home office building, which Atlanta Life had occupied for sixty years.[31] Similarly, the spectacularly sleek new building gave a needed face-lift to Auburn Avenue, which had in the last decade began suffering from the blight associated with encroaching urban renewal and declining business activity. Atlanta Life's construction of its new headquarters building was one of the first major efforts to revitalize this historic black business street. The building, located at the corner of Auburn Avenue and Courtland Street close to the heart of the downtown business center, was viewed by many as the westernmost anchor of a resurrected Auburn Avenue.[32]

The completion of Herndon Plaza and the new headquarters complex represented a grand triumph for the new leadership. In addition to its importance as a symbol of community revitalization, the new complex serves as concrete evidence of the enterprise's maturation. After eight decades of operation, Atlanta Life stands firmly among black business institutions and enterprises with significant resources and possibilities for future expansion and economic service to the community.

It remains for the future, however, to assess fully the efforts and achievements of the new generation of leaders. Preliminary indications are encouraging, especially as they point to the firm's growing coffers and widening markets. Industrial insurance is coming under the careful scrutiny of consumer and legislative groups with critics labeling the nickel-and-dime insurance as a costly prey upon the poor.[33] Atlanta Life is beginning to make significant inroads into the ordinary and group markets. At the end of 1982, industrial insurance represented only approximately 37 percent of the total volume of business, down significantly from the 1973 percentage.[34]

For Atlanta Life, expanded growth and productivity is at the heart of the agenda for the 1980s. This goal has propelled the firm to improve its image with more modern, efficient methods and facilities as well as more attractive portfolios. The agenda also stresses new acquisitions, including additional life insurance companies and even the possibility of noninsurance firms.[35] In general, the challenges for the firm are to maintain its standing as one of the nation's outstanding examples of black economic development and to continue to assist black America in dealing with problems growing out of the economic conditions of the times.

The firm's heritage as one of the guardians of black economic dignity is important for Atlanta Life. In the 1980s, even as the present leaders are concerned with the future, probing new markets and new mergers, they are very mindful of the heritage and obligations of a race

Mrs. Helen Johnson Collins, Board Chairwoman, 1984–Present (Courtesy of Atlanta Life Insurance Company)

enterprise. As the officers grapple with the problem of expanding the markets in the twelve states in which the firm now operates, it is expected that the important areas of concern will remain the declining number of black insurance companies, the need for jobs and employment opportunities for blacks, and the necessity of providing needed services to the black community. Despite the dilemma of changing markets and cultural settings, the firm has not forsaken these traditions. Atlanta Life has chosen to maintain faith with its traditions and ethnic identity, to seek to make itself more attractive to the black market, and, at the same time, to search for viable formulas to help meet the challenges of the 1980s, especially those involving the need to capture a larger share of the total market.

Notes

Preface

1. General sources for a review of black business efforts include John Henry Harmon, Jr., Arnett G. Lindsay, and Carter Godwin Woodson, *The Negro as a Business Man* (College Park, Md.: McGrath, 1929); Abram Lincoln Harris, *The Negro as Capitalist: A Study of Banking and Business Enterprise among American Negroes* (New York: Haskell House, 1936); Vishnu V. Oak, *The Negro's Adventure in General Business* (1949; rpt. Westport, Conn.: Negro Universities Press, 1970); Booker T. Washington, *The Negro in Business* (1907; rpt. Chicago: Afro-American Press, 1969). Several studies provide insight into black economic and entrepreneurial activities in the pre–Civil War era. A few of these sources include Letitia Woods Brown, *Free Negro in the District of Columbia, 1790–1846* (New York: Oxford University Press, 1972), pp. 129–65; Rhoda Golden Freeman, "The Free Negro in New York City in the Era before the Civil War" (Ph.D. dissertation, Columbia University, 1966), pp. 267–314; Luther Porter Jackson, *Free Negro Labor and Property Holding in Virginia, 1830–1860* (1942; rpt. New York: Atheneum, 1969); H. E. Sterkx, *The Free Negro in Antebellum Louisiana* (Rutherford, N.J.: Fairleigh Dickinson University Press, 1972), pp. 200–239; Edward F. Sweat, "The Free Negro in Ante-Bellum Georgia" (Ph.D. dissertation, Indiana University, 1957); Ivy Marina Wilramanayaki, "The Free Negro in Antebellum South Carolina" (Ph.D. dissertation, University of Wisconsin, 1966), pp. 126–49; James Martin Wright,

207

The Free Negro in Maryland (New York: Columbia University Press, 1921), pp. 149–97; Richard R. Wright, Jr., *The Negro in Pennsylvania: A Study in Economic History* (1912; rpt. New York: Arno Press, 1969), pp. 126–49. In addition, see Leonard P. Curry, *The Free Black in Urban America, 1800–1950: The Shadow of the Dream* (Chicago: University of Chicago Press, 1981), pp. 15–48; Ira Berlin, *Slaves without Masters: The Free Negro in the Antebellum South* (New York: Pantheon Books, 1975); Leon F. Litwack, *North of Slavery: The Negro in the Free States, 1790–1860* (Chicago: University of Chicago Press, 1961); W. Sherman Savage, *Blacks in the West* (Westport, Conn.: Greenwood Press, 1976), pp. 120–38; Juliet E. K. Walker, *Free Frank: A Black Pioneer on the Antebellum Frontier* (Lexington: University Press of Kentucky, 1983). The post–Civil War era is also covered in several state studies, including Lester C. Lamon, *Black Tennesseans, 1900–1930* (Knoxville: University of Tennessee Press, 1977), pp. 167–206; Frenise A. Logan, *The Negro In North Carolina, 1876–1894* (Chapel Hill: University of North Carolina Press, 1964), pp. 97–116; George Brown Tindall, *South Carolina Negroes, 1877–1900* (Columbia: University of South Carolina Press, 1952), pp. 124–52; David A. Gerber, *Black Ohio and the Color Line, 1860–1915* (Urbana: University of Illinois Press, 1976), pp. 60–92; Laurence D. Rice, *The Negro in Texas, 1874–1900* (Baton Rouge: Louisiana State University Press, 1971), pp. 184–208; *The Negro in Virginia*, A Study Compiled by Workers of the Writers' Program of the Works Projects Administration in the State of Virginia, Sponsored by Hampton Institute (New York: Hastings House, 1940), pp. 292–305.

2. See Edward Franklin Frazier, *Black Bourgeoisie* (New York: Free Press, 1965).

1: A Heritage of Mutual Aid

1. Minutes of Board of Directors Meeting, Atlanta Life Insurance Company, 1 July 1927, Atlanta Life Insurance Company Files, Atlanta, Georgia; hereafter cited as ALCF.

2. Ibid.; see also 4 April, 3 May, 1 June 1927.

3. *New York World*, 31 July 1927.

4. For an excellent discussion of the role of benevolent societies in the development of black institutional life, see Robert L. Harris, Jr., "Early Black Benevolent Societies, 1780–1830," *Massachusetts Review* 20 (Autumn 1979): 603–25.

5. William Johnson Trent, Jr., "Development of Negro Life Insurance Enterprises" (Master's thesis, University of Pennsylvania, 1932), pp. 8–9. See also Carter Godwin Woodson, "Insurance Business among Negroes," *Journal of Negro History* 14 (April 1929): 202; William Edward Burghardt Du Bois, ed., *Some Efforts of American Negroes for Their Own Social Bet-*

terment, Atlanta University Publication 3 (Atlanta: Atlanta University Press, 1898), and *Economic Cooperation among Negro Americans,* Atlanta University Publication 12 (Atlanta: Atlanta University Press, 1907); Monroe Nathan Work, "The Negro in Business and the Professions," *Annals of the American Academy of Political and Social Sciences* 140 (November 1928): 142.

6. John W. Blassingame, ed., *Slave Testimony: Two Centuries of Letters, Speeches, Interviews, and Autobiographies* (Baton Rouge: Louisiana State University Press, 1977), p. 377.

7. Woodson, "Insurance Business among Negroes," p. 202.

8. Harris, "Early Black Benevolent Societies," pp. 609–10.

9. Charles Harris Wesley, *Richard Allen: Apostle of Freedom* (Washington, D.C.: Associated Publishers, 1935), p. 58.

10. Ibid., pp. 59–63; Trent, "Development of Negro Life Insurance Enterprises," pp. 2–3; Wright, *Negro in Pennsylvania,* pp. 31–32.

11. James B. Browning, "The Beginnings of Insurance Enterprise among Negroes," *Journal of Negro History* 22 (October 1937): 417; Trent, "Development of Negro Life Insurance Enterprises," p. 2.

12. Articles of the Free African Society, quoted in Wesley, *Richard Allen,* p. 61; see also Trent, "Development of Negro Life Insurance Enterprises," p. 2; and Wright, *Negro In Pennsylvania,* p. 31.

13. Wright, *Negro in Pennsylvania,* pp. 30–33; Browning, "Beginnings of Insurance Enterprise among Negroes," pp. 417–18.

14. August Meier and Elliott Rudwick, *From Plantation to Ghetto* (New York: Hill and Wang, 1966), pp. 90–91; see also William Edward Burghardt Du Bois, *The Philadelphia Negro: A Social Study* (Philadelphia: University of Pennsylvania, 1899), p. 222.

15. Harris, "Early Black Benevolent Societies," p. 611.

16. E. Horace Fitchett, "The Traditions of the Free Negro in Charleston, South Carolina," *Journal of Negro History* 25 (April 1940): 139.

17. Quoted in Robert L. Harris, Jr., "Charleston's Free Afro-American Elites: The Brown Fellowship Society and the Humane Brotherhood," *South Carolina Historical Magazine* 82 (October 1981): 292.

18. Fitchett, "Traditions of the Free Negro In Charleston," pp. 144–45.

19. Browning, "Beginnings of Insurance Enterprise among Negroes," p. 424.

20. See Harris, "Charleston's Free Afro-American Elites," pp. 298–301.

21. Trent, "Development of Negro Life Insurance Enterprises," p. 8; see also Browning, "Beginnings of Insurance Enterprise among Negroes," pp. 428–29.

22. Du Bois, ed., *Some Efforts,* p. 5.

23. William Patrick Burrell and D. E. Johnson, *Twenty-Five Years History of the Grand Fountain of the United Order of True Reformers, 1881–1905* (Richmond: N.p., [1909]), pp. 38–39.

24. Harris, *Negro as Capitalist*, p. 46; see also Burrell and Johnson, *Twenty-Five Years*, p. 116; Walter B. Weare, *Black Business in the New South: A Social History of the North Carolina Mutual Life Insurance Company* (Urbana: University of Illinois Press, 1973), p. 13.

25. Trent, "Development of Negro Life Insurance Enterprises," pp. 20–21.

26. Weare, *Black Business in the New South*, pp. 14, 48, 67–68.

27. Merah Stevens Stuart, *An Economic Detour: A History of Insurance in the Lives of American Negroes* (New York: Wendell Malliett and Company, 1940), pp. 311, 234–35; James B. Mitchell, *The Collapse of the National Benefit Life Insurance Company: A Study in High Finance among Negroes* (Washington, D.C.: Howard University Press, 1939); *Southern Aid Society of Virginia, Inc.*, p. 22, pamphlet in possession of the author.

28. Harry Herbert Pace, "The Business of Insurance among Negroes," *Crisis* 32 (September 1926): 222.

29. Isabel Dangaix Allen, "Negro Enterprise: An Institutional Church," *Outlook* 88 (17 September 1904): 179–83; T. W. Walker, "Negro Coal Mining Company," speech presented at a meeting, National Negro Business League, *Proceedings* (Boston: J. R. Hamm, 1900), p. 106; Trent, "Development of Negro Life Insurance Enterprises," p. 33.

30. Stuart, *Economic Detour*, p. 9.

31. Ibid., pp. 9, 36; Walker, "Negro Coal Mining Company," p. 111.

32. *Atlanta Independent*, 30 January 1904, 4 March, 9 October 1905.

33. The earliest independent black church in Atlanta, organized by black Methodists, was set up about 1853 (the date is disputed). See Edward Randolph Carter, *The Black Side: A Partial History of the Business, Religious, and Educational Side of the Negro in Atlanta, Ga.* (Atlanta: N.p., 1894), pp. 14–15; *A Century of Progress and Christian Service*, a historical booklet prepared by Bethel A.M.E. Church, Atlanta, Georgia, August 1968, in possession of the author.

34. Carter, *Black Side*, pp. 21, 246–49; Clarence Albert Bacote, *The Story of Atlanta University: A Century of Service, 1865–1965* (Atlanta: Atlanta University Press, 1969), p. 4.

35. Carter, *Black Side*, p. 249.

36. Ibid.; Du Bois, ed., *Some Efforts*, p. 53.

37. U.S. Bureau of the Census, *Thirteenth Census of the U.S., 1910, Abstract of the Census with Supplement for Georgia* (Washington, D.C.: U.S. Government Printing Office, 1913), p. 95.

38. Alexa Benson Henderson, "Alonzo Herndon and Black Insurance in Atlanta," *Atlanta Historical Bulletin* 21 (Spring 1977): 36; W. A. Jordan, speech, National Negro Insurance Association, *Proceedings* (Richmond: Quality Printing Company, 1926).

39. Stuart, *Economic Detour*, p. 117, Trent, "Development of Negro Life

Insurance Enterprises," p. 30; Interview with the Reverend William Holmes Borders, Atlanta, Georgia, 1 November 1974.

40. *Atlanta Independent*, 15 October 1910; *Voice of the Negro* 3 (July 1906): 512; Interview with Borders.

41. *Voice of the Negro* 2 (March 1905): 192; Interview with Borders. No records are extant for the association.

42. Du Bois, ed., *Some Efforts*, p. 47.

43. *Atlanta Independent*, 9 October 1905.

44. Lucian L. Knight, *History of Fulton County, Georgia, Narrative and Biographical* (Atlanta: A. H. Cawston, 1930), p. 399. See also Jack Blicksilver, "Life Insurance Company of Georgia: The Formative Years, 1891–1918," in Louis B. Cain and Paul J. Uselding, eds., *Business Enterprise and Economic Change* (Kent, Ohio: Kent State University Press, 1973), pp. 265–66.

45. *Acts and Resolutions of the General Assembly of the State of Georgia, 1905* (Atlanta: Franklin Printing Company, 1906), pp. 96–97.

46. William H. A. Carr, *From Three Cents a Week: The Story of the Prudential Insurance Company of America* (Englewood Cliffs, N.J.: Prentice-Hall, 1975), pp. 113–16; Earl Chapin May and Will Oursler, *The Prudential: A Story of Human Security* (Garden City, N.Y.: Doubleday, 1950), p. 12; Louis I. Dublin, *A Family of Thirty Million: The Story of the Metropolitan Life Insurance Company* (New York: Metropolitan Life Insurance Company, 1943), p. 121.

47. Carr, *From Three Cents a Week*, pp. 14–15.

48. Dublin, *A Family of Thirty Million*, p. 43.

49. Ibid., pp. 64–66; May and Oursler, *The Prudential*, pp. 129–41.

50. Morton Keller, *The Life Insurance Enterprise, 1885–1910: A Study of the Limits of Corporate Power* (Cambridge, Mass.: Belknap Press of Harvard University Press, 1963), pp. 251–58. In 1912 Georgia, along with Colorado, Indiana, and South Carolina, organized a Department of Insurance. See *Acts and Resolutions, Georgia*, 1912, p. 119.

51. James Arthur Hopkins, *Atlanta—You Ought to Know Some Pioneers of Atlanta*, in National Negro Business League Directory and Souvenir Program, 1937, pp. 18–19, Atlanta-Fulton Public Library, Atlanta. Whites who may have submitted bids were not identified.

52. Alonzo Franklin Herndon, "Atlanta Life: Past, Present, Future," an address delivered 22 January 1924, in ALCF; "A Brief History of the Company, 1905–1923," in ALCF. The purchase price is given as from $140 to $200 in various accounts.

53. *Atlanta Independent*, 23 September 1905.

54. Truman Kella Gibson, "The History of Industrial Insurance and the Story of Atlanta Mutual," in Du Bois, ed., *Economic Cooperation among Negroes in Georgia*, p. 38.

2: Alonzo Herndon: Barber and Businessman

1. For a discussion of the early twentieth-century responses to segregation, see August Meier, *Negro Thought in America, 1880–1915: Racial
Ideologies in the Age of Booker T. Washington* (Ann Arbor: University of
Michigan Press, 1969), pp. 42–58; C. Vann Woodward, *Origins of the New
South, 1877–1913* (Baton Rouge: Louisiana State University Press, 1971),
pp. 350–68; John Hope Franklin, *From Slavery to Freedom: A History of Negro Americans*, 6th ed. (New York: Knopf, 1988), pp. 251, 264, 303; Weare,
Black Business in the New South, pp. 22–26.
2. Interview with Kathleen Redding Adams, Atlanta, Georgia, 22 June
1979; *Atlanta Independent*, 7 September 1918.
3. Herndon, "Atlanta Life."
4. "An Open Letter to Atlanta Life Workers Everywhere" [1928], p. 1, in
ALCF; *New York World*, 31 July 1927 (clipping), in Herndon Family Papers,
Atlanta, Georgia; hereafter cited as HFP; Robert W. Chamblee, "Alonzo
Franklin Herndon," *Vision*, June 1928, p. 7. For data on members of the
Herndon family household, see the U.S. Census, Population Schedule, 1870,
Walton County, Georgia, pp. 376–77, in Georgia Department of Archives
and History (microfilm).
5. Obituary, *Vision*, June 1928, p. 8; "The Atlanta Life Insurance Company," *Underwriters' Forum*, January 1947, p. 7; Stuart, *Economic Detour*,
p. 7.
6. Chamblee, "Alonzo Franklin Herndon," p. 7; *Atlanta Journal*, 10
May 1914; see also *Atlanta City Directory*, 1883–1904 (Atlanta: Foote and
Davies, 1884–1911).
7. *Atlanta Journal*, 10 May 1914; undated news release in ALCF.
8. *Atlanta Journal*, 10 May 1914; see also Franklin M. Garrett, *Atlanta
and Environs: A Chronicle of Its People and Events*, 2 vols. (New York:
Lewis Historical Publishing Company, 1954), 1:609.
9. *New York World*, 31 July 1927.
10. John Henry Harmon, "The Negro as a Local Businessman," *Journal of
Negro History* 14 (April 1929): 119–20; Harris, *The Negro as Capitalist*, pp.
9–10.
11. *New York World*, 31 July 1927.
12. See order of funeral services for Alonzo Herndon, in *Atlanta Independent*, 28 July 1927.
13. "Atlanta Massacre," *Independent*, 4 October 1906, p. 799.
14. *New York World*, 31 July 1927; "Famous Herndon Barbershop Given
to Employees," undated news release, in ALCF.
15. Interview with Edward Lloyd Simon, Atlanta Georgia, 12 November
1974; Interview with Robert W. Chamblee, Atlanta, Georgia, 14 August
1974; Alonzo F. Herndon to O. O. Hamilton, president of Real Estate Ex-
change, 5 May 1925, in HFP; *Atlanta Journal*, 22 July 1927; *New York*

World, 31 July 1927; see also General Index to Deeds, to April 1901, pp. 83–84; 1901–10, pp. 97–98, Fulton County Court House, Atlanta.
16. Preliminary Statement of Assets and Liabilities of Estate of A. F. Herndon, Deceased, 19 August 1927, copy in HFP.
17. U.S. Census, Population Schedule I, 1880, Chatham County, Georgia, p. 19, microfilm in Georgia Department of Archives and History, Atlanta; Clarence Albert Bacote, "Theater at Atlanta University," *Atlanta University Bulletin,* September 1974, p. 18.
18. *Bulletin of Atlanta University,* June 1891, p. 6. For a discussion of legislative action leading to the establishment of a state school for blacks, see Bacote, *Story of Atlanta University,* pp. 70–77, 86–101.
19. Juanita Paschal Toomer, "Miracle on Auburn Avenue" (unpublished manuscript, 1980), p. 5, in ALCF; Taped interview with Mrs. Eugene Martin and Mrs. Lorimer D. Milton, Atlanta, Georgia, 27 May 1981.
20. Anna B. Curry to Alonzo F. Herndon, 6 September 1901, in HFP.
21. *Boston Daily Advertiser,* 29 January 1904.
22. *Boston Transcript,* 23 January 1904; *Boston Traveler,* 25 January 1904; Bacote, *Story of Atlanta University,* p. 129.
23. "Postscript by W. E. B. Du Bois," *Crisis* 34 (September 1927): 239.
24. Alonzo Herndon to Martha A. McNeil, Baden-Baden, [1912], in HFP.
25. Toomer, "Miracle on Auburn Avenue," p. 26.
26. Bacote, "Theater at Atlanta University," pp. 19–20. For discussion of Adrienne Herndon's views on theater, see Adrienne Elizabeth Herndon, "Shakespeare at Atlanta University," *Voice of the Negro* 3 (July 1906): 282, 285.
27. Adrienne McNeil Herndon to Booker T. Washington, 12 February 1907, in Louis R. Harlan and Raymond W. Smock, eds., *The Booker T. Washington Papers,* vols. 8–9 (Urbana: University of Illinois Press, 1979–80), 9:216–17.
28. Bacote, "Theater at Atlanta University," p. 20; Bacote, *Story of Atlanta University,* p. 129.
29. Alonzo F. Herndon to Jessie Gillespie, undated, in HFP.
30. For details of honeymoon plans see Alonzo F. Herndon to Mary and Emma Gillespie, 25 April 1912, in HFP.
31. Ibid.
32. John O. Holzhueter, "Ezekiel Gillespie, Lost and Found," *Wisconsin Magazine of History* 60 (Spring 1977): pp. 179–84.
33. William Edward Burghardt Du Bois, ed., *The Negro in Business,* Atlanta University Publication 4 (Atlanta: Atlanta University Press, 1899), pp. 56–60.
34. Ibid., pp. 5, 56–60.
35. Ibid., p. 5.
36. National Negro Business League, *Proceedings,* 1900 (Boston: J. R. Hamm, 1900), pp. 7–8; see also Booker T. Washington, *The Negro in Business* (1907; rpt. Chicago: Afro-American Press, 1969), pp. 268–69; Vishnu V.

Oak, *The Negro's Adventure in General Business* (1949; rpt. Westport, Conn.: Negro Universities Press, 1970), pp. 104–5; William Edward Burghardt Du Bois, "The Growth of the Niagara Movement," *Voice of the Negro*, January 1906, pp. 43–45.

37. Albon L. Holsey, "The National Negro Business League: Forty Years in Review," *Crisis* 48 (April 1941): 104.

38. *Atlanta Independent*, 20 December 1913.

39. Alonzo F. Herndon to Emmett J. Scott, 2 July 1915, in Booker T. Washington Papers, Library of Congress.

40. Herbert Aptheker, *A Documentary History of the Negro People in the United States*, 2 vols. (New York: Citadel Press, 1951) 2:901; Dittmer, *Black Georgia*, p. 170.

41. Harlan and Smock, eds., *Washington Papers*, 8:386–87.

42. Booker T. Washington to Henry A. Rucker, 20 March 1906, ibid., pp. 552–53.

43. Henry A. Rucker to Emmett J. Scott, 16 October 1905; Annie L. Rucker to Scott, 7 December 1905, in Washington Papers.

44. In a letter to Booker T. Washington, Mrs. Herndon talked about the riot's effect on her family. See Adrienne Herndon to Booker T. Washington, 12 February 1907, in Harlan and Smock, eds., *Washington Papers*, 9:216–17.

45. "Postscript by W. E. B. Du Bois," p. 239.

46. Bacote, "Negro in Georgia Politics," pp. 497–98; Dittmer, *Black Georgia*, pp. 97–98; *Atlanta Constitution*, 28 July 1907.

47. "Postscript by W. E. B. Du Bois," p. 239.

48. At his death, Herndon left bequests to all of these organizations; see Last Will and Testament of Alonzo F. Herndon, Will no. 15390, Will Book I, p. 114, Fulton County Court House, Atlanta.

49. Louise Delphia Davis Shivery, "History of Organized Social Work among Atlanta Negroes, 1890–1935" (Master's thesis, Atlanta University, 1936), pp. 6–11.

50. Homer C. McEwen, Sr., "First Congregational Church, Atlanta," *Atlanta Historical Bulletin* 21 (Spring 1977): 134. For information on the early social work activities of the First Congregational Church, see ibid., pp. 134–38; Edyth Lively Ross, "Black Heritage in Social Welfare: A Case Study of Atlanta," *Phylon* 37 (Winter 1976): 302.

51. Du Bois, ed., *Some Efforts*, p. 51.

52. *Atlanta Journal*, 22 July 1927; *Vision*, June 1926.

53. Interview with Borders.

54. *Atlanta Independent*, 26 February 1925.

55. Toomer, "Miracle on Auburn Avenue," p. 26.

56. *Atlanta Independent*, 26 February 1925.

57. Herndon, "Atlanta Life," p. 22.

3: Faith in the Enterprise

1. *Atlanta Independent*, 26 February 1925.
2. Interview with Chamblee, 14 August 1974.
3. *Atlanta Independent*, 5 August 1905.
4. "Epitome of Atlanta Life Ins. Co.," *Atlanta Life Bulletin*, undated issue, p. 2, in ALCF.
5. *Atlanta Independent*, 23 September 1905.
6. Ibid.
7. Ibid.
8. Ibid., 6 November 1910.
9. The building, situated on the northeast corner of Auburn Avenue and Bell Street, was purchased on 5 June 1900 at public sale for $825. Deed Book, No. 144, Fulton County, p. 676. See also *Atlanta Independent*, 23 September 1905; "The Atlanta Life Insurance Company."
10. The number of agents varies from one to three in different accounts. See Herndon, "Atlanta Life"; *A Brief History of the Company, 1905–1923*, p. 1, pamphlet in ALCF; Atlanta Life Insurance Company, Minutes of Stockholders Meeting, 24 January 1923, in ALCF.
11. *Report of the Insurance Department of the Comptroller-General's Office for Year Ending 31 December 1906* (Atlanta: Franklin Printing and Publishing Company, 1907), p. 504, hereafter cited as *Comptroller-General's Report*.
12. *Atlanta Independent*, 8 July, 16 September, 23 December 1905, 20 January 1906; Trent, "Development of Negro Life Insurance Enterprises," p. 34.
13. *Scroll*, November 1911; Interview with Simon, 19 November 1974.
14. The term *debit* refers to the agent's weekly collection as well as to the route he covered.
15. Interview with Chamblee, 14 August 1974.
16. Ibid.; see also Margaret Shannon, "Wealthy Atlanta Negroes . . . How They Did It," *Atlanta Journal and Constitution Magazine*, 9 March 1969, p. 30.
17. Interview with Chamblee, 14 August 1974.
18. Woodward, *Origins of the New South*, pp. 351–52.
19. Dewey W. Grantham, Jr., *Hoke Smith and the Politics of the New South* (Baton Rouge: Louisiana State University Press, 1958), pp. 158–62; see also John Dittmer, *Black Georgia in the Progressive Era, 1900–1920* (Urbana: University of Illinois Press, 1977), p. 100.
20. Jesse Max Barber, "The Atlanta Tragedy," *Voice*, November 1906, pp. 473–79; "Atlanta Massacre," *Independent*, 4 October 1906, pp. 799–800; Ray Stannard Baker, *Following the Color Line: American Negro Citizenship in the Progressive Era* (New York: Harper & Row, 1908), pp. 3–18; Dittmer, *Black Georgia*, pp. 124–31.

21. *Atlanta Journal*, 14 July 1907; Dittmer, *Black Georgia*, p. 135.

22. Clarence A. Bacote, "The Negro in Georgia Politics, 1880–1908" (Ph.D. dissertation, University of Chicago, 1955), p. 497; Bacote, "Some Aspects of Negro Life in Georgia," *Journal of Negro History* 43 (July 1958): 200–201.

23. Interview with Gilbert Earl DeLorme, Atlanta, Georgia, 28 August 1974.

24. *Atlanta Independent*, 22 June 1907, 12 February, 4 June 1910.

25. *Acts and Resolutions of the General Assembly of the State of Georgia*, 1909, p. 169. A policy reserve is defined as that amount which together with future premiums, interest, and the benefit of survivorship is assumed to be sufficient to pay future claims. See Solomon S. Huebner and Kenneth Black, Jr., *Life Insurance*, 7th ed. (New York: Appleton-Century-Crofts, 1969), p. 358.

26. See *Comptroller-General's Report*, 1908–10.

27. *Atlanta Independent*, 4 June 1910.

28. See Knight, *History of Fulton County*, p. 399; Blicksilver, "Life Insurance Company of Georgia," pp. 265–66.

29. *Acts and Resolutions*, 1909, p. 171.

30. "Epitome of Atlanta Life," p. 2; Annual Report of Officers of Atlanta Mutual Insurance Co., [1919], p. 3, in ALCF.

31. "Epitome of Atlanta Life," p. 2.

32. Ibid.; W. Carroll Latimer to Alonzo Herndon, 30 June 1917, in HFP.

33. Stuart, *Economic Detour*, pp. 84–85.

34. Ibid., pp. 150–51.

35. "Epitome of Atlanta Life," p. 2.

36. "Sketches of the Lives of Atlanta Business Leaders," *Atlanta World*, 8 August 1930; Toomer, "Miracle on Auburn Avenue," p. 30.

37. *Atlanta Independent*, 9 September 1911.

38. "Epitome of Atlanta Life," p. 3.

39. Stuart, *Economic Detour*, p. 285. A legal reserve life insurance company is defined as one that operates under state insurance laws specifying the minimum reserves the company must maintain on its policies.

40. Stuart, *Economic Detour*, pp. 284–88; Trent, "Development of Negro Life Insurance Enterprises," p. 39.

41. Stuart, *Economic Detour*, p. 306; see also Comradge Leroy Henton, "Heman E. Perry: Documentary Materials for the Life History of a Business Man" (Master's thesis, Atlanta University, 1948); Papers of Thomas W. Jarrett, Atlanta, Georgia; Alexa Benson Henderson, "Heman E. Perry and Black Enterprise in Atlanta, 1908–1925," *Business History Review* 61 (Summer 1987): 216–42; Eric Walrond, "The Largest Negro Commercial Enterprise in the World," *Forbes*, February 1924, pp. 503–5, 523, 525, 533; Judy D. Simmons, "Heman E. Perry: The Commercial Booker T. Washington," *Black Enterprise*, April 1978, pp. 41–49.

42. Harry Herbert Pace, "A New Business Venture," *Crisis* 8 (January 1914): 142–44.

43. "Epitome of Atlanta Life," p. 3.

44. Pace, "New Business Venture," p. 144; Trent, "Development of Negro Life Insurance Enterprises," p. 39; Henderson, "Heman E. Perry," p. 224.

45. *Atlanta Independent*, 28 June, 20 December 1913, 6 June, 8 August 1914.

46. See Dittmer, *Black Georgia*, p. 49. Several attempts to locate the source cited by Dittmer in Washington papers have failed.

47. *Atlanta Independent*, 26 December 1914.

48. Ibid., 9 October 1905, 14 June 1913, 24 January, 4, 11, 18, 25 April, 1 August 1914.

49. Ibid., 30 October 1915.

4: A Matter of Survival

1. Harmon, "The Negro as a Local Business Man," p. 122.

2. For a discussion of early spurts of growth in the industry affecting black companies, see Pace, "Business of Insurance among Negroes," p. 219; *Atlanta Life Bulletin*, undated, p. 4.

3. *Acts and Resolutions*, 1912, p. 142.

4. Trent, "Development of Negro Life Insurance Enterprises," p. 22; Du Bois, ed., *Economic Cooperation*, p. 109; Weare, *Black Business in the New South*, p. 15.

5. For a discussion of mutual versus stock companies, see Huebner and Black, *Life Insurance*, pp. 635–42; David Lynn Bickelhaupt, *General Insurance*, 10th ed. (Homewood, Ill.: Richard D. Irwin, 1979), p. 118; Joseph B. McClean, *Life Insurance*, 9th ed. (New York: McGraw-Hill, 1962), pp. 340–53.

6. *Acts and Resolutions*, 1912, pp. 127–28.

7. Interview with Chamblee, 13 August 1974.

8. Report of the Association Examination of Atlanta Life Insurance Company by States of Georgia, Kansas, and Tennessee, 31 December 1953–31 December 1956, pp. 2, 4 (mimeographed), ALCF; *Atlanta Life Bulletin*, undated, p. 4.

9. "Epitome of Atlanta Life," p. 4.

10. Trent, "Development of Negro Life Insurance Enterprises," p. 47.

11. "Epitome of Atlanta Life," p. 4; *Atlanta Independent*, 25 March 1916; Interview with Chamblee, 13 August 1974.

12. *Atlanta Independent*, 25 March 1916; see also ibid., 1 July 1911, 17 April 1915.

13. "Epitome of Atlanta Life," p. 4; Interview with Chamblee, 13 August 1974.

14. L. C. Stewart to Alonzo Herndon, 16 July 1917, HFP; Annual Report of Officers, Atlanta Mutual Insurance Company, [1919], p. 7, in ALCF; Interview with Chamblee, 13 August 1974.

15. "Epitome of Atlanta Life," p. 4; Annual Report of Officers, [1919], p. 7. Conflicting reports exist regarding the reinsuring company. Two firms, the Cotton States Life Insurance Company of Memphis and Interstate Life of Chattanooga, are cited in the sources. As the meeting between the principals took place in Memphis, it is probable that the former was the reinsuring firm.

16. Stewart to Herndon, 16 July 1917.

17. Annual Report of Officers, [1919], p. 7.

18. Ibid., pp. 8–9.

19. Ibid., pp. 9–11.

20. Ibid., p. 9.

21. Ibid., p. 11; Interview with Chamblee, 13 August 1974.

22. *Atlanta Independent*, 6 March 1915.

23. Examination of Atlanta Mutual Insurance Company, 1 January 1917–31 December 1919, p. 3, in ALCF; see also *Atlanta City Directory*, 1921.

24. See Alexa Henderson and Eugene Walker, *Sweet Auburn: The Thriving Hub of Black Atlanta* (Denver: U.S. Department of Interior/National Park Service, 1983); Michael L. Porter, "Black Atlanta: An Interdisciplinary Study of Blacks on the East Side of Atlanta, 1890–1930" (Ph.D. dissertation, Emory University, 1974).

25. Henderson and Walker, *Sweet Auburn*, p. 19.

26. Emmet John Hughes, "The Negro's New Economic Life," *Fortune* 54 (September 1956): 248.

27. Henderson and Walker, *Sweet Auburn*, pp. 4–10; Porter, "Black Atlanta," pp. 166–68.

28. Henderson and Walker, *Sweet Auburn*, p. 15.

29. Ibid., pp. 19–41.

30. Benjamin Griffith Brawley, *A Social History of the American Negro* (1921; rpt. New York: Collier Books, 1970), p. 344.

31. Emmett J. Scott, *Negro Migration during the War* (1920; rpt. New York: Arno Press, 1969), pp. 38–41.

32. Ibid., p. 61.

33. Report of H. S. Miller and Company to Hon. Frank N. Julian, 1 June 1923, in ALCF.

34. E[ugene] M. Martin to J[efferson] G. Ish, 28 April 1937, in ALCF.

35. Dittmer, *Black Georgia*, pp. 196–97.

36. Walter Francis White, " 'Work or Fight' in the South," *New Republic*, 1 March 1919, p. 145.

37. Examination of Atlanta Mutual Insurance Company, 1 January 1917–31 December 1919, p. 7, in ALCF; Interview with Chamblee, 14 August 1974.

38. Alonzo F. Herndon to District Managers and Agents, 18 November 1920, in ALCF.

39. *Atlanta Independent*, 23, 30 December 1920, 6 January, 3, 10 February 1921. The shortage of $22,000 reported in the newspapers seems excessive and is not verified in any other source.

40. Atlanta Mutual Secretary (unsigned) to William A. Wright, 26 January 1921, in ALCF.

41. Interview with Chamblee, 14 August 1974.

42. George Washington Lee, "Hail to the Memory of the Founder," an address given in June 1970, Atlanta, Georgia, copy in possession of the author.

43. *Acts and Resolutions*, 1920, p. 213; William A. Wright to Atlanta Mutual Life Insurance Company, 20 December 1920, 24 January 1921, in ALCF.

44. Interview with J. D. Bansley, Jr., January 1975.

45. "Epitome of Atlanta Life," p. 5; Minutes of Board of Directors Meeting, 10 October 1921, 20 October 1922, in ALCF.

46. Minutes of Board of Directors Meeting, 20 October 1922; Eugene M. Martin to M. D. Whatley, stockholder, 30 October 1922; Minutes of Stockholders Meeting, 24 January 1923, all in ALCF.

47. Minutes of Board of Directors Meeting, 30 August, 20 October 1922, 23 May 1923, 28 May 1924, in ALCF.

5: An Emphasis on Expansion

1. Harmon, "The Negro as a Local Businessman," pp. 132–39.

2. See Vishnu V. Oak, *The Negro's Adventure in General Business*; Lerone Bennett, "Money, Merchants, Markets: The Quest for Economic Security," *Ebony* 29 (November 1973): 72–82; (December 1973): 56–65; (February 1974): 66–78.

3. Minutes of the Board of Directors Meeting, 20 October 1922; E. M. Martin to Frank J. Haight, 28 September 1922, in ALCF.

4. Minutes of the Board of Directors Meeting, 16 February 1923, in ALCF.

5. Frederick Lewis Allen, *Only Yesterday: An Informal History of the 1920s* (New York: Harper & Row, 1964), pp. 225–33.

6. Minutes of Board of Directors Meeting, 25 April, 19 July 1923, in ALCF. Figures for the black population of the states into which Atlanta Life expanded are taken from Henderson H. Donald, "The Negro Migration of 1916–1918," *Journal of Negro History* 6 (October 1921): 383–498.

7. E. M. Martin to J. C. Luning, 26 September 1923; W. W. Blocker to E. M. Martin (telegram), 7 October, 10 October 1923, in ALCF.

8. Report of the First Quarterly Line-up, Atlanta Life Insurance Company, May 1924, in ALCF.

9. David M. Tucker, *Lieutenant Lee of Beale Street* (Nashville: Vanderbilt University Press, 1971), pp. 43–45; Tucker, "Black Pride and Negro Business in the 1920's," *Business History Review* 43 (Winter 1969): 435–37.

10. Stuart, *Economic Detour*, pp. 288–302; Interview with George W. Lee, Atlanta, Georgia, 3 October 1974; Trent, "Development of Negro Life Insurance Enterprises," p. 41; Tucker, *Lieutenant Lee*, pp. 50–51.

11. Tucker, *Lieutenant Lee*, p. 51; Tucker, "Black Pride and Negro Business," p. 441; Interview with Lee; George W. Lee, *Beale Street: Where the Blues Began* (New York: Robert O. Ballou, 1934), p. 187.

12. Interview with Lee; Stuart, *Economic Detour*, pp. 303–4; Lee, *Beale Street*, p. 190; Tucker, *Lieutenant Lee*, p. 52.

13. Minutes of Board of Directors Meeting, 23 April 1924, in ALCF; Interview with Lee; Lee, "Alonzo Franklin Herndon—Moulder of Men," undated manuscript in possession of the author; see also *Atlanta Life Bulletin*, 1924–25, in ALCF.

14. Harmon, "The Negro as a Local Business Man," p. 150; Donald, "Negro Migration of 1916–1918," p. 476.

15. Minutes of Board of Directors Meeting, 23 April 1924; see also *Atlanta Life Bulletin*, 1924–28, in ALCF.

16. Minutes of the Board of Directors Meeting, 26 September 1923, 23 January 1924, in ALCF.

17. Nell Irvin Painter, *Exodusters: Black Migration to Kansas after Reconstruction* (New York: Knopf, 1977), p. 260; see also Randall B. Woods, "C. H. J. Taylor and the Movement for Black Political Independence, 1882–1896," *Journal of Negro History* 67 (Summer 1982): 123–24, which sheds light on the activities of one Kansas migrant and the impact of men such as Taylor on the community; Roy Garvin, "Benjamin Singleton and His Followers," *Journal of Negro History* 33 (January 1948): 7–23; Billy D. Higgins, "Negro Thought and the Exodus of 1879," *Phylon* 32 (Spring 1971): 39–52; Glen Schwendemann, "St. Louis and the 'Exodusters' of 1879," *Kansas Historical Quarterly* 26 (Autumn 1960): 233–49; Robert G. Athearn, *In Search of Canaan: Black Migration to Kansas, 1879–1880* (Lawrence: Regents Press of Kansas, 1978).

18. "Business Enterprises Owned and Operated by Negroes in Houston, Texas," Special Report of the Project to Study Business and Business Education among Negroes, p. 6; see also "Business Enterprises Owned and Operated by Negroes in St. Louis, Missouri," Special Report of the Project to Study Business and Business Education among Negroes, pp. 5–6; both MSS in Division of Archives and Special Collections, Robert W. Woodruff Library, Atlanta University Center, Atlanta.

19. Harmon, "The Negro as a Local Business Man," p. 150.

20. Stuart, *Economic Detour*, pp. 63, 72–74; Harmon, "The Negro as a Local Business Man," p. 149.

21. Minutes of Board of Directors Meeting, 25 March 1924, in ALCF; *Vision*, June 1926; Examination Report of Books, Records, and Securities, 31

December 1940, in ALCF; Interview with Simon, 24 June 1975; Interview with Pritchett H. Willard, Atlanta, Georgia, 3 October 1974.

22. "Epitome of Atlanta Life," p. 5; Minutes of Board of Directors Meeting, 17 August 1923; see also Benjamin M. Gilmore to Alonzo Herndon, 29 October 1926; Eugene M. Martin to Benjamin M. Gilmore, 19 November 1926, all in ALCF.

23. *Vision*, July 1926, pp. 4, 10; Interview with Simon, 24 June 1975.

24. Interview with DeLorme.

25. See Marquis James, *The Metropolitan Life: A Study in Business Growth* (New York: Viking Press, 1947), p. 340; May and Oursler, *The Prudential*, p. 53. In 1920 the United States Census Bureau reported 3,095 black insurance officials and agents.

26. See Joseph A. Pierce, *Negro Business and Business Education: Their Present and Prospective Development* (New York: Harper and Brothers, 1947).

27. Minutes of Stockholders Meeting, 24 January 1923, in ALCF.

28. Ibid.; Interviews with Chamblee, 13 August 1974, DeLorme, 20 August 1974, and Simon, 12 November 1974.

29. Souvenir Program, Managers and Agents Conference, 22, 23, and 24 January 1924, in ALCF.

30. Whole life insurance is payable to a beneficiary at the death of the policyholder. The premiums may be payable for a specified number of years (limited payment life) or for life (straight life). Endowment is life insurance that is payable to the policyholder, if he is living, on the maturity date stated in the policy or to a beneficiary if the policyholder dies before that date. See *Life Insurance Fact Book, 1974* (New York: Institute of Life Insurance, 1974), pp. 118, 126.

31. Interview with Simon, 24 June 1975. The case of the interviewee is illuminating on the matter of salary. With a group of forty-nine men, all but four of whom were college graduates, he completed the salesmanship course in the early 1930s and was assigned to a special team. He earned a base salary of $12.50 per week plus the usual commissions for this class of salesmen.

32. A. F. Herndon Scrapbook entitled "Application Shower," 30 June 1917, in HFP.

33. Minutes of Board of Directors Meeting, Special Session, 25 March 1924; Minutes of Stockholders Meeting, 28 January 1925; Program for Senatorial Conference, all in ALCF.

34. Program for Senatorial Conference, in ALCF.

35. *Atlanta Life Bulletin*, 30 May, 13, 20 June 1925, in ALCF.

36. Norris Herndon, welcome address for Twentieth Anniversary Conference, *Atlanta Life Bulletin*, [July 1925], pp. 1, 5, in ALCF.

37. Minutes of Board of Directors Meeting, 28 October 1925, 1 June 1926, in ALCF.

38. Robert L. Chamblee, "Building Program for 1926," Amendment to

Blue Book, 15 March 1926, in ALCF.

39. "The Atlanta Life Insurance Company, 1905–1923," p. 12, in HFP.

40. Eugene M. Martin to Cyrus Campfield, 5 August 1921; Minutes of Stockholders Meeting, 24 January 1923, in ALCF; see also Bacote, "Some Aspects of Negro Life," p. 198.

41. National Negro Insurance Association, *Proceedings of the First Annual Session*, 27 October 1921, p. 23; "The Atlanta Life Insurance Company, 1905–1923," p. 12.

42. Minutes of Stockholders Meeting, 24 January 1923; Minutes of Board of Directors Meeting, 25 April 1923, in ALCF.

43. Interview with Borders.

44. Pace, "Business of Insurance among Negroes," p. 224, and "The Attitude of Life Insurance Companies toward Negroes," *Southern Workman*, January 1928, p. 3.

45. For a discussion of participating and nonparticipating policies, see Huebner and Black, *Life Insurance*, pp. 636–38, 643–46.

6: A Great Racial Burden

1. Ridgley Torrence, *The Story of John Hope* (New York: Macmillan, 1948), p. 249.

2. Bennett, "Money, Merchants, Markets," p. 75; see also Pierce, *Negro Business and Business Education*, pp. 210–11; Harris, *Negro as Capitalist*, pp. 144–64, 178–79.

3. *Comptroller-General's Report, 1922*; see also Ira De A. Reid, "A Research Memorandum of the Negro in the American Economic System—The Standard Life Insurance Company," in Henton, "Heman E. Perry," p. 254, hereafter cited as "Documentary Materials."

4. "History of the Standard Life Insurance Company," in *The Standard Life Year Book, 1923* (Atlanta: Service Printing Company, 1923); Jesse B. Blayton to Dr. W. E. B. Du Bois, Re: Standard Life Insurance Company and Affiliates, Heman Perry et al., 16 December 1935, both in "Documentary Materials," pp. 95–98, 231–37.

5. Blayton to Du Bois, 16 December 1935, in "Documentary Materials," pp. 234–35; Jesse B. Blayton, "Phylon Profile: Heman E. Perry," p. 2; draft in Jarrett Papers; *Baltimore Afro-American*, 24 January 1925.

6. "Minutes of Conference of Black Business and Professional Men," 18 July 1924, Atlanta, Georgia, in Jarrett Papers. The specific amount of the loan or Perry's indebtedness was not ascertained. Rumors were prevalent at the time which greatly influenced reporting of the loan. The agreement itself does not indicate the sum loaned.

7. See "Memorandum of Agreed Basis of Financial Statement and Readjustment between the Service Realty Company, the Standard Life Insurance

Company, the Citizens Trust Company, and the Southeastern Trust Company," 24 July 1924, Exhibit "A," in *Charles H. Brown, et al. v. Southeastern Trust Company, et al.,* Fulton Superior Court, File No. 68732, 29 June 1926; James B. Mitchell, "The Collapse of the National Benefit Life Insurance Company—A Study in High Finance among Negroes," both in "Documentary Materials," pp. 31–32, 134–35.

8. "Draft of Proposed Contract of Merger between Southern Life Insurance Company and Standard Life Insurance Company," 15 January 1924, in "Documentary Materials," p. 138.

9. *Baltimore Afro-American,* 24 January 1925; see also *Savannah Tribune,* 22 January 1925.

10. Torrence, *Story of John Hope,* pp. 248–50.

11. See *Atlanta Independent,* 29 January 1925.

12. Quoted in ibid., also in "Documentary Materials," p. 224.

13. R. R. Moton to George Peabody, 27 August 1924; Julius Rosenwald to R. R. Moton (telegram), 4 November 1924, in Robert Russa Moton Papers, Hollis Burke Frissell Library, Tuskegee University, Tuskegee, Alabama; James Mitchell, "The Collapse of National Benefit Life Insurance Company: A Study in High Finance among Negroes," in "Documentary Materials," p. 37; Transcript of interview with J. B. Blayton, 18 April 1952, in Jarrett Papers; *Baltimore Afro-American,* 13 December 1924; see also Henderson, "Heman E. Perry," pp. 234–35.

14. "Minutes of Conference of Black Business and Professional Men," 18 July 1924; *Baltimore Afro-American,* 13 December 1924, 17 January 1925.

15. Minutes of Stockholders Meeting, 28 January 1925, in ALCF.

16. See Walrond, "Largest Negro Commercial Enterprise in the World."

17. Transcript of interview with J. B. Blayton, 18 April 1952, p. 4, in Jarrett Papers.

18. Interview with Simon, 24 June 1975.

19. Blayton to Du Bois, 16 December 1935, in "Documentary Materials," p. 235; Eugene M. Martin to William J. Trent, Jr., 16 May 1933, in ALCF; Transcript of interview with J. B. Blayton, 18 April 1952, p. 4, in Jarrett Papers; see also claims of plaintiffs in *Brown v. Southeastern Trust,* in "Documentary Materials," pp. 108–32.

20. Lee, *Beale Street,* p. 187; see also Tucker, *Lieutenant Lee,* p. 51.

21. *Savannah Tribune,* 18 December 1924; see also ibid., 2 March 1918, 18 January, 22 March, 12 April 1919, 3, 17 January 1920; Minutes of Board of Directors Meeting, 22 December 1924, in ALCF.

22. Alonzo F. Herndon II, to Eugene M. Martin, 2 June 1925, in ALCF.

23. Minutes of Board of Directors Meeting, 5 June 1930; *Vision,* July 1930; Examination Report of Books, Records, and Securities, 1931, p. 6, in ALCF; Atlanta Life press release, n.d., in ALCF; *Best's Life Insurance Report, 1930* (New York: Alfred M. Best Company, 1931), p. 103.

24. *Birmingham World,* 1 July 1931, reprinted in *Vision,* July 1931, p. 6; Handwritten notes of Union Central Relief and Atlanta Life Alabama Man-

agers' Conference, 20 June 1931, in ALCF.

25. E. S. Peters to E. M. Martin, 15 October 1932; *Press Forum Weekly* (clipping), 21 January 1933, both in ALCF.

26. E. M. Martin to E. S. Peters, 2 November 1932, in ALCF.

27. E. M. Martin to R. T. Jackson, 3 February 1933, in ALCF.

28. Martin to Peters, 2 November 1932.

29. Eugene M. Martin to Atlanta Life Managers, 11 December 1934, in ALCF.

30. Minutes of Board of Directors Meeting, 20 June, 4 August 1932; Newspaper clipping from unidentified Houston paper, 27 August 1932; C. N. Walker (Texas state manager) to Western Mutual Agency Force, 20 August 1932; W. A. Tarver (Texas Insurance Commission chairman) to Atlanta Life, 7 October 1932; State Examination Report of Books, Records, and Securities, 1932, all in ALCF.

31. Newspaper clipping from unidentified Houston paper, 27 August 1932; *Press Forum Weekly*, 21 January 1933.

32. Mitchell, "Collapse of National Benefit," in "Documentary Materials," pp. 16–17, 21.

33. Ibid., pp. 21, 32, 44, 49; Stuart, *Economic Detour*, p. 316.

34. Mitchell, "Collapse of National Benefit," in "Documentary Materials," pp. 69–71.

35. Ibid., p. 82; Stuart, *Economic Detour*, p. 317; *Baltimore Afro-American*, 27 June, 4, 18 July, 1 August 1931.

36. Martin to Pinkett, 11 July 1931, in ALCF.

37. Merah S. Stuart to Black Insurance Executives, 28 July 1931, in ALCF.

38. Martin to Pinkett, 8 August 1931, in ALCF.

39. E. M. Martin (secretary) to Pritchett Willard (manager), 8 April 1932; Thomas B. Lee to Eugene Martin, 9 April 1932, in ALCF.

40. William J. Kennedy, Jr., *The Negro's Adventure in the Field of Life Insurance* (Durham: North Carolina Mutual Insurance Company, 1934), p. 11; Stuart, *Economic Detour*, p. 170, see also pp. 146–47, 169, 186, 273–74.

41. Stuart, *Economic Detour*, pp. 94–97.

42. See Pierce, *Negro Business and Business Education*, pp. 210–11; Harris, *The Negro as Capitalist*, pp. 144–64, 178–79; Bennett, "Money, Merchants, Markets," pp. 74–75.

43. Bennett, "Money, Merchants, Markets," p. 75.

44. "Some Suggestions with Respect to Business and the Depression," *Negro History Bulletin*, January 1940, p. 57.

45. Trent, "Development of Negro Life Insurance Enterprises," p. 62.

46. Eugene M. Martin, Draft of Annual Message as President of the National Negro Insurance Association [1934], in ALCF.

7: The Legacy of Leadership

1. *Atlanta Daily World*, 8 August 1930.
2. Toomer, "Miracle on Auburn Avenue," p. 30.
3. Stuart, *Economic Detour*, pp. 128–29.
4. Interview with Simon, 19 November 1974; Toomer, "Miracle on Auburn Avenue," pp. 48–50.
5. *Atlanta Independent*, 19 March, 12 November 1904.
6. Toomer, "Miracle on Auburn Avenue," p. 102.
7. Minutes of Board of Directors Meeting, 1 June 1933, 6 March 1934, in ALCF; *Atlanta World*, 11, 13 February 1936; Stuart, *Economic Detour*, pp. 122–23.
8. *Vision*, June 1927, p. 10; *Atlanta World*, 2, 4 February 1947.
9. Minutes of Board of Directors Meeting, 6 March 1934, in ALCF.
10. "The Negro in Business," *Ebony* 18 (September 1963): 214.
11. Interview with Chamblee, 13 August 1974; *T. K. Gibson* v. *A. F. Herndon*, Fulton Superior Court, Docket No. 41618, vol. P-2, p. 214. The original suit has been signed out and was not returned at this writing. See also *Atlanta Independent*, 28 December 1918.
12. *Vision*, May 1968, p. 5; *Atlanta Daily World*, 8 August 1930.
13. Eugene Martin to Walter Francis White, 19 October 1938, in ALCF; *Vision*, May 1968, p. 4.
14. Stuart, *Economic Detour*, p. 126.
15. Minutes of Board of Directors Meeting, 7 May 1947, in ALCF.
16. Tucker, *Lieutenant Lee*, pp. 40–42.
17. Ibid., pp. 57, 81.
18. Toomer, "Miracle on Auburn Avenue," pp. 60–61.
19. Ibid.; Cyrus Campfield to Eugene Martin, 7 March, 29 November 1932, in ALCF; *Atlanta Daily World*, 8 August 1930.
20. William Edward Burghardt Du Bois, "The Cultural Mission of Atlanta University," *Phylon* 3 (Second Quarter 1942): 106; see also George A. Towns, "The Sources of the Tradition of Atlanta University," *Phylon* 3 (Second Quarter 1942): 117.
21. Bacote, *Story of Atlanta University*, p. 23.
22. Du Bois, ed., *Economic Cooperation*, pp. 5–6.
23. Du Bois, "Cultural Mission of Atlanta University," p. 114.
24. Du Bois, ed., *Economic Cooperation*, p. 11.
25. Toomer, "Miracle on Auburn Avenue," p. 14; Interview with DeLorme.
26. Alonzo Herndon to Norris Herndon, 7 December 1921, in HFP.
27. Atlanta Life news release, undated, pp. 1–2, in ALCF; *Atlanta Life Bulletin*, 2 August 1924, p. 1; *Vision*, May 1930, pp. 11–12, July 1931, p. 9; *Atlanta Daily World*, 8 August 1930; "Atlanta University Graduates in Life Insurance," *Atlanta University Bulletin*, March 1928, p. 2.

28. Eugene M. Martin, speech before district managers, special agents, auditors, and workers of Atlanta Life, 3 October 1925, in ALCF.

29. E. Emerson Waite, "Social Factors in Negro Business Enterprise" (Master's thesis, Duke University, 1940), p. 60.

30. Stuart, *Economic Detour*, p. 123. The complete order of service appeared in the *Atlanta Independent*, 28 July 1927.

31. *Vision*, June 1928, p. 9.

32. Resolution of the Special Team of Florida and the Agency Force of Jacksonville, 22 July 1927, ALCF.

33. *Atlanta Independent*, 25 December 1915, 8 June 1914.

34. Ibid., 8 September 1906, 4 April, 6 June 1914.

35. Ibid., 28 July 1927.

36. *Atlanta Georgian*, 29 July 1927; Preliminary Statement of Assets and Liabilities of A. F. Herndon, Deceased, 19 August 1927; Last Will and Testament of Alonzo F. Herndon, No. 15390, Will Book I, p. 114, Fulton County Court House, Atlanta.

37. "Postscript by W. E. B. Du Bois, p. 239.

38. Minutes of Stockholders Meeting, 24 January 1923, in ALCF.

8: Depression and War Years

1. Minutes of Stockholders Meeting, 26 January 1927, 25 January 1928; Minutes of Board of Directors Meeting, 1 June 1927, in ALCF; *Atlanta Independent*, 27 January, 17 February 1927; *Vision*, June 1927.

2. Minutes of Board of Directors Meeting, 25 January 1928, in ALCF.

3. See Examination Report of Books, Records, and Securities, 1924–34, in ALCF; *Report of Insurance Department, State of Georgia*, 1924–32 (formerly *Comptroller-General's Report*) (Atlanta: Index Printing Company, 1924–32).

4. Minutes of Board of Directors Meeting, 6 December 1933, 2 July 1928, 13 June, 1 July 1929, in ALCF.

5. See Examination Report of Books, Records, and Securities, 1929–33, in ALCF.

6. Ibid., 1930.

7. Minutes of Board of Directors Meeting, 10 September, 9 December 1930; Minutes of Stockholders Meeting, 27 January 1932, in ALCF.

8. Minutes of Board of Directors Meeting, 8 August 1930, in ALCF.

9. Ibid., 23 January, 10 April, 13 June 1929; Examination Report of Books, Records, and Securities, 1 January–31 December 1929, in ALCF.

10. *Vision*, January 1930.

11. Minutes of Stockholders Meeting, 27 January 1932, in ALCF.

12. Minutes of Board of Directors Meeting, 17 November 1937, 24 July 1939, in ALCF.

13. "Investments of Georgia Insurance Companies: An Act," 27 August 1929, in ALCF.

14. Examination Report of Books, Records, and Securities, Selected Years, 1921–35, in ALCF.

15. James E. Stamps, "A Survey of Negro Life Insurance Companies," December 1935, p. 7 (mimeographed), in ALCF.

16. Examination Reports—Books, Records, and Securities, Selected Years, 1921–35; Minutes of Administrative Staff Meetings, Atlanta Life Insurance Company, 5 April 1960, in ALCF; Examination Report of Books, Records, and Securities, 1940, in ALCF; L. A. Irons to Eugene Martin, 7 March 1935, Record Group 8, Georgia Department of Archives and History, Atlanta; Interview with Henry Neal Brown, Atlanta, Georgia, 15 November 1974.

17. See *Best's Life Insurance Report*, 1935 (New York: Alfred M. Best Company, 1935), p. x.

18. Robert Christian Puth, *Supreme Life: The History of a Negro Life Insurance Company* (New York: Arno Press, 1976), p. 112.

19. *Birmingham Weekly Review*, 21 July 1935, clipping in ALCF.

20. Eugene M. Martin to C. L. Sharpe, 23 May 1933, in ALCF.

21. J. S. Himes, Jr., "Forty Years of Negro Life in Columbus, Ohio," *Journal of Negro History* 27 (April 1942): 133–54.

22. Interview with Simon, 19 November 1974.

23. Minutes of Board of Directors Meeting, 11 July 1935; C. L. Sharpe to Eugene M. Martin, 18 May 1933, in ALCF. One such request came from Port-au-Prince, Haiti; see Edward Mathons to Eugene M. Martin, 26 June 1941, in ALCF.

24. Asa T. Spaulding, "Charting Our Course for the Future," in National Negro Insurance Association, *Proceedings* (Richmond: Quality Printing Company, 1936), pp. 139–40.

25. Minutes of Board of Directors Meeting, 17 October 1938, 17 December 1941, in ALCF.

26. Eugene Martin to Cyrus Campfield, 7 November 1944, in ALCF.

27. Interview with Simon, 19 November 1974.

28. Minutes of Board of Directors Meeting, 22 November 1940, in ALCF.

29. See Louis Ruchames, *Race, Jobs, and Politics: The Story of FEPC* (New York: Columbia University Press, 1953).

30. "Salary Standardization and Classifications," 29 January 1945, in ALCF.

31. Minutes of Board of Directors Meeting, 25 July 1942; see also ibid., 19 April 1944, 29 January 1945, in ALCF.

32. Ibid., 24 March 1926.

33. Stuart, *Economic Detour*, pp. 93, 116–17, 152, 156, 288–89, 326–27; see also Souvenir Silver Jubilee Year Program, Mammoth Life and Accident Company, 1915–40, Vertical File, Woodruff Library, Atlanta University Center.

34. Toomer, "Miracle on Auburn Avenue," pp. 177–78.

35. See the *Vision*, April 1927, June 1932.

36. Eugene Martin to C. N. Walker, 12 May 1942, in ALCF.

37. Minutes of Board of Directors Meeting, 29 September 1942, 19 April 1944; Minutes of Stockholders Meeting, 25 March 1942; Ralph E. Shikes to Eugene M. Martin, 18 November 1942; Martin to Ira de A. Reid, 4 October 1944, all in ALCF.

38. *Pittsburgh Courier*, 10 May 1941, p. 22.

39. Minutes of Board of Directors Special Meeting, 24 February 1941; Eugene Martin to Walter White, 1 May 1941, in ALCF.

40. Minutes of Stockholders Meeting, 24 March 1937, in ALCF; *Vision*, June 1932.

41. Eugene M. Martin to C. N. Walker, 14 May 1941, in ALCF.

42. Minutes of Stockholders Meeting, 4 May 1931; Minutes of Board of Directors Meeting, 19 October 1943, in ALCF; *Best's Life Insurance Reports*, 1939, pp. 78–79; ibid., 1943, p. 63.

9: An Anxious New Era

1. Minutes of Stockholders Meeting, 25 January 1928, in ALCF.

2. Toomer, "Miracle on Auburn Avenue," p. 90.

3. Ibid., pp. 120–21.

4. *Weekly Reporter*, 28 March 1955, in ALCF.

5. "The Millionaire Nobody Knows," *Ebony* 10 (October 1955): 43.

6. George W. Lee to Eugene M. Martin, 16 January 1933, in ALCF.

7. Minutes of Board of Directors Meeting, 19 July 1944; Minutes of Stockholders Meeting, 22 May 1947, in ALCF.

8. Minutes of Board of Directors Meeting, 31 January, 12 April, 31 October 1946, in ALCF.

9. Minutes of Stockholders Meeting, 31 January 1946, in ALCF.

10. Ibid.

11. Minutes of Board of Directors Meeting, 12 March 1947, in ALCF.

12. Ibid., 10 November 1948.

13. Neil A. Wynn, *The Afro-American and the Second World War* (New York: Holmes & Meier, 1976), p. 62.

14. Minutes of Board of Directors Meeting, 6 October 1944, 2 May 1948; Minutes of Stockholders Meeting, 18 May 1949, in ALCF.

15. Minutes of Stockholders Meeting, 24 May 1950, in ALCF.

16. Minutes of Board of Directors Meeting, 3 November 1949, 13 July 1950, in ALCF.

17. Examination Report of Books, Records, and Securities, 1955, 1956, in ALCF.

18. Puth, *Supreme Life*, p. 170. Puth notes that laws prohibiting the designation of an applicant's race preclude absolute proof of this contention.

19. For a discussion of urban conditions and blacks in the postwar era, see Wynn, *The Afro-American and the Second World War*, pp. 60–78.

20. See *Best's Life Insurance Report*, 1940–60.

21. May and Oursler, *The Prudential*, p. 176.

22. Jesse Edward Gloster, *North Carolina Mutual Life Insurance Company: Its Historical Development and Current Operations* (New York: Arno Press, 1976), p. 97.

23. May and Oursler, *The Prudential*, p. 228.

24. On 25 September 1945, Atlanta Life instituted a noncontributory welfare plan for its employees. The plan, which provided for retirement benefits at age sixty-five, included life insurance, disability, and accident and health insurance with all costs borne by the company. A spokesman for the enterprise described the plan as "the most important factor in attracting and keeping capable agents and clerks" (Minutes of Stockholders Meeting, 19 May 1948, in ALCF).

25. May and Oursler, *The Prudential*, pp. 220–29.

26. Minutes of Administrative Staff Meeting, 28 May 1958, in ALCF.

27. *Best's Life Insurance Report*, 1950–60.

28. Minutes of Board of Directors Meeting, 23 January, 10 April, 13 June 1929, 19 October 1943, 30 June, 8, 28 September 1948, 31 May 1955, 4 September 1962; Minutes of Stockholders Meeting, 4 May 1939, in ALCF.

29. Figures based on data gathered from *Best's Life Insurance Report*, 1940–73.

30. Minutes of Stockholders Meeting, 2 May 1948, in ALCF.

31. Ibid.

32. Ibid.

33. Last Will and Testament of Norris B. Herndon, 25 November 1955, No. 144, Fulton County Court House, Atlanta; *Vision*, December 1974, p. 4; Interview with Simon, 19 November 1974.

34. Toomer, "Miracle on Auburn Avenue," p. 233.

35. Undated press release, in ALCF.

36. Minutes of Stockholders Meeting, 25 March 1942; Minutes of Executive Committee Meeting, 24 February 1942, in ALCF.

37. Interview with Simon, 19 November 1974.

38. Minutes of Board of Directors Meeting, 4 March, 3 April, 9 June 1936, 29 January, 3 May 1944, in ALCF.

10: Civil Rights and Social Responsibility

1. Martin Luther King, Jr., *Where Do We Go from Here: Chaos or Community?* (New York: Harper & Row, 1968), p. 164.

2. In 1950 seven of the nine directors of Atlanta Life were graduates or former students of Atlanta University: Fred Toomer (1911), Eugene Martin (1912), Norris Herndon (1919), Walter Smith (1919), William Charles

Thomas (1922–23, A.B. Amherst 1926), Dr. Henry Lang (1925), and Gilbert DeLorme (1923–27, A.B. Fisk University 1928). Only George Lee and Lemuel Haywood had not matriculated at the institution. For a discussion of Atlanta's black leadership class, see August Meier and David Lewis, "History of the Negro Upper Class in Atlanta, Georgia, 1890–1958," *Journal of Negro Education* 28 (Spring 1959): 128–39; see also Eugene Martin to Eslande Robeson, 5 December 1941, in ALCF.

3. Du Bois, "Cultural Mission of Atlanta University," pp. 106, 108, 110; Bacote, *Story of Atlanta University,* pp. 90–94.

4. Bacote, *Story of Atlanta University,* pp. 405–25, quotation on p. 407.

5. Eugene Martin to Eslande Robeson, 5 December 1941.

6. Herndon's various contributions seemed to be generally well known, although specific documentation of his philanthropy is unavailable.

7. *Atlanta Journal,* 10 June 1977.

8. Interview with Dr. Samuel N. Nabrit, Atlanta, Georgia, 1 July 1975.

9. Eugene Martin to Eslande Robeson, 5 December 1941.

10. Walter Francis White, *A Man Called White* (New York: Arno Press, 1969), pp. 135–36.

11. Mayor Roy Lecraw to Marion S. Doom, 8 July 1941, in ALCF.

12. Eugene Martin to Wesley Winons Stouts, 16 December 1940, in ALCF.

13. Eugene Martin to Hale Holden, 10 July 1939, in ALCF.

14. Ibid.

15. Ibid.; see also Minutes of Board of Directors Meeting, 24 July 1939, in ALCF.

16. Eugene Martin to Dr. Gypsy Smith, Sr., 24 June 1935, in ALCF.

17. Eugene Martin to Eslande Robeson, 5 December 1941.

18. Eugene Martin to Walter White, 19 January 1938, in ALCF.

19. Ibid., 23 July 1941.

20. See White, *A Man Called White.*

21. Roy Wilkins to Eugene Martin, 17 August 1939, in ACLF.

22. Walter White to Eugene Martin, 29 October, 16 December 1935, 17 November 1937, 3 May 1939; Martin to White, 30 October 1935, 6 January, 15 March, 3, 24 June 1938; Martin to Allan Knight Chalmers, 14 March 1939; Roy Wilkins to Martin, 17, 31 August 1939; Martin to Roy Wilkins, 22 August 1939, all in ALCF.

23. "An Open Letter to the President and the Senate of the United States of America," 13 February 1938, in ALCF.

24. Walter White to Eugene and Helen Martin, 25 February 1938, in ALCF.

25. Eugene Martin to Walter White, 15 March 1938, 1 October 1940, in ALCF.

26. White, *A Man Called White,* p. 163; see also *Atlanta Daily World,* 18, 19 February 1942.

27. *Atlanta Daily World,* 19 February 1942, 31 October 1943; White, *A*

Man Called White, pp. 114, 163.

28. *Atlanta Daily World,* 18 February 1942; see also *William H. Reeves v. E. S. Cook, et al.,* CA 2538, General Index 24864, U.S. District Court, Northern District of Georgia, Atlanta Division.

29. *Atlanta Daily World,* 25 November 1942; Toomer, "Miracle on Auburn Avenue," pp. 183, 241–42; *Vision,* May 1968.

30. *Atlanta Daily World,* 19 February, 7 April 1942.

31. Ibid., 1, 3, 25 November 1942; *Reeves* v. *Cook.*

32. *Reeves* v. *Cook; Atlanta Daily World,* 30 November, 1 December 1942, 3 July 1943.

33. *Samuel L. Davis* v. *E. S. Cook, et al.,* CA 2682, General Index 27117, U.S. District Court, Northern District of Georgia, Atlanta Division; Toomer, "Miracle on Auburn Avenue," pp. 244–45.

34. Interview with Benjamin Elijah Mays, Atlanta Georgia, 3 May 1975.

35. Interview with Mays.

36. Interview with Jesse Hill, Jr., Atlanta, Georgia, 24 April 1975; William Schemmel, "Profile of Jesse Hill, Jr.," *Atlanta Magazine,* July 1971, p. 19; Robert J. Sye, "Jesse Hill, Jr.: Atlanta's Human Dynamo," *Sepia,* June 1978, pp. 75–80; *Atlanta Inquirer,* 1 August 1970.

37. *Atlanta Inquirer,* 1 August 1970.

38. Ibid.; Interview with Donald Hollowell, 9 August 1983; *Atlanta Daily World,* 10 January 1961. Two days after being admitted to the university, the two students were suspended following a riot on the Athens campus. They were reinstated under court order on 16 January 1961.

39. Jack Lamar Walker, Jr., "Protest and Negotiation: A Study of Negro Political Leaders in a Southern City" (Ph.D. dissertation, University of Iowa, 1963), pp. 70–80, 96, 106–12.

40. Schemmel, "Profile of Jesse Hill, Jr.," p. 19; Sye, "Jesse Hill, Jr.," p. 77; *Atlanta Constitution,* 13 May 1973, 8 April 1977; Interview with Nabrit.

41. Interview with Nabrit.

42. Samuel N. Nabrit, "Natal Day Address," given at Atlanta Life, 26 June 1974, copy in possession of the author.

43. Tucker, *Lieutenant Lee,* pp. 57, 67.

44. Ibid., p. 82.

45. Ibid., pp. 82–85.

46. Ibid., pp. 169–71.

47. Ibid., pp. 203–4.

48. Interview with Alonzo C. Touchstone, Griffin, Georgia, 28 May 1975; *Atlanta Daily World,* 4 November 1945.

49. Minutes of the Montgomery Improvement Association, Transportation Committee, 18 June, 10 July, 18 July 1956, copy in possession of Johnnie R. Carr.

50. Martin Luther King, Jr., to Johnnie R. Carr, 1 September 1967, in possession of Carr.

51. Interview with Nabrit.
52. Interview with Mays.
53. Nabrit, "Natal Day Address"; Interview with Nabrit; *Atlanta Inquirer,* 1 August 1970.

11: Challenges of a New Era

1. Atlanta Life Insurance Company, Minutes of Administrative Staff Meeting, 11 June 1958, in ALCF.
2. Ibid.; Minutes of Meeting of Board of Directors, 15 December 1953, 31 May 1955, in ALCF.
3. Interview with Simon, 12 November 1974; Eugene Martin to President [Norris Herndon] and Executive Committee, undated memo in ALCF.
4. Harding B. Young and James M. Hund, "Negro Entrepreneurship in Southern Economic Development," in Melvin L. Greenhut and W. Tate Whitman, eds., *Essays in Southern Economic Development* (Chapel Hill: University of North Carolina Press, 1964), p. 130.
5. Robert C. Puth, "Can Black Insurance Companies Survive?" *Challenge* 17 (May–June 1974): 52.
6. Ibid., pp. 55, 58; Linda Pickthrone Fletcher, *The Negro in the Insurance Industry* (Philadelphia: University of Pennsylvania Press, 1970), p. 129.
7. Puth, "Can Black Insurance Companies Survive?" p. 53; see also Robert C. Puth, "From Enforced Segregation to Integration: Market Factors in the Development of a Negro Life Insurance Company," in Louis B. Cain and Paul J. Uselding, eds., *Business Enterprise and Economic Change* (Kent, Ohio: Kent State University Press, 1973), pp. 295–98.
8. Ibid., pp. 54–57.
9. "The GMS Store: A Brief History of the Founding and Development of Golden State Mutual Life," January 1972, n.p.; Golden State Mutual, Annual Report to the Board of Directors for Year Ending 31 December 1972, pp. 3, 9, in possession of the author.
10. Weare, *Black Business in the New South,* pp. 284–85.
11. See *Best's Life Insurance Reports,* 1970–80.
12. Jesse Hill, Jr., to Norris B. Herndon, undated memo in ALCF.
13. *Best's Life Insurance Report,* 1973, p. 184.
14. Minutes of Stockholders Meeting, 6 May 1959, in ALCF.
15. See *Best's Life Insurance Report,* 1948–75.
16. Weare, *Black Business in the New South,* p. 280; Shannon, "Wealthy Atlanta Negroes," p. 12; Faye McDonald Smith, "Atlanta Life: 75 Years Old and Still Looking Ahead," *Black Enterprise* 7 (June 1977): 133.
17. See Weare, *Black Business in the New South,* pp. 265–66.

18. Folder on Herndon Foundation, in ALCF; *Vision*, December 1974, pp. 3–4.

19. *Vision*, December 1974, p. 4; Smith, "Atlanta Life," p. 137.

20. *Vision*, December 1974.

21. Folder on Herndon Foundation, in ALCF; Smith, "Atlanta Life," pp. 137, 139.

22. Testimony of Jesse Hill, Jr., before Congressional Committee, March 1973, in Folder on Herndon Foundation, ALCF.

23. Smith, "Atlanta Life," p. 139.

24. Interview with Hill.

25. See Atlanta Life Insurance Company, 69th Annual Statement, 1 January 1974, in ALCF.

26. Smith, "Atlanta Life," p. 133.

27. Statement of Guaranty Life Insurance Company, 31 December 1961, in ALCF.

28. Interview with Hill; Interview with Brown; *Vision*, December 1974, p. 29; see also *Best's Life Insurance Reports*, 1963–83.

29. Smith, "Atlanta Life," p. 133.

30. "Atlanta Life Turns 75," *Ebony* 36 (June 1981): 109; *Vision*, May 1980, p. 3; *Atlanta Constitution*, 22 September 1980.

31. Smith, "Atlanta Life," p. 133.

32. See Hughes, "The Negro's New Economic Life," p. 248.

33. *Atlanta Constitution*, 29 June, 6 July, 26 August 1980; see *Atlanta Journal*, 30 June–2 July 1980.

34. *Best's Life Insurance Report*, 1983.

35. *Vision*, May 1980, p. 3.

Selected Bibliography

Manuscript Sources

Atlanta-Fulton Public Library, Atlanta, Georgia

Hopkins, James Arthur. "Atlanta—You Ought to Know Some Pioneers of Atlanta." In *National Negro Business League Directory and Souvenir Program*, 1937, pp. 18–19.

Martin, Eugene Marcus. "Atlanta—You Ought to Know Your Own Insurance Companies." In *National Negro Business League Directory and Souvenir Program*, 1937, pp. 21–22.

Atlanta Life Insurance Company Files

Annual Report of Officers. Atlanta Mutual Insurance Company [1919].

Annual Statements. Atlanta Mutual Life Insurance Company. 1916–22.

Atlanta Life Bulletin, 1924–26.

"Epitome of Atlanta Life," *Atlanta Life Bulletin* [1925].

Examination of Atlanta Mutual Insurance Company, 1 January 1917–31 December 1919.

Examination Report of Books, Records, and Securities, 1916–56.

Herndon, Alonzo Franklin. "Atlanta Life: Past, Present, Future." An address delivered 22 January 1924, Atlanta, Georgia.
———. "Cooperation in Business." Speech given before the Atlanta Life Clerical Staff, 31 May 1926, Atlanta, Georgia.
Lee, George Washington. "Alonzo Franklin Herndon—A Molder of Men." Address given on 8 June 1971, Atlanta, Georgia.
———. "Hail to the Founder." Address given in June 1970, Atlanta, Georgia.
Minutes of Administrative Staff Meetings, 1940–66.
Minutes of Board of Directors' Meetings, 1922–62.
Minutes of Executive Committee Meetings, 1940–66.
Minutes of Stockholders Meetings, 1922–62.
"Report on Association Examination of the Atlanta Life Insurance Company by States of Georgia, Kansas, and Tennessee, 1953–1956."
Secretary's Files, 1922–73.
Stamps, James E. "A Survey of Negro Life Insurance Companies," December 1935. Mimeographed.

Fulton County Court House, Atlanta, Georgia

Deed Book. No. 144.
General Index to Deeds, 1890–1910.
Herndon, Alonzo Franklin. Last Will and Testament. No. 15390. Atlanta, Georgia.
Herndon, Norris Bumstead. Last Will and Testament. No. 144. Atlanta, Georgia.

Georgia Department of Archives and History, Atlanta, Georgia

Annual Report to the Georgia Insurance Department. Atlanta Life Insurance Company, 1923–73. Record Group 8.
Tax Digest. 1905, 1926. Fulton County, Georgia.
U.S. Bureau of the Census. Population Schedule, 1880. Chatham County, Georgia. Microfilm.
———. Population Schedule, 1880. Clayton County, Georgia. Microfilm.
———. Population Schedule, 1870. Walton County, Georgia. Microfilm.

Herndon Museum, Atlanta, Georgia

Herndon Family Papers.

Hollis Burke Frissell Library, Tuskegee University, Tuskegee, Alabama

Robert Russa Moton Papers.

Library of Congress, Washington, D.C.

Booker T. Washington Papers.

Robert W. Woodruff Library, Atlanta University Center, Division of Archives, Special Collections, Atlanta, Georgia

"Business Enterprises Owned and Operated by Negroes in Houston, Texas."
  Special Report of the Project to Study Business and Business Education
  among Negroes.
"Business Enterprises Owned and Operated by Negroes in St. Louis, Missouri." Special Report of the Project to Study Business and Business Education among Negroes.

Thomas W. Jarrett Papers, Atlanta, Georgia

Minutes of Conference of Black Business and Professional Men, 18 July 1924.
Transcript of interview with Jesse B. Blayton, Atlanta, Georgia, 18 April 1952.
Transcript of interview with A. M. Carter, Atlanta, Georgia [1952].
Transcript of interview with Dr. George W. Howell, Atlanta, Georgia [1952].
Transcript of interview with Olive Perry, Houston, Texas [1952].
Transcript of interview with John Pinkett, Washington, D.C. [1952].

Published Public Documents

Acts and Resolutions of the General Assembly of the State of Georgia. Atlanta: Franklin Printing Company, 1905–18.
Atlanta City Directory, 1883–1910. Atlanta: Foote and Davies, Publishers,
  1884–1911.
Best's Life Insurance Reports, 1927–85. New York: Alfred M. Best Company,
  1928–86.
Report of the Insurance Department, 1924–85. (*Report of the Insurance Department of the Comptroller-General's Office,* 1905–23.) Atlanta: Franklin
  Printing and Publishing Company, 1906–24.

U.S. Bureau of the Census. *Negro Population, 1790–1915.* Washington, D.C.: U.S. Government Printing Office, 1918.

———. *Thirteenth Census of the United States, 1910. Abstract of the Census with Supplement for Georgia.* Washington, D.C.: U.S. Government Printing Office, 1913.

U.S. State Department of Commerce. *Report of Insurance Companies Owned and Operated by Negroes,* 1940, 1949. Washington, D.C.: U.S. Government Printing Office, 1940, 1949.

Newspapers and Other Periodicals

Atlanta Constitution, 28 July 1907; 13 May 1913; 22, 23 July 1927; 13 May 1973; 8 April 1977; 29 June, 6 July, 26 August, 22 September 1980.

Atlanta Daily World, 8 August 1930; 6 January 1935; 11, 13 February 1936; 18, 19 February, 7, 9 April, 2 August, 1, 13, 25, 30 November, 1 December 1942; 3 July, 31 October 1943; 4 November 1945; 2, 4 February 1947; 12 January, 4 June 1950; 10 January 1961; 13 August 1978.

Atlanta Georgian, 22, 29 July 1927.

Atlanta Independent, 1904–28.

Atlanta Inquirer, 1960–70.

Atlanta Journal, 14 July 1907; 10 May 1914; 22, 27 July 1927; 10 June 1977; 30 June, 2 July 1980.

Baltimore Afro-American, 13 December 1924; 17, 24 January 1925; 27 June, 4, 18, 25 July, 1 August 1931.

Birmingham Weekly Review, 21 July 1935.

Bulletin of Atlanta University, June 1891.

Crimson and Gray, July 1913.

New York World, 31 July 1927.

Pittsburgh Courier, 10 May 1941.

Savannah Tribune, 2 March 1918; 18 January, 22 March, 12 April 1919; 3, 17 January 1920; 18 December 1924; 22 January 1925.

Scroll, November 1911; March 1917.

Vision, 1926–32; 1968–74; 1980.

Voice of the Negro, 1904–6.

Interviews

Adams, Kathleen Redding. 22 June 1979. Atlanta, Georgia.
Borders, Reverend William Holmes. 1 November 1974. Atlanta, Georgia.
Brown, Henry Neal. 15 November 1974. Atlanta, Georgia.
Chamblee, Robert W. 13–14 August 1974. Atlanta, Georgia.
DeLorme, Gilbert Earl. 28 August 1974. Atlanta, Georgia.

Hill, Jesse, Jr. 24 April 1975. Atlanta, Georgia.
Hollowell, Donald. 9 August 1983. Atlanta, Georgia.
Lee, George Washington. 3 October 1974. Atlanta, Georgia.
Martin, Mrs. Eugene M. 27 May 1981. Atlanta, Georgia.
Mays, Benjamin Elijah. 3 July 1975. Atlanta, Georgia.
Milton, Mrs. Lorimer D. 27 May 1981. Atlanta, Georgia.
Nabrit, Samuel N. 1 July 1975. Atlanta, Georgia.
Simon, Edward Lloyd. 12–19 November 1974, 24–27 June 1975. Atlanta, Georgia.
Touchstone, Alonzo C. 28 May 1975. Griffin, Georgia.
Willard, Pritchett Hydal. 3 October 1974. Atlanta, Georgia.

Books

Allen, Frederick Lewis. *Only Yesterday: An Informal History of the 1920s.* New York: Harper & Row, 1964.
Allen, Richard. *The Life, Experience, and Gospel Labors of the Rt. Rev. Richard Allen.* Philadelphia: F. Ford and M. A. Riply, 1880.
Aptheker, Herbert. *A Documentary History of the Negro People in the United States.* 2 vols. New York: Citadel Press, 1951.
Athearn, Robert G. *In Search of Canaan: Black Migration to Kansas, 1879–80.* Lawrence: Regents Press of Kansas, 1978.
Bacote, Clarence Albert. *The Story of Atlanta University: A Century of Service, 1865–1965.* Atlanta: Atlanta University Press, 1969.
Baker, Ray Stannard. *Following the Color Line: American Negro Citizenship in the Progressive Era.* New York: Harper & Row, 1908.
Bickelhaupt, David Lynn. *General Insurance.* 10th ed. Homewood, Ill.: Richard D. Irwin, 1979.
Blassingame, John W., ed. *Slave Testimony: Two Centuries of Letters, Speeches, Interviews, and Autobiographies.* Baton Rouge: Louisiana State University Press, 1977.
Bragg, George F. *Richard Allen and Absalom Jones.* Baltimore: Church Advocate Press, 1915.
Brawley, Benjamin Griffith. *A Social History of the American Negro.* 1921. Reprint. New York: Collier Books, 1970.
Burrell, William Patrick. *Twenty-Five Years History of the Grand Fountain of the United Order of True Reformers, 1881–1905.* Richmond, Va.: N.p. [1909].
Carr, William H. A. *From Three Cents a Week: The Story of the Prudential Insurance Company of America.* Englewood Cliffs, N.J.: Prentice-Hall, 1975.
Carter, Edward Randolph. *The Black Side: A Partial History of the Business, Religious, and Educational Side of the Negro in Atlanta, Ga.* Atlanta: N.p., 1894.

Dittmer, John. *Black Georgia in the Progressive Era, 1900–1920.* Urbana: University of Illinois Press, 1977.

Dublin, Louis I. *A Family of Thirty Million: The Story of the Metropolitan Life Insurance Company.* New York: Metropolitan Life Insurance Company, 1943.

Du Bois, William Edward Burghardt. *The Philadelphia Negro: A Social Study.* Philadelphia: University of Pennsylvania, 1899.

————, ed. *Economic Cooperation among Negro Americans.* Atlanta University Publication 12. Atlanta: Atlanta University Press, 1907.

————, ed. *Economic Cooperation among Negroes in Georgia.* Atlanta University Publication 19. Atlanta: Atlanta University Press, 1917.

————, ed. *The Negro in Business,* Atlanta University Publication 4. Atlanta: Atlanta University Press, 1899.

————, ed. *Some Efforts of American Negroes for Their Own Social Betterment.* Atlanta University Publication 3. Atlanta: Atlanta University Press, 1898.

Fletcher, Linda Pickthrone. *The Negro in the Insurance Industry.* Philadelphia: University of Pennsylvania Press, 1970.

Franklin, John Hope. *From Slavery to Freedom: A History of Negro Americans.* 4th ed. New York: Knopf, 1974.

Garrett, Franklin M. *Atlanta and Environs: A Chronicle of Its People and Events.* 2 vols. New York: Lewis Historical Publishing Company, 1954.

Gloster, Jesse Edward. *North Carolina Mutual Life Insurance Company: Its Historical Development and Current Operations.* New York: Arno Press, 1976.

Grantham, Dewey W., Jr. *Hoke Smith and the Politics of the New South.* Baton Rouge: Louisiana State University Press, 1958.

Harlan, Louis R., and Raymond Smock, eds. *The Booker T. Washington Papers.* Vols. 8–9. Urbana: University of Illinois Press, 1979–80.

Harris, Abram Lincoln. *The Negro as Capitalist: A Study of Banking among Negroes.* New York: Haskell House, 1936.

Henderson, Alexa Benson, and Eugene Walker, *Sweet Auburn: Thriving Hub of Black Atlanta, 1900–1960.* Denver: U.S. Department of Interior/National Park Service, 1983.

Huebner, Solomon S., and Kenneth Black, Jr. *Life Insurance.* 7th ed. New York: Appleton-Century-Crofts, 1969.

James, Marquis. *The Metropolitan Life: A Study in Business Growth.* New York: Viking Press, 1947.

Jones, Edward N. *Blacks in Business.* New York: Grosset & Dunlap, 1971.

Keller, Morton. *The Life Insurance Enterprise, 1885–1910: A Study of the Limits of Corporate Power.* Cambridge, Mass.: Belknap Press of Harvard University Press, 1963.

King, Martin Luther, Jr. *Where Do We Go from Here: Chaos or Community?* New York: Harper & Row, 1968.

Knight, Lucian L. *History of Fulton County, Georgia, Narrative and Bibliographical*. Atlanta: A. H. Cawston, 1930.

Lee, George Washington. *Beale Street: Where the Blues Began*. New York: Robert O. Ballou, 1934.

Life Insurance Fact Book, 1974. New York: Institute of Life Insurance, 1974.

McClean, Joseph B. *Life Insurance*. 9th ed. New York: McGraw-Hill, 1962.

May, Earl Chapin, and Will Oursler. *The Prudential: A Story of Human Security*. Garden City, N.Y.: Doubleday, 1950.

Meier, August. *Negro Thought in America, 1880–1915: Racial Ideologies in the Age of Booker T. Washington*. Ann Arbor: University of Michigan Press, 1969.

Meier, August, and Elliott Rudwick. *From Plantation to Ghetto*. New York: Hill and Wang, 1966.

Mitchell, James B. *The Collapse of the National Benefit Life Insurance Company: A Study in High Finance among Negroes*. Washington, D.C.: Howard University Press, 1939.

National Negro Business League. *Proceedings, 1900*. Boston: J. R. Hamm, Publishers, 1900.

National Negro Insurance Association. *Proceedings, 1921–1960*. Richmond: Quality Printing Company, 1921–60.

Oak, Vishnu V. *The Negro's Adventure in General Business*. 1949. Reprint. Westport, Conn.: Negro Universities Press, 1970.

Painter, Nell Irvin. *Exodusters: Black Migration to Kansas after Reconstruction*. New York: Knopf, 1977.

Pierce, Joseph A. *Negro Business and Business Education: Their Present and Prospective Development*. New York: Harper and Brothers, 1947.

Puth, Robert Christian. *Supreme Life: The History of a Negro Life Insurance Company*. New York: Arno Press, 1976.

Ruchames, Louis. *Race, Jobs, and Politics: The Story of FEPC*. New York: Columbia University Press, 1953.

Scott, Emmett J. *Negro Migration during the War*. 1920. Reprint. New York: Arno Press, 1969.

Stuart, Merah Stevens. *An Economic Detour: A History of Insurance in the Life of American Negroes*. New York: Wendell Malliett and Company, 1940.

Torrence, Ridgley. *The Story of John Hope*. New York: Macmillan, 1948.

Tucker, David M. *Lieutenant Lee of Beale Street*. Nashville: Vanderbilt University Press, 1971.

Washington, Booker Taliaferro. *The Negro in Business*. 1907. Reprint. Chicago: Afro-American Press, 1969.

Weare, Walter B. *Black Business in the New South: A Social History of the North Carolina Mutual Life Insurance Company*. Urbana: University of Illinois Press, 1973.

Wesley, Charles Harris. *Richard Allen: Apostle of Freedom*. Washington, D.C.: Associated Publishers, 1935.

White, Walter Francis. *A Man Called White*. New York: Arno Press, 1969.

Woodward, C. Vann. *Origins of the New South, 1877–1913*. Baton Rouge: Louisiana State University Press, 1971.
Wright, Richard Robert, Jr. *The Negro in Pennsylvania: A Study in Economic History*. 1912. Reprint. New York: Arno Press, 1969.
Wynn, Neil A. *The Afro-American and the Second World War*. New York: Holmes & Meier, 1976.

Articles

Allen, Isabel Dangaix. "Negro Enterprise: An Institutional Church." *Outlook* 88 (17 September 1904): 179–83.
"The Atlanta Life Insurance Company." *Underwriters' Forum*, January 1947, p. 7.
"Atlanta Life Turns 75." *Ebony* 36 (June 1981): 108–16.
"Atlanta Massacre." *Independent*, 4 October 1906, pp. 799–800.
"Atlanta University Graduates in Life Insurance." *Atlanta University Bulletin*, March 1928, pp. 11–14.
Bacote, Clarence Albert. "Some Aspects of Negro Life in Georgia." *Journal of Negro History* 43 (July 1958): 186–213.
———. "Theater at Atlanta University." *Atlanta University Bulletin*, September 1974, pp. 18–21.
Barber, Jesse Max. "The Atlanta Tragedy." *Voice* (formerly *Voice of the Negro*), November 1906, pp. 473–79.
Bennett, Lerone. "Money, Merchants, Markets: The Quest for Economic Security." *Ebony* 29 (November 1973): 72–82; (December 1973): 56–65; (February 1974): 66–78.
Blicksilver, Jack. "Life Insurance Company of Georgia: The Formative Years, 1891–1918." In Louis B. Cain and Paul J. Uselding, eds., *Business Enterprise and Economic Change*, pp. 248–79. Kent, Ohio: Kent State University Press, 1973.
Browning, James Blackwell. "The Beginnings of Insurance Enterprise among Negroes." *Journal of Negro History* 22 (October 1937): 417–32.
Donald, Henderson H. "The Negro Migration of 1916–1918." *Journal of Negro History* 6 (October 1921): 383–498.
Du Bois, William Edward Burghardt. "The Cultural Mission of Atlanta University." *Phylon* 3 (Second Quarter 1942): 104–15.
———. "The Growth of the Niagara Movement." *Voice of the Negro*, January 1906, pp. 43–45.
Fitchett, E. Horace. "The Traditions of the Free Negro in Charleston, South Carolina." *Journal of Negro History* 25 (April 1940): 139–52.
Garvin, Roy. "Benjamin Singleton and His Followers." *Journal of Negro History* 33 (January 1948): 7–23.
Gibson, Truman Kella. "The History of Industrial Insurance and the Story of Atlanta Mutual." In William Edward Burghardt Du Bois, ed. *Economic Co-*

242   Selected Bibliography

operation among Negro Americans, pp. 37–38. Atlanta University Publication 12. Atlanta: Atlanta University Press, 1907.

Harmon, John Henry. "The Negro as a Local Businessman." *Journal of Negro History* 14 (April 1929): 116–55.

Harris, Robert L., Jr. "Charleston's Free Afro-American Elites: The Brown Fellowship Society and the Humane Brotherhood." *South Carolina Historical Magazine* 82 (October 1981): 289–310.

———. "Early Black Benevolent Societies, 1780–1830." *Massachusetts Review* 20 (Autumn 1979): 603–25.

Hawkins, Homer C. "Trends in Black Migration from 1863–1960." *Phylon* 34 (June 1973): 140–52.

Henderson, Alexa Benson. "Alonzo Herndon and Black Insurance in Atlanta." *Atlanta Historical Bulletin* 21 (Spring 1977): 34–47.

———. "Heman E. Perry and Black Enterprise in Atlanta, 1908–1925." *Business History Review* 61 (Summer 1987): 216–42.

Herndon, Adrienne Elizabeth. "Shakespeare at Atlanta University." *Voice of the Negro* 3 (July 1906): 482–85.

Higgins, Billy D. "Negro Thought and the Exodus of 1879." *Phylon* 32 (Spring 1971): 39–52.

Himes, J. S., Jr. "Forty Years of Negro Life in Columbus, Ohio." *Journal of Negro History* 27 (April 1942): 133–54.

Holsey, Albon Lucius. "The National Negro Business League: Forty Years in Review." *Crisis* 48 (April 1941): 104–5.

Holzhueter, John O. "Ezekiel Gillespie, Lost and Found." *Wisconsin Magazine of History* 60 (Spring 1977): 179–84.

Hughes, Emmet John. "The Negro's New Economic Life." *Fortune* 54 (September 1956): 127–31, 248, 251–63.

McEwen, Homer C., Sr. "First Congregational Church, Atlanta." *Atlanta Historical Bulletin* 21 (Spring 1977): 129–41.

Meier, August, and David Lewis. "History of the Negro Upper Class in Atlanta, Georgia, 1890–1958." *Journal of Negro Education* 28 (Spring 1959): 128–39.

"The Millionaire Nobody Knows." *Ebony* 10 (October 1955): 43–46.

"The Negro in Business." *Ebony* 18 (September 1963): 211–18.

Pace, Harry Herbert. "The Attitude of Life Insurance Companies toward Negroes." *Southern Workman* 57 (January 1928): 3–7.

———. "The Business of Insurance among Negroes." *Crisis* 32 (September 1926): 219–24.

———. "A New Business Venture." *Crisis* 8 (January 1914): 142–44.

Palmer, Edward Nelson, "Negro Secret Societies." *Social Forces* 23 (October 1944): 207–12.

"Postscript by W. E. B. Du Bois." *Crisis* 33 (September 1927): 239.

Puth, Robert C. "Can Black Insurance Companies Survive?" *Challenge* 17 (May–June 1974): 51–59.

———. "From Enforced Segregation to Integration: Market Factors in the Development of a Negro Life Insurance Company." In Louis B. Cain and Paul J. Uselding, eds., *Business Enterprise and Economic Change*, pp. 295–98. Kent, Ohio: Kent State University Press, 1973.

Ross, Edyth Lively. "Black Heritage in Social Welfare: A Case Study of Atlanta." *Phylon* 37 (Winter 1976): 297–307.

Schemmel, William. "Profile of Jesse Hill, Jr." *Atlanta Magazine*, July 1971, pp. 19–23.

Schwendemann, Glen. "St. Louis and the 'Exodusters' of 1879." *Kansas Historical Quarterly* 26 (Autumn 1960): 233–49.

Shannon, Margaret. "Wealthy Atlanta Negroes . . . How They Did It." *Atlanta Journal and Constitution Magazine*, 9 March 1969.

Simmons, Judy D. "Heman E. Perry: The Commercial Booker T. Washington." *Black Enterprise* 8 (April 1978): 41–49.

Smith, Faye McDonald. "Atlanta Life: 75 Years and Still Looking Ahead." *Black Enterprise* 7 (June 1977): 133–39, 187.

"Some Suggestions with Respect to Business and the Depression." *Negro History Bulletin*, January 1940, p. 57.

Sye, Robert J. "Jesse Hill, Jr.: Atlanta's Human Dynamo." *Sepia*, June 1978, pp. 75–80.

Towns, George Alexander. "The Sources of the Tradition of Atlanta University." *Phylon* 3 (Second Quarter 1942): 117–34.

Tucker, David M. "Black Pride and Negro Business in the 1920's." *Business History Review* 43 (Winter 1969): 435–51.

Walrond, Eric. "The Largest Negro Commercial Enterprise in the World." *Forbes* 13 (February 1924): 503–5, 523, 525, 533.

White, Walter Francis. " 'Work or Fight' in the South." *New Republic*, 1 March 1919, pp. 144–46.

Woods, Randall B. "C. H. J. Taylor and the Movement for Black Political Independence, 1882–1896." *Journal of Negro History* 67 (Summer 1982): 123–24.

Woodson, Carter Godwin. "Insurance Business among Negroes." *Journal of Negro History* 14 (April 1929): 202–26.

Work, Monroe Nathan. "The Negro in Business and the Professions." *Annals of the American Academy of Political and Social Sciences* 140 (November 1928): 138–44.

Young, Harding B., and James M. Hund. "Negro Entrepreneurship in Southern Economic Development." In Melvin L. Greenhut and W. Tate Whitman, eds., *Essays in Southern Economic Development*, pp. 112–57. Chapel Hill: University of North Carolina Press, 1964.

Theses, Dissertations, and Other Unpublished Works

Bacote, Clarence Albert. "The Negro in Georgia Politics, 1880–1908." Ph.D. dissertation, University of Chicago, 1955.

Bryson, Winfred Octavius, Jr. "Negro Life Insurance Companies: A Comparative Analysis of the Operating and Financial Experience of Negro Legal Reserve Life Insurance Companies." Ph.D. dissertation, University of Pennsylvania, 1948.

Henton, Comradge Leroy. "Heman E. Perry: Documentary Materials for the Life History of a Business Man." Master's thesis, Atlanta University, 1948.

Kennedy, William J., Jr. "The Negro's Adventure in the Field of Life Insurance." Durham: North Carolina Mutual Insurance Company, 1934.

Porter, Michael Leroy. "Black Atlanta: An Interdisciplinary Study of Blacks on the East Side of Atlanta, 1890–1930." Ph.D. dissertation, Emory University, 1974.

Shivery, Louise Delphia Davis. "History of Organized Social Work among Atlanta Negroes, 1890–1935." Master's thesis, Atlanta University, 1936.

Toomer, Juanita Paschal. "A Miracle on Auburn Avenue." Atlanta: Atlanta Life Insurance Company, 1980.

Trent, William Johnson, Jr. "Development of Negro Life Insurance Enterprises." Master's thesis, University of Pennsylvania, 1932.

Waite, E. Emerson. "Social Factors in Negro Business Enterprise." Master's thesis, Duke University, 1940.

Walker, Jack Lamar, Jr. "Protest and Negotiation: A Study of Negro Political Leadership in a Southern City." Ph.D. dissertation, University of Iowa, 1963.

Index

245